Property of

That, excepting in rare cases, you might as well send to the Foundling Hospital and borrow a baby as to borrow a book with the idea of its being any great satisfaction. We like a baby in our cradle, but prefer that one which belongs to the household. We like a book, but want to feel it **is** ours. We never yet got any advantage from a borrowed book. We hope those never reaped any profit from the books they borrowed from us, but never returned.—

* * *

Don't worry your friends **by** borrowing this book. Buy one.

* * *

For sale by all book-dealers or by mail on receipt of price by publisher.

Peschel Press ~ **P.O. Box 132** ~ **Hershey, PA 17033** ~ **www.PeschelPress.com**

I0388976

The 223B Casebook Series
Sherlock Holmes Victorian Parodies and Pastiches:
1888-1899
Sherlock Holmes Edwardian Parodies and Pastiches I:
1900-1904
Sherlock Holmes Edwardian Parodies and Pastiches II:
1905-1909
Sherlock Holmes Great War Parodies and Pastiches I:
1910-1914
Sherlock Holmes Great War Parodies and Pastiches II:
1915-1919
Sherlock Holmes Jazz Age Parodies and Pastiches I:
1920-1924
Sherlock Holmes Jazz Age Parodies and Pastiches II:
1925-1930
The Early Punch Parodies of Sherlock Holmes

The Rugeley Poisoner Series
The Illustrated Life and Career of William Palmer
The Times Report of the Trial of William Palmer
The Life and Career of Dr. William Palmer of Rugeley

Annotated Editions
The Complete, Annotated Secret Adversary
By Agatha Christie
The Complete, Annotated Mysterious Affair at Styles
By Agatha Christie
The Complete, Annotated Whose Body?
By Dorothy L. Sayers

Other Books
The Dictionary of Flowers and Gems
Suburban Stockade

Also by Bill Peschel
Hell's Casino
Writers Gone Wild (Penguin)
The Casebook of Twain and Holmes

THE ILLUSTRATED
Life and Career
OF
WILLIAM PALMER

THE ONLY AUTHENTIC LIKENESS OF WILLIAM PALMER.

THE ILLUSTRATED
Life and Career
OF
WILLIAM PALMER

(The Rugeley Poisoner, Vol. 1)

CONTAINING

DETAILS OF HIS CONDUCT AS SCHOOL-BOY, MEDICAL-STUDENT, RACING-MAN, AND POISONER;

WITH

ORIGINAL LETTERS OF WILLIAM AND ANNE PALMER,

AND

OTHER AUTHENTIC DOCUMENTS.

TOGETHER WITH

THE WHOLE OF HIS PRIVATE DIARY UP TO THE HOUR OF HIS ARREST, AND THE FULLEST PARTICULARS RESPECTING HIS EXECUTION AT STAFFORD.

ILLUSTRATED

With Views, Portraits, And Representations Of The Chief Incidents In His Career,

REPUBLISHED WITH ANNOTATIONS AND ADDED MATERIAL

By Bill Peschel

PESCHEL PRESS ~ HERSHEY, PA.

THE ILLUSTRATED LIFE AND CAREER OF WILLIAM PALMER. (The Rugeley Poisoner series, Vol. 1). Book format, modified artwork, and footnotes copyright 2016 by Bill Peschel. All rights reserved. Printed in the United States of America.

No part of the footnotes may be used or reproduced in any manner without written permission except in cases of brief quotations embodied in critical articles or reviews. For information, email peschel@peschelpress.com or write to Peschel Press, P.O. Box 132, Hershey, PA 17033.

Cover design by Bill Peschel. Cover artist unknown.

www.peschelpress.com

ISBN-13: 978-1530827114
ISBN-10: 1530827116

Library of Congress Control Number: 2016904592

First printing: April 2016

Table of Contents

CHAPTER I.
Palmer's Ancestors — The Founder of the Palmer Family — His Widow and her reputed Lovers 21

CHAPTER II.
The Childhood and School-days of William Palmer — His Apprenticeship to Evans and Sons of Liverpool — The Missing Letters, and the Abstracted Money 30

CHAPTER III.
Palmer Apprenticed to Mr. Tylecote, the Surgeon — How he Borrows Five Pounds — The Footman at "The Abbey" — Sham Patients — How He served the Assistant, and How He Ran Away 42

CHAPTER IV.
Palmer is Walking Pupil at the Stafford Infirmary — Death of Abley at the Lamb and Flag — Palmer goes to London — Passes his Examination 47

CHAPTER V.
Palmer comes to London — His Medical "Grinder" — Palmer a Student at Bartholomew's — His Extravagant Mode of Life 49

CHAPTER VI.
Colonel Brookes and Mrs. Thornton — "Good Annie Brookes" 61

CHAPTER VII.
Palmer's Courtship at Abbot's Bromley — Some Love-Letters 66

CHAPTER VIII.
The Town of Rugeley 73

CHAPTER IX.
Palmer's Married Life — His Show of Religion 81

CHAPTER X.
Palmer quits Physic for the Turf — His Racing Establishment 89

CHAPTER XI.
Palmer as a Racing and Betting Man 103

CHAPTER XII.
Some suspected Cases of Poisoning — An Illegitimate Child — Mrs.

Thornton (Palmer's Mother-in-Law) — Bladon, the Sporting Bagman — Beau Bentley — The Chickens and the Pills — The young Man named Bly 112

CHAPTER XIII.
The Illness and Death of Palmer's Wife — £13,000 netted by the Transaction 120

CHAPTER XIV.
Palmer freed from his Pecuniary Difficulties — His Maid-Servant, Eliza Tharm — A Fashionable "Hell" and Casino 127

CHAPTER XV.
Palmer's Brother Walter — His Habits — His Illness — The Insurances on his Life — The Bottles of Poison in the Stables of the Junction Inn — Walter Palmer's Death 141

CHAPTER XVI.
William Palmer visits Walter's Wife — Sends the Insurance Policy to Pratt — The Offices refuse Payment — Makes a Demand on Walter's Wife — Proposes to insure the Life of George Bates, Esq. — More "Hot" Brandy 155

CHAPTER XVII.
Palmer's Connexion with Mr. Pratt, the West End Bill Discounter and Solicitor 166

CHAPTER XVIII.
Shrewsbury Races — Polestar, the winning Horse — "Burning" Brandy and Water 169

CHAPTER XIX.
Cook and Palmer at Rugeley — Cook's Illness — The Pills — A Death-bed Scene 174

CHAPTER XX.
Cook's Step-Father comes to Rugeley — The Missing Betting Book — Post-mortem Examination — Palmer Attempts to Bribe the Postboy — Is more Fortunate with the Postmaster — Tries It On with the Coroner — Is Arrested for Debt — Is Found Guilty of Wilful Murder 181

CHAPTER XXI.
Palmer's Farewell — Palmer in Prison — His Voluntary Starvation

— His Furniture Seized and Sold 190

CHAPTER XXII.
The Sale of Palmer's Stud at Tattersall's 195

CHAPTER XXIII.
Palmer's House at Rugeley 199

CHAPTER XXIV.
Verdicts of Wilful Murder in the Cases of Ann Palmer and Walter Palmer — Palmer as a Witness at Westminster — He Charges his Wife with Forgery 204

CHAPTER XXV.
William Palmer is Tried for Murder 208

CHAPTER XXVI.
The Execution 214

CHAPTER XXVII.
Palmer's Character and Peculiarities — Personal Appearance — Resemblance to Manning — The Poisoner's Hand — Extreme Neatness — Hospitality and Generosity — General Character — Fear of Sleeping Alone 225

William Palmer's private Diary for the Year 1855 230

ADDED MATERIAL.
The Jane Letters 263
    William Palmer
On Duty with Inspector Field 273
    Charles Dickens
Judge Hawkins' Memoirs 288
    Sir Henry Hawkins
Judge Kenealy's Memoirs 291
    Edward Kenealy
Jorrick Goes to the Races 296
    Robert Smith Surtees
The Physiology of the London Medical Student 304
    Albert Richard Smith
Key Dates in William Palmer's life 331
Bibliography 336
About the Editor 337

Introduction

"When a doctor does go wrong, he is the first of criminals. He has nerve and he has knowledge. Palmer and Pritchard were among the heads of their profession."
 Sherlock Holmes, *The Adventure of the Speckled Band*

"Look at the scores and scores of murders that have gone unproved and unsuspected till the fool of a murderer went too far and did something silly which blew up the whole show. Palmer, for instance. His wife and brother and mother-in-law and various illegitimate children, all peacefully put away—till he made the mistake of polishing Cook off in that spectacular manner."
 Lord Peter Wimsey, *Unnatural Poison*

IT WAS INEVITABLE THAT THE good doctor and I would meet. He appears at the intersection of several of my long-standing interests: history, the Victorian era, true crime, Sherlock Holmes, and Lord Peter Wimsey. I just didn't think it would be as his publisher.

I founded Peschel Press in 2010 with the intention of publishing my fiction. But inspiration intervened, as well as the lack of a suitable manuscript. I needed something to sell. I had been annotating the Wimsey stories at my website (www.planetpeschel.com). When I turned to Sayers' first novel, *Whose Body?*, I discovered that a quirk in the copyright law left the book in the public domain in the U.S. I decided to publish it as a book. Going through the process from editing to proofing would let me hone my skills in the practical side of book-making as well as make a little money.

Palmer appeared only as one of Sayers' few footnotes in *Whose Body?* Lord Peter Wimsey and his friend, police inspector Parker, were discussing whether a suspect's decades-long jealousy was a strong enough motive for murder. Parker thought not, laconically calling it — "Very old — and not much of a motive." Wimsey replied:

"People have been known to do that sort of thing."

The footnote to this consisted of a long quotation from Lord Chief Justice Campbell's summing-up of the evidence in *Regina vs. Palmer.* Being a dutiful researcher, I read up on the case and footnoted the footnote. Being an aficionado of Victorian true crime, I also wrote a short essay for the back of the book describing the case in more detail.

That's when I learned that the Palmer case was the Crime of the Century, or at least the Crime of Mid-Century Britain. News of his arrest, with intimations that he had also done in his wife, mother-in-law, several children, and his fellow gamblers, created a sensation. The trial at London's Old Bailey (which itself was unprecedented, requiring an act of Parliament to move it from Staffordshire) lasted for 12 days, at a time when even murder trials lasted for one.

The trial was also notable for the introduction of the expert witness. Not much was known about poisons and how they acted on the body. A test was developed for strychnine, but no one was certain if it could be found after it was absorbed into the body. The only way to find out what worked and what didn't was for researchers to poison animals — rabbits, dogs, and cats in particular — and see what happened, both outside and inside the body. The result was a lot of discussion in the press and medical journals about, to use Donald Rumsfeld's phrase, the known-knowns, the known-unknowns, and the unknown-unknowns of poisons.

All this was a consequence of advances made possible by the Industrial Revolution, when a host of inventions swept Britain, causing massive disruptions everywhere. Changes in manufacturing and transportation made drugs more readily available on the open market. Arsenic, prussic acid, and strychnine were sold over the counter. A reduction in the paper tax and advances in presses dropped the price of newspapers and magazines to the point where everyone could afford one. Universal schooling created a generation of readers, and publishers raced to give them what they enjoyed.

What people wanted to read about most, it seems, was crime. It was a popular genre during the Victorian era. The stories of burglars, highwaymen, and cutthroats followed a familiar path that always led to their hanging, complete with their last confession, followed by a moralistic plea not to follow them.

The most popular crime was murder by poison, which struck

at the heart of Victorian concerns. It was a personal act inflicted by a family member, relative, or friend on the innocent and involved a betrayal of trust. It took place in the home, that sanctum sanctorum of Victorian life. Frequently, it was motivated by sexual desire or the consequences of it. One of the more notorious cases, for example, was that of a genteel Scotswoman, Madeleine Smith, who at 21 poisoned her ex-lover when he threatened to send her love letters to her family.

(There were two elements to this case that added a thrilling *frisson* to Victorian newspaper readers: the victim was a dastardly Frenchman — which appealed to British xenophobia — and that the jury returned a verdict of "not proven" — a decision unique to Scotland that meant "we think ye did it, lassie, but the evidence didna prove it.")

Many cases never moved off the newspaper page, and it was left to later writers to reconstruct them. Palmer, however, had inspired three books that I wanted to see back in print: this one, the *Times'* edition of the trial transcript, and Dr. George Fletcher's *The Life and Career of Dr. William Palmer of Rugeley.*

Dr. Fletcher's book was published in 1925. It went through one edition and then fell out of print. This was a pity, because he had a personal interest in Palmer that's reflected in his writing. Like Palmer, he was born in the county of Staffordshire and even knew many of the people involved in the case, including John Parsons Cook:

"My earliest recollections begin with Cook coming to Bromsgrove (where my father practised as a doctor), when I was a schoolboy, and I carried his cricket-bag to the ground in the summer of 1855. And I remember my father strongly upbraiding him, a fine young man about twenty-seven years of age, telling him he was wasting his substance and his health in riotous living, racing, and general dissipation, adding, 'Even now you are on your way to Worcester Races with a set of blacklegs and idlers, the worst of whom is that dissolute Dr. Palmer, who will rob you again and again'; and mother chimed in with a lot more to the same effect."

This memory and the aftermath inspired Fletcher to explore the case. He visited Rugeley several times and spoke to anyone who knew anything about the case. Late in his life, his friends encouraged him to publish what he had learned. His *Life and Career* follows the familiar story, but it's told from a personal perspective.

As for the trial transcript, there were several good candidates, including the official record available online at the Old Bailey website. But the *Times* version was accompanied by a wealth of woodcuts specially produced for the newspaper. Making woodcuts was an expensive, time-consuming process, and publishers rarely created them only for books. You'll see that in the *Illustrated Life;* many were clearly made for previous books, and the thrifty publisher reused a few for *The Yelverton Marriage Case* (1861).

But the *Times* had covered the trial; their artist had already created the illustrations for the newspaper, so reusing them for the book was not only cost-effective, but gave the reader something they wouldn't find in other books: a window into Palmer's world and its inhabitants. Reading Elizabeth Mills' testimony about Cook's agonies as he slowly, fearfully died from strychnine is riveting. Seeing her as the courtroom artist saw her resurrects her. She stands in the dock in her best dress, bonnet tied firmly in place, gripping a book (the Bible she swore an oath on?) and pointing (to Palmer, who from her elevated position she could see across the courtroom?).

Her sallow, thin face hints at a lifetime of physical labor. She could have stepped from the pages of Dickens. Considering that what she saw in that candlelit room rivaled Bill Sykes' murder of Nancy in *Oliver Twist* for sheer terror, she might as well have.

Admittedly, *The Times Report of the Trial of William Palmer* can be a slog. All trials are inherently dull, and even with a man's life in the balance, Palmer's was no exception. After the prosecution witnesses described the events leading up to the murder and Palmer's behavior, the defense relied solely on a parade of medical experts of varying quality arguing that Cook died from anything, seemingly everything, instead of from poison. Was it apoplexy? Was it syphilis? Was it something in his spine? The only fun comes from seeing Jeremiah Smith, Palmer's longtime friend and co-conspirator, squirming on the stand, trying to explain why he spent so many nights at the home of Mrs. Palmer (his mother, then in her 60s) rather than walking home to his bachelor bed. One wonders why the defense didn't object to this line of questioning, but one doesn't object.

After that, there was the judge's day-long summing up of the evidence — old Campbell wanted to see Palmer swing and didn't he make every effort to hint that to the jury! — and then the Attorney-General got his turn. By law, the defense was obliged to remain silent, so we can forgive Palmer's note to his attorney that he'd like to give the judge a dose of strychnine. I would have, too.

Compared to the length and complexity of editing the *Times* book, working on *The Illustrated Life* was sheer fun. It was an "instant book" published quickly after Palmer's hanging. The story was efficiently told, without the curlicues and digressions common to Victorian fiction, and the sidelights into horse racing, the education of medical students, and London nightlife are detailed and knowing.

With Palmer dead, they could throw in everything they heard about him, but the book doesn't read as a collection of fictions. Exaggerations, surely; one can't see Palmer as a lusty, drunken medical student and the later country doctor with his soft-soap manners and phlegmatic temperament. But the book conveys what it was like to live in those times, where a country lad in Rugeley could be awed by the delights of London, accurately described by Dr. Watson as "that great cesspool into which all the loungers and idlers of the Empire are irresistibly drained!"

Accompanied by Stephen Bates' *The Poisoner* (2014) as a chaser, the Rugeley Poisoner series covers every aspect of the Palmer case, with revealing details about the discreet pleasures and passions of the mid-Victorian-era gentleman. And when you're done, maybe you'll understand the countryside as Sherlock Holmes did in "The Copper Beeches," as a place that hides "deeds of hellish cruelty, the hidden wickedness which may go on, year in, year out, in such places, and none the wiser."

Bill Peschel
Hershey, Pa.
March 24, 2016

How This Book Was Edited

The text was taken from Google Books, which scanned a printed copy using optical-character recognition and converted it into text. The quality was scattershot, as anyone who has bought a printed copy of the PDF file will see. So the manuscript was read four times, twice on the computer screen and twice in the printed version by myself and a copy editor. Problem areas were identified and corrected after comparison to the PDF.

That was the easy part. We had to decide how faithful this edition should be to the first edition. Should we recreate the book or should it be improved, and if so, how far? Should we ignore factual errors, footnote them or silently correct them? Should the illustrations be kept in their original locations, even when they're clearly out of place? How far should we go to make the book useful to modern readers without losing the flavor of how the language was used at the time?

To find an answer, we had to decide between preserving the past, mistakes and all, and providing an edition that would provide a better reading experience. At first the choices were made piecemeal, as they arose, but as the decisions piled up, it became clear that we wanted to sell a definitive, but edited version. We decided to make minor corrections to the text silently.

After that, the editing process fell into place. Words that were capitalized that wouldn't be today were retained, but we removed the spaces before semi-colons and question and exclamation marks. Spaces were inserted around long dashes. Long blocks of text were broken into paragraphs as a concession to the reader's eyes.

Then there were questions of fact. Palmer's hired man was spelled Bate here but Bates in other books. I used Bates. Walter Palmer's "bottle-holder" responsible for keeping him from drink is known elsewhere as Walkenden, so that is the case here.

The illustrations were cleaned up as best they could be. Some from *The Times Report of the Trial of William Palmer* were moved here, where they could illustrate scenes mentioned in the text. Others were added from other books and websites.

The Value of a Pound

Converting a pound in 1856 to today that would have any meaning is difficult. There's inflation and deflation to consider. Some products, such as computers, modern drugs, and digital watches, didn't exist in 1856. Lower energy prices and international trade have dramatically changed the value of goods such as clothing and out-of-season produce. The factors that go into setting wages have changed as well. Today's business owners must take into account taxes, pensions, insurance, and other costs that were not considered in Palmer's time. There were also marked differences in wages paid to skilled workers, semi-skilled workers, and laborers.

The Measuring Worth website (www.measuringworth.com) offers several methods of determining the true value of a pound. They show that the relative value of an 1856 pound ranges from £82 (how much that pound would buy today) to £2,060 (the economic power of that pound when compared to the gross domestic product). Since we want to know how valuable that pound would be to us, we'll use the historic standard of living measurement, in which a pound then would be worth £82 or $134, rounded off, as of Sept. 3, 2014 (when £1 is worth $1.64). That was the value we used in the *Trial* volume.

Shameless Self-Promotion

Before I go, I'd like to make a personal request. If you like this book, tell your friends. Mention it on your social network or the website where you bought this book. If you like, email me at peschel@peschelpress.com or write to the Press at P.O. Box 132, Hershey, PA 17033-0132. Tell me I'm not alone in thinking annotations and extras helped you enjoy the book.

Word of mouth spurs sales, helps me support my family and encourages me to publish more annotations.

Dedication

To Teresa, for not getting any ideas after proofing these books.

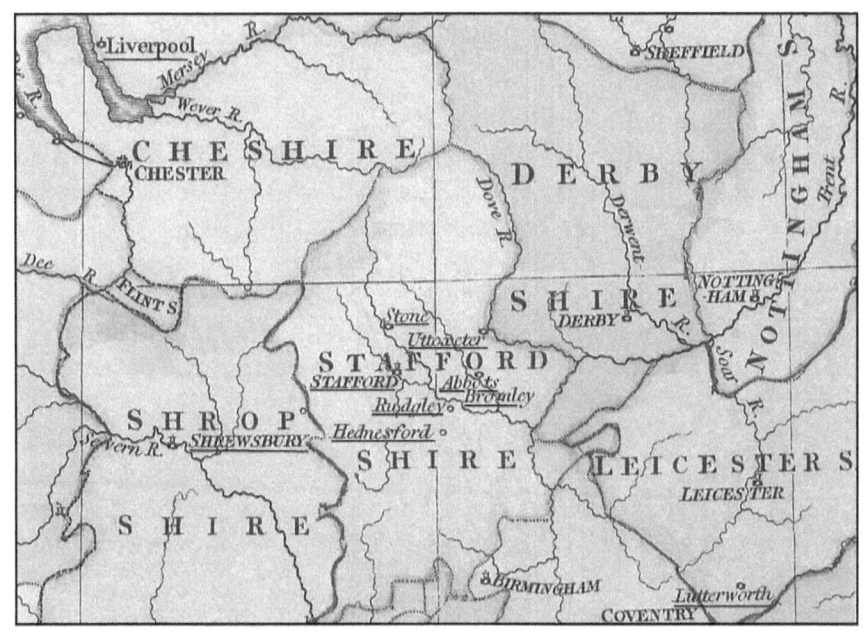

LIVERPOOL, STAFFORDSHIRE AND RUGELEY IN PALMER'S TIME.

LIVERPOOL AND RUGELEY IN RELATION TO LONDON.

Preface.

WILLIAM PALMER, THE POISONER, HAS passed by a terrible and opprobrious death to the bar of a more awful tribunal, and to the presence of a mightier audience than that before which he publicly stood for so many days in London.

For what other deeds he has to be there arraigned we shall never know in this world. Enough, however, has been proved, to the satisfaction of all thinking minds, to consign him to a doom which could not have been aggravated on earth had everything of which he was guilty been adduced.

It is no subtle or recondite moral that his fate inculcates. More than once of late years, he has had large sums of money in his possession, and yet, from the moment of his first frauds, he never regained a chance of independence or of solvency; since the same epoch, he endeavoured to parry immediate and pressing dangers, by incurring progressively higher and worse risks, which were not to be so instantaneously encountered, but which were inevitable in their own time — until, from the fraud of a bill which there was no rational prospect of meeting when due, he advanced to the deeper fraud of forged acceptances, continually renewed by fresh forgeries; and so, step by step, to the plunder of insurance companies by means of polices made available through the assassination of the insured; and, lastly, to robbery with his own hand at the death-bed of the man whom he had murdered.

Not for one instant, in spite of the enormous amounts for which he laid his schemes, could he see his way towards clearing himself; and not for one instant, despite of a certain superficial popularity among his coarse associates, could he say to himself that he was safe. Had he purchased by that certainty of ruin, more or less speedy, in which he involved his affairs, and by those still more terrible and more fatal uncertainties with which he begirt the duration of his existence, as well as the mode of its close — had he thus purchased some of the most exquisite delights and the chief enjoyments of which man is susceptible, the cost would still have been insensate.

But — having started with fair opportunities and ample means — it was for the sake of that hideous and dark career to which we have alluded — it was for the sake of that life of forlorn makeshifts, of mysterious expedients, of unintermitted alarm, struggle, and anxiety — for the sake of this wretched, troublous, crazed, hurrying, and desperate existence, that he chose to bring himself at the age of thirty-two, or very little more, to the terrible and ignominious death which he publicly underwent on the gallows in front of Stafford gaol.

The moral is trite and obvious. It is not on every nature that the influences which led Palmer to destruction would have proved so malign: but they were not the less evil in themselves, and they are not the less a danger. The unbridled impatience to grow rich quickly, the excitement of a gambling life and the ever deepening debasement of unprincipled companionship, will produce their natural fruit in a great many characters who might otherwise have remained innocent of at least the more dreadful forms of crime.

As to the guilt of the wretched man, the certainty of it is such as may safely set the public conscience at rest. It is true, the proofs in this case were exclusively circumstantial.[1] But we would remind all who may not have accurately reflected on this interesting subject, that no proofs can possibly be so satisfactory as those derived from circumstantial evidence, where the chain of that evidence is really complete.

And why? Because, however trustworthy witnesses may be, they still are liable, when deposing to the fact itself at issue, itself controverted (instead of to a multiplicity of seemingly minor circumstances) — however trustworthy witnesses may be, they are liable to be swayed by a thousand feelings — by pity, terror, hope, fear, by likes and dislikes; — whereas circumstances have neither likes nor dislikes, no passions, no emotions, no interests to warp their testimony or cloud their judgment.

It may be said that it is living witnesses, after all, who depose to those circumstances themselves. True; but so far as each is severally concerned, these circumstances do not appear necessarily connected with the actual deed, or with its

---

[1] The legal definition means evidence that requires an inference to connect it to a fact. For example, it is circumstantial evidence if a forensic scientist testifies that the bullet that killed a man came from the defendant's gun, because it does not prove that it was the defendant who pulled the trigger.

disturbing spectacle. No one individual circumstance would of itself convict the accused; it is the chain of them which involve him, and that chain is formed out of the depositions of a multitude of different persons, who not only could not possibly have concerted such a mutually explaining body of proofs, but who are many of them strangers to each other, and are, like all numerous masses of individuals, actuated by various interests, objects, and passions.

The obvious impossibility of jointly inventing this complete plot of inferential proof — an impossibility inherent in the very nature of circumstantial evidence — where every fact would be indifferent only for its perfect concordance with every other fact, and where each of these facts is attested by a distinct witness unconnected, and often unacquainted, with his fellow deponents; this impossibility constitutes the superior strength of circumstantial evidence, in comparison with that direct testimony about the main issue itself, which testimony can be, and too often is, suborned on either side.

WILLIAM PALMER

CHAPTER I.

PALMER'S ANCESTORS — THE FOUNDER OF THE PALMER FAMILY — HIS WIDOW AND HER REPUTED LOVERS.

IF THE LIVES OF THE great and good are deserving of being written for the admiration of succeeding generations, and to excite those who study them to the practice of brave and virtuous actions, the careers of great criminals are equally worthy of being recorded, that their misdeeds may become the abhorrence of posterity, and that all who ponder over their wretched courses may take warning by the rapid progress with which, after the first false step, they too surely enter upon their downward path of crime.

Among this class of lives, few are so pregnant with warning as that of the man whose name has hung incessantly on the lips of people of all classes and conditions, for weeks —

nay, for months past; the long catalogue of whose victims, as one fresh case after another emerged into the light, sent a thrill of indignant horror throughout the land; and whose conviction has calmed that just apprehension which existed in the minds of all thoughtful men, with regard to the security of life in this country, against the insidious arts of the skilled secret poisoner. Need we say that we allude to the notorious William Palmer, of Rugeley

This wretched man seems to have sprung from a bad stock, for it is currently reported throughout the midland counties that old Bentley, William Palmer's grandfather, by the mother's side, was a kind of bully to a woman who kept a brothel in a back street in Derby. She is represented as being an ignorant woman of somewhat faded attractions, who, with an eye to the main chance, was continually sending Bentley (then a young man) with money to the bank. But Bentley, who had also an eye to the main chance, put it in his own name, and thus, in the course of a few years, contrived to amass a large sum of money. In the meanwhile, Bentley had not been true to the dubious attractions of his mistress, and as she had a very foul tongue and a rather heavy hand. In the course of mutual explanations they fell to blows, the consequences of which were that he drew out *his* money (as he now called it) from the bank to the alarm and consternation of Miss Margaret Taff, or, as she was more familiarly styled, Pegg Taff, of Mickleover.[1] At her threats of prosecution he merely laughed, like a pleasant man as he was; and in the end, or rather in the very night following, he decamped, taking with him the spoil which amounted in round numbers to £560.[2]

With this sum we find Mr. Bentley turning up at Longway House,[3] near Lichfield with a wife and a daughter; the wife, a lady of whose antecedents nothing is known, except that she was a Mrs. Sharrod; the daughter, the present Mrs. Palmer, sen., who it is reported used to visit Lichfield market with

---

[1] A village in Derbyshire that is now a suburb of Derby. It is about 30 miles northeast of Rugeley.

[2] Worth nearly £46,000 or $75,000 today.

[3] A home built southeast of Rugeley in the 1750s and demolished in the late 19th century. The name lives on in a converted 3-story barn that was sold in 2010 for £650,000.

poultry, butter, and eggs, the produce of the farm which her father occupied. From Longway House the family removed to Cleat Hill, and thence to Ashton Hays in the parish of Kings Bromley. Mr. Bentley, by the judicious use which he had made of Pegg Taff's round hundreds, was now to all appearances a respectable man, well to do in the world. In this position we will leave him to say a few words about his son-in-law, the father of the present Palmer generation.

Bentley's daughter was a prudent young lady, who thought it not amiss to have a couple of strings to her bow.[4] She was courted by Mr. Hodson, the Marquis of Anglesey's[5] steward, and by a young sawyer[6] of the name of Palmer. The sawyer, whom everybody speaks of as a coarse, vulgar fellow, fancying that the Marquis's steward was almost fond enough of Sarah Bentley to marry her, saved him the trouble by marrying her himself. Mr. Hodson is said to have proved none the less fond of Sarah Palmer than he had been of Sarah Bentley; and while he was paying his court to her, her husband was quietly marking the Marquis of Anglesey's timber, which is a very innocent practice in itself, but when by marking them 1,1; 2, 2; 3, 3; instead of 1, 2, 3, Palmer could get six at the price of three, or better still, ten at the price of one, for we were informed by an old man who carted timber for old Palmer, that he had seen ten No. tens come in one day from Stroughborough Park[7] — you can imagine that, even after "going snags"[8] with the steward

---

[4] To keep another man interested in her if the relationship fell apart. From the practice of archers to keep a spare bowstring handy, in case the first one snaps or loosens in wet weather.

[5] A peerage that was created in 1815 for Henry Paget (1768-1854), who served with distinction at the battle of Waterloo. In addition to other offices, he was twice Lord Lieutenant of Ireland.

[6] A man who saws wood for a living. Part of his job was to number the trees that would be cut and sold. The steward was supposed to make sure the count was correct so the Marquis would get his fair share of the proceeds. As we shall see, this was not always done.

[7] The author might have confused the Marquis's family seat at Beaudesert, a few miles away from Rugeley with the nearby Shugborough Estate that was owned by the Earl of Lichfield. It is now open to the public as a self-described "working historic estate."

[8] Dividing the profits among the participants. More commonly called "going snacks." One slang dictionary attributed the phrase to a body-

Hodson, he still was in a fair way to make his fortune.[9]

He evidently thought so, for he took extensive premises at Rugeley, built a fine house, began to keep servants, and, in fact, accumulated money. Then he fell in with the steward of the Bagot estate,[10] with whom he was also in the habit of "going snags," and these sums of compound addition were worked out again with similar results.

Finally, he fell in with the lease of the East Collieries at Brereton[11] and might now be considered a rich and prosperous gentleman.

But one day this rich and prosperous gentleman came in from his timber-yard to dinner; he ate heartily, seemed to be quite well, and to be enjoying himself. He was just finishing his dinner when he fell back with his bread and cheese clutched in his hand — dead, without a word.

This happened, we believe, in 1837. The will which old Palmer left behind him was unsigned, and it is understood that Joseph, the eldest son, who would have taken all the freehold property[12] in his own right, executed a deed to the effect that he and his brothers should have £7,000 each,[13] and that the old

---

snatcher named Snacks, who was so swamped with work during one of London's many plagues that he shared his proceeds with anyone willing to help dig up corpses to sell to medical schools.

[9] Timber scams such as mismarking trees are still in use today. A 2000 article in *Massachusetts Woodland Steward* magazine warned that a "significant minority" of loggers intend to cheat landowners out of paying the fair market value of their timber. A 1988 study found undertallying on timber sales was "extremely widespread, and constitutes a very significant abuse of the property rights of landowners."

[10] The Bagot family has owned land in Staffordshire since the 11th century. The family still lives at Blinthfield Hall, five miles north of Rugeley.

[11] A colliery is a British word for a coal mine. Brereton was a village that has now been incorporated into Rugeley.

[12] In the U.K., land can be held as a leasehold or a freehold. In a leasehold, the property is rented from the owner for a period of time. At the end of the period, depending on the contract, the property could revert to the owner, or be leased for another period of time. In a freehold, the home's occupant owns the property outright

[13] Each share was worth £574,000 or $938,000 today. The total estate was valued at £70,000, or 10 times those amounts.

PALMER FAMILY VAULT IN RUGELEY CHURCHYARD.

lady should have the remainder, and the landed property, for her lifetime; she, however, engaging not to marry.

Mrs. Palmer's solicitor repeatedly told Joseph that he would repent it some day, and in fact refused to have the deed executed by which Joseph dispossessed himself of so much property unless another solicitor was called in. Joseph then had his own solicitor, and for some time had thoughts of backing out, but eventually he signed the deed.

The body of the old man was laid in Rugeley church yard, and a tomb erected above his grave. He had risen to wealth and respectability, and deserved, according to the notions of his heirs, to have a Grecian tomb placed over his "dust and ashes," with iron rails to keep off the curious intruder. A man that leaves £70,000 behind him deserves something better than a grass mound to mark his last resting-place. He sprang from nothing, but he mustn't end so. He must be made a good deal of.

On the stone slab above the tomb — that kind of death's visitor's-book, where all who enter have their names written down, — is inscribed, in deeply-cut letters that will bear much wear and tear before they are worn away, "In a vault beneath are interred the remains of Joseph Palmer," together with his age, and the date of his death.[14]

The sawyer's widow, in course of time, consoled herself for the loss of her spouse by other attachments. One of her favoured swains was a strapping linendraper,[15] named Duffy; and at the "Shoulder of Mutton" public-house,[16] in the Market-place of Rugeley, and close to the Town Hall, there could be seen, until recently seized by the police, the love-letters which the youthful, fascinating, and unfortunate Duffy is said to have received from the aged, giddy, and wealthy Mrs. Palmer.

The "Shoulder of Mutton" is a cottage with a tall roof, from which the bedroom windows look out upon the street. Over the entrance-door is the painting of an immense shoulder of mutton, only to be matched by the enormous dried hams showing through the passage window. In the front portion of the premises, the shelves are ornamented with sample-bottles of wines and spirits, which at the first glance have the appearance of medicine bottles. There is also a plaster cast of a cow, although no milk is to be purchased on the premises; and, unless the image should refer to "cream of the valley," it is totally out of place, and without meaning.

The taproom looks as if it had lately been added to the other portions of the house, for it has a small slate roof of its own, and is glazed with heavy white sashes and small panes of glass, twelve to the square yard, and is entirely out of character with the remainder of the building.

Thomas Clewley, the landlord, is a fine-looking man, with white hair and a cherry-red face, that puts one in mind of "trifle" at an evening party.[17] The statement he makes to his

---

[14] The Palmer family vault can still be found in the rear of St. Augustine's churchyard, but time has not been kind to it. Originally, it was a stone slab supported by side and end pieces and surrounded by an ironwork railing. The railing was donated to a scrap drive during World War II, and sometime after 1980 vandals destroyed the supporting pieces, leaving the top on the ground.

[15] A dealer in fabrics.

[16] The inn still exists on Yoxall Road northeast of Rugeley. On its web site, the owners make no mention of its connection to Palmer.

[17] A sponge cake with a fruit filling covered with layers of custard, jelly, and cream. Soaking the cake in fortified wine or sherry gives it a distinctive kick.

THE SHOULDER OF MUTTON INN, RUGELEY.

customers, respecting Duffy and Mrs. Palmer, senior, is as follows:—

"There was a strapping chap of the name of Duffy — a good-looking fellow — who used to come to lodge with me. He was rather a dull chap in the house, and he'd sit still and drink. He did not run up a very big shot. The first time he came here, Mr. William Palmer paid for him. The second time he came, Mr. William Palmer told me he wouldn't pay, so I gave Duffy the bill, but he did not pay me then; he said he should have some money coming in a day or two.

"Soon after, he went out of the house without saying anything, and I never set eyes on him again. We gave him three or four years for coming back again; but as he didn't come, and his boxes began to smell very bad, my missus opened them — there was only a lot of dirty shirts and things. He hadn't no clothing only what he had on his back. In the trunks I found some letters, not put by with any care, as if they were particular valuable, but just careless. They were only courting letters, and were from Mrs. Palmer (the old lady), written to him.

"I should think Duffy was about forty years old, and Mrs. Palmer was from about fifty-five to sixty. She has sons now as is above forty. I think Duffy was in the linendrapery line. I never paid no more attention to him than that he was a traveller. The police has been here, and got Duffy's traps.[18]

"The letters finished off with loving and kissing. They made appointments to meet at a many different places; but I was in no way interested in their loves, and I never troubled my head about it; it was the women as exposed the whole business — nobody would have seen 'em or known anything about the letters if it had not been for them. I should have burned 'em, or kept 'em secret. No, I never charged sixpence a-head to see 'em; I only showed 'em for a lark.

The way in which they came to be seen was this — My missus got speaking of 'em, and one or two young chaps came here and gammoned the missus to show 'em. They spent one or two shillings in grog to have a look; then come another and another, and at last I took 'em away; but the missus got 'em again. There's no keeping the women quiet in these matters.

Mr. Jerry Smith has long enjoyed the honour among the Rugeley people of being considered the fortunate successor of the truant Duffy; and it will be remembered, that, during his examination at Palmer's trial, the Attorney-General pressed him very closely on the point. As, however, when he was asked whether any improper intimacy existed between Mrs. Palmer and himself, he went to the extent of saying, that he hoped not — that there ought not to be any pretence for saying there was — with sundry other such-like denials, we suppose we may take it for granted that there is really no foundation for the reports current in the town of Rugeley, and that all the talk concerning Mrs. Palmer, sen., and Mr. Jerry Smith is a string of base fabrications from beginning to end.[19]

---

[18] Belongings or luggage. Possibly a contraction of "trappings," a word meaning the objects and adornments that symbolize a condition. For example, owning a fabulous home and a fleet of Corvettes could represent "the trappings of success."

[19] Jeremiah Smith's testimony at the trial is a model of equivocation, evasion, and bald-faced lying, especially when the prosecutor, Alexander Cockburn, pressed him about his relationship with William Palmer's mother:

Q: I ask you, upon your oath, whether you were not intimate with her; you know what I mean?

A: I was not; no more intimate with her than the proper intimacy that ought to exist.

Then, he had to admit that he paid two or three overnight visits a week to the house despite living less than a 15-minute walk away. After hectoring him further on this point, the attorney-general asked again:

Q: Having stated all that, do you mean to say before this jury that there was nothing but a proper intimacy between you and Mrs. Palmer?

A: I do.

Or, to quote a recent president, "I did *not* have sex with that woman."

CHAPTER II.

THE CHILDHOOD AND SCHOOL-DAYS OF WILLIAM PALMER — HIS APPRENTICESHIP TO EVANS AND SONS OF LIVERPOOL — THE MISSING LETTERS, AND THE ABSTRACTED MONEY.

WHEN OLD PALMER DIED HE left behind him seven children, the issue of his marriage with Sarah Bentley.

Joseph, the eldest son, was placed as an apprentice to the firm of Halhead, Fletcher, and Co., timber merchants, of Liverpool, in whose establishment he remained for between five and six years. He then left Liverpool, and returned to Rugeley, where he commenced business in his father's trade, combining with it that of a dealer in foreign timber. Not long afterwards he was introduced to the family of Mr. Milcrest, of Liverpool, and ere long married the eldest daughter, with whom he obtained a considerable fortune. Three years since he gave up the business of a timber merchant, and purchased a colliery at Cannock Chase near Walsall,[1] but after working this colliery for a short time, and losing a few thousand pounds by it, he ultimately disposed of it, retired from business altogether, and now resides with his family in Liverpool. The second son is William, the subject of the present memoir.

George, the next brother, is an attorney in Rugeley. He is also, by marriage, connected with a Liverpool family, having married Miss Clarke, a daughter of Mr. Clarke, of Seacombe, formerly an iron merchant in Liverpool.

Walter was the fourth son: of him we shall have to speak more particularly as our narrative advances.

The youngest son, Thomas, who is now a clergyman of the Established Church,[2] is at the present time twenty-eight years

---

[1] An industrial town in the West Midlands region, about 15 miles south of Rugeley.
[2] The Church of England founded by Henry VIII in 1534 after he

of age, and is also an exceedingly pious young man. Like the rest of his brothers, he was identified with Liverpool in his more youthful days, for he finished an apprenticeship commenced by his brother William, to Evans and Sons, chemists, of that place. He showed early indications of a studious disposition, and displayed evidences of a serious and religious turn of mind. He was not long before he formed a determination to enter the church, and became a divinity student at St. Bees College.[3] Here he remained for two years, and at the expiration of that time he entered into holy orders, and is now residing at Coton Elms, in Derbyshire.[4] He it is who has recently published a pamphlet in defence of his brother William, in which he speaks of him, as "that darling brother, the playmate of my infancy, the companion of my youthful sports, in whom my heart's-blood circulates, and with whom my love is entwined; whose tongue never spoke falsely to one of us, but to whose language we listened ever with full assurance

---

separated the nation's Catholic churches from the Roman Catholic Church's authority.

[3] An independent theological college in Cumberland founded in 1816. It was closed in 1895. St. Bees is a village whose name is a corruption of the local Saint Bega, an Irish princess from the early Middle Ages.

[4] A county to the east of Staffordshire.

in its integrity and its faith."[5]

The eldest daughter married Mr. Heywood, of Haywood, and drank herself to death; she is represented as a very bad character, and horrible rumours are circulated concerning her, which decency will not allow us even to allude to in print.[6]

The youngest daughter in no respect resembles her sister. Against her the finger of scandal has never dared to point. She is a very quiet, unassuming, charitable girl, and is a general favourite; she is lady-like in appearance, and is well-informed and accomplished. There was a rumour that she had gone mad since the termination of her brother's trial, but we are glad to find that it is not true.[7]

The house in which most, if not all, of these children were born, and in which the prosperous old sawyer — the founder of the Palmer family — resided at the time of his death, and which his widow still occupies, has been thus described by a clever correspondent of the *Illustrated Times*.[8]

"It is," he tells us "a handsome, comfortable-looking place, built of red brick. On one side, next the graveyard, it is patched with a splendid ivy tree, that grows up to the very roof, and makes the walls look thick and smooth about the little window where the blind looks so white from contrast with the dark foliage. On the other side, next the canal,[9] it is patched with a

---

[5] From *A Letter to the Lord Chief Justice Campbell*, a polemic attacking Campbell for his conduct of the trial. Although credited to the Rev. Thomas Palmer, he denied any connection with it. It is suspected that one of Palmer's lawyers, Edward Kenealy, was behind it.

[6] This was Mary Ann Palmer (1816-?), the eldest child, about which we know nothing else.

[7] Sarah Palmer (1832-1907) did indeed live an unblemished life. She married Alexander Brodie in London in 1856, settled down to become a vicar's wife and gave birth to eight children.

[8] The house across the street from St. Augustine's still exists. The Palmer house, then called the Yard, as of 2015 was occupied by a computer data storage business. The graveyard next door belongs to the ruins of a church called The Old Chancel that dates from the 12th century and was partially demolished in 1823. It still stands today.

[9] The Trent and Mersey Canal that connects the two rivers was built in 1777 and was instrumental in the early growth of Rugeley. The hand-dug 93-mile canal connects the ports of Hull on the east coast with Liverpool on the west.

MRS. PALMER'S HOUSE.

big, bulging, two-storeyed bow window, built of stone, which has no business to be there, for it is not in character, and looks tawdry. It is as if some idea had struck the tenant to improve the premises. The windows have sheets of plate-glass, and gay wire blinds, and rich silken curtains, a good deal in the public-house style of "fancy." The other bow window behind has a much better effect, with its little panes, like those we see represented in the sterns of old ships, and agrees with the countryfied look of the remaining portions of the house.

"Over the entrance-door is a white verandah, big enough to be a summer-house, if there were any creeping plants about it; but it is naked and carefully painted white. The Palmers are evidently people to like the respectable look of fresh paint. The garden in front is planted with large evergreens, clipped into a round form, and having a highly stiff and cultivated look, which lets everybody know that a gardener is kept. Where the old timber-yard-used to be, and what was once a large wharf, has been converted into an attempt at a sloping lawn leading down to the canal. A few shrubs have been planted along the carriage drive, but they are growing brown at the tips, and look unhealthy. The old crane which once creaked under the weight of heavy timber, now rests idly at the water's edge, with a kind of wooden casing over him to keep him from the rain. A long narrow barge passes in the canal, drawn by a horse forced slantways by the strain upon the rope. The man at the helm turns round to look at Mrs. Palmer's house, and keeps on gazing until the trees at the bend hide him from the sight.

"At the other end of the timber-yard are the remains of the late stock-in-trade of the late sawyer. The few planks have grown black, and are piled up together, and form a convenient roosting-place for the fowls, and for hanging up linen to dry.

"If the front of the house has an imposing aspect, the back part, at least, lets you into the mystery of the attempt that has been made to obtain the admiration of the passer-by in the road. The back premises are dirty, and full of dirt. The garden is uncultivated, and the mould trodden under foot until it has grown as hard as the remains of the gravel walks that surround them. A few dish cloths hang up to dry; and there are a water-butt, with rusty hoops, and a coach-house and stable that a London cabman would not occupy. Here the carriage was kept; here the man in livery used to put to when ordered to 'come round.' Nobody who saw the handsome vehicle sweeping round the carriage-drive would imagine that it had just come out of such a hovel of a stable, with the black thatch dropping away, and the woodwork looking too rotten even to burn.

"In this house William Palmer was born, with two churches looking down upon him, and gravestones around and about. 'The nearer the church, the farther from God.'[10] As he played among the tombs, he could learn that men sometimes lived, like William Cope and John Dawson, to be 85 years old before they died. He could take such reading lessons as that on the monument near the gate, with the carved letters now filled in with green moss:—

> 'Praises on tombs are trifles vainly spent;
> A man's good name is his best monument.'"

---

[10] From *Proverbs* (c.1538) by John Heywood (c.1497-c.1580).

The morning after Palmer's birth, the apprentice of a grocer, carrying on business very nearly opposite the house at Rugeley, where William Palmer first saw the light, was sent by his mistress with her respectful compliments to know how Mrs. Palmer and the baby were.

Some thirty-two years afterwards, this apprentice rises to be a London alderman, takes his seat, in his official capacity, on the bench at the Central Criminal Court during the trial of William Palmer for murder!

It is the nearest approach that we have yet met with in real life, towards realising the climax of Hogarth's glorious series of the "Apprentices,"[11] where the "industrious apprentice, arrived at the dignity of a Judge, has the idle apprentice brought before him, charged with murder."

The Alderman to whom our anecdote refers is Mr. Thomas Sidney, late M.P. for Stafford.[12]

William Palmer, as a child, was noted for a great display of amiability and kindness, but he was also noted for great cruelty towards animals and for indulging in general mischief in a sly underhand way; he has been known to torture animals, and even insects, and to play tricks with aged people, when he thought there was no opportunity of being detected; but in public, he was always officiously helping somebody, as though it were his wish to make himself generally agreeable.

He was born, in the year 1824, at the house in Rugeley which his mother now occupies, and was christened on the 21st of October, according to the following certificate:—

---

[11] William Hogarth (1697-1764) was a printer, printmaker, and social critic who was a pioneer in creating sequential art. He created series of intricate, symbolic woodcuts with morals in mind such as "The Four Stages of Cruelty" and "The Harlot's Progress." In the "Industry and Idleness" series (1747), Hogarth traced the lives of two apprentices, one of whom through idleness and crime ended up on the gallows, and the other through hard work became Lord Mayor of London.

[12] Sir Thomas Sidney (1805-1889) attended the first day of the trial. Born in Stafford as the son of a woolen draper, he became a tea dealer and importer in London before moving into politics, becoming alderman and sheriff in quick succession. He was member of Parliament for Stafford (1847-1852) and London's mayor (1853-54). In 1889, a fountain honoring him was erected in Stafford. It was destroyed after a van crashed into it in 1928.

"BAPTISM.

"*October* 21st, 1824 — WILLIAM, son of JOSEPH and SARAH PALMER, Rugeley, *Timber Merchant.*

"CHARLES INGE, *Vicar.*"

"The above is a true copy, taken from the parish register, this 9th day of June, 1856.

"T. D. ATKINSON, *Vicar.*"

Littler, a sawyer, an old man who was working in Palmer's father's yard when each of the children were born, and knew the whole of the family, and who has, moreover, nursed William Palmer many a time, furnishes the following particulars of his early days. He says, "the father was very strict with his children generally; made them play in the yard, and would not let them go into the village; but they were allowed to go wild after the father's death.

"The father never flogged William so much as he did the others! No, sir, William was not a particular favourite, but he was not so wild as the others, Walter in particular.

"Old Mrs. Palmer was very fond of her children, but especially fond of Joseph.

"Well, perhaps, he was a little sly. You see young men will be young men, and William was quieter like! Yes, sir, Walter was very racketty — and not so good-natured as William.

"William was the best-natured of all the brothers; in fact, sir, the people round about used to say he was the best of the bunch. I've often carried him through the fields in my arms; we used to play together at marbles. I never saw him in a bad temper. No, sir, a better tempered or more generous child there never was; he was a very nice young gentleman.

"When a baby he was very fat and lust — but the family were all very fat and lust.[13] None of them could walk before sixteen or eighteen months. No, sir, William Palmer never played at the racketty games like his other brothers, Walter for instance. William was very fond of marbles, ball, and

---

[13] He meant "lusty," meaning stout, strong and sturdy. The word was not commonly used as a noun, which has a completely different and more common meaning.

sometimes tipcat. Oh, yes, he played very well with them; he was a capital aim at marbles.

"Yes, sir, he did go to Bonney's, and he went to Clark's before that, sir. You see Clark had the grammar school before Bonney; but Clark died, and then Bonney came. William and his brothers were day-scholars; the school is the next house to Mrs. Palmer's. Bonney was reckoned a very clever schoolmaster.

"Yes, William Palmer was just as generous when he grew up; he never forgot an old face. Why he never met me but he said 'Littler, will you have a glass of something to drink.' He gave a deal to the poor, he was very charitable and kind."

Several of Palmer's schoolfellows, with whom we have spoken, describe him while at Bonney's, as having been "always up to his tricks;" and mention that it was a frequent habit of his to borrow money under false pretences, from the men who were employed in his father's timber-yard. He would go to them in his plausible way, and induce them to believe that his father had no change, and wanted sixpence or a shilling, as the case might be, which no sooner had he procured but he would spend amongst his schoolfellows indiscriminately.

Yet none of his schoolfellows liked him; and although they would readily associate with the other brothers, most of them were very distant to William. One schoolfellow now resident at Bilston, speaks somewhat better of him, for he says, "that in the case of a school row, he was in the habit of protecting the weaker side."

T. Sherrit, for many years connected with Rugeley church, and now acting as parish-clerk, says of William Palmer:—

"I knew him when a lad; I never knew any harm of him; I gave him singing lessons; he came to me of his own accord, because he thought he should like it. He was a very good boy with me, but then I would not have anybody in the class unless he was; but the boys used to tell tales about him — that he was given to swearing, and other tricks. Mr. Bonney could tell you something about him, if he was alive, for he was a man of great discrimination; he could tell a boy's character directly. We had as many as eighty-three scholars when he was alive; we have only twenty-four now, and, some time ago, it had dwindled down to sixteen."

But when William Palmer left school he must have been an indifferent character, for not many months after that he went to be apprenticed to a wholesale chemist at Liverpool, where he behaved himself very badly, and where he is reported to have seduced a girl, and where it is quite certain that he robbed his masters.

The firm Palmer was apprenticed to was that of Messrs. Evans and Sons, wholesale druggists, of Lord-street, Liverpool.[14] When he first entered upon this situation he conducted himself with all seeming propriety, was attentive to his various duties, and for a long time there was not the slightest shadow of a suspicion of anything wrong in the conduct of the apprentice.

At length, however, unaccountable complaints arise. Various customers of Messrs. Evans begin to write to the effect that they have remitted money to the firm, in payment of their several accounts, of which they have had no acknowledgment. Inquiries are made without effect. No cash has come to hand

---

[14] Only 30 years old by the time Palmer darkened its doors, Evans, Sons and Co. was a growing concern as a manufacturer and retailer of pharmaceuticals, with branches in London and Liverpool. Its founder, John Evans, was still alive at that time, but his son Edward Evans seems to have been in charge. The Liverpool office was on Lord-street in the city's shopping district. A 1905 profile of the company noted that the company, still controlled by Evans' descendants, had added branches in Toronto and Montreal, and several laboratories and mills in London.

from the complaining customers. They, in their turn, are positive that it was sent. The matter seems to rest between them and the post-office; no one suspected Palmer, whose duty it was to go every day to the Liverpool post-office to fetch the letters of the firm. It may be as well here to remark that it is customary in Liverpool, as in other important towns of England, for merchants to have letter-boxes of their own at the post-office, into which all letters directed to the firm are placed, and whence they are fetched by clerks or other *employes*; soon after the arrival of the mails, and are thus received much earlier than they would be if delivered by the letter-carriers.

Finding that these complaints of money lost became more frequent, Messrs. Evans and Sons wrote to the General Post-office, in London, on the subject. Accordingly the Post-office authorities sent an inspector down to Liverpool, to make inquiries into the matter. Every plan was tried that could be thought of to detect the thief, who it was believed must be some one in the Post-office, at Liverpool or elsewhere. Traps were laid for them, and letters traced from the moment of their being posted till they were delivered, but in vain. The missing letters still remained a mystery, and still complaints came pouring in that money had been sent by post, but had not come to hand; one customer declaring that he had remitted £60, another £90, and so on.

One day, however, it occurred to Mr. Evans, junior, one of the partners of the firm, that, though the inspector sent from London had done all that could be done in tracing letters from one office to another, it yet remained to trace them from the Liverpool post-office to the counting-house in Lord-street.

So he went out one day, just after Palmer had gone to the post-office, as usual, to fetch the letters, and resolved to keep his eye on the apprentice. Palmer received the correspondence of the day — a good large batch, as generally happened — and walked off with it, little suspecting that a keen eye followed all his movements. Soon after he had left the post-office, he was observed to feel the letters, one by one, as though to ascertain if any of them had enclosures in them. Coming to one more bulky than the rest, he stopped deliberately and opened it. But he was disappointed this time; the letter that he opened had no money in it so cramming it carelessly into his pocket, and having ascertained that there was little prospect of anything of value in the others, he presented himself with the unopened letters in the counting-house of his employer.

The gentleman who had watched him had arrived before him.

"But, Palmer," he exclaimed, when he received the letters, "these are not all that came to day; are they?"

"Certainly, sir," said Palmer boldly.

"Where then," asked Mr. Evans, "is the letter that I saw you open in the street, and put into your pocket?"

Even when charged thus positively, Palmer still held out; boldly denying that he had been guilty of the deed imputed to him. The evidence, however, was too strong against him to admit of doubt. Messrs. Evans and Sons immediately discharged him, and wrote to acquaint his mother with his conduct.

The old lady came over to Liverpool at once, accompanied by the brother of the culprit, and implored the Messrs. Evans to be merciful to him. These gentlemen very properly observed it did not rest with them. It was not they who had been robbed, but their customers, whose money he had stolen. It was with them that she must deal. Mrs. Palmer was accordingly furnished with the addresses of all those who had complained of their remittances not having come to hand, and the indulgent mother went round to them, and made good the defalcations[15] of her son.

Palmer confessed his guilt when there was no further chance of his denying it; and on his expressing extreme penitence, his mother begged that Messrs. Evans would allow him to remain with them until the term of his apprenticeship expired. To this, of course, these gentlemen could not assent. But to prevent the public scandal that would arise from the cancelling of the young man's Indentures, were the reason of it known, they acceded to the mother's solicitations so far as to consent to take another son to finish the apprenticeship. So William Palmer was dismissed, and his brother Thomas, now the clergyman, took his place for the remainder of the term,

---

[15] A more formal word meaning to embezzle. From the medieval Latin *defalcat* for "lopped."

conducting himself during his stay with them in the most exemplary manner.

Even at this early stage of his career, it would seem that William Palmer had contracted the evil habit of gambling, which ultimately led to his ruin; for we understand that, while in the service of Messrs. Evans and Sons, a very large portion of his ill-gotten gains was expended in betting on the Liverpool and Chester races. Another portion — not by any means an inconsiderable one — went in the society of females of the worst character, with whom, unfortunately, Liverpool, like most large seaport towns, abounds.

He managed, however, to conceal these vices from his masters, for he was an out-door apprentice, not residing in the house with them; and, during the whole time that he served as their apprentice, he bore a good character for steadiness and attention to business. How well deserved this character was, his conduct proved.

It is after this, when he is getting on for eighteen, that he has one more chance given him. He is apprenticed to Tylecote, of Haywood.

STAFFORDSHIRE POTTERY SOUVENIR OF WILLIAM PALMER'S HOUSE.

CHAPTER III.

PALMER IS APPRENTICED TO TYLECOTE THE SURGEON — HOW HE BORROWS FIVE POUNDS — THE FOOTMAN AT "THE ABBEY" — SHAM PATIENTS — HOW HE SERVED THE ASSISTANT, AND HOW HE RAN AWAY.

WILLIAM PALMER, AT THE AGE of eighteen, was apprenticed for five years, to Edward T. Tylecote,[1] surgeon, of Haywood, near Rugeley, and while there became notorious for certain bad habits which it will be hardly possible to narrate here; but so far as we may allude to them, (and inasmuch as we think it of very great importance to do so,) we will.

Haywood[2] is a little village, lying between Shoughborough Park and the Ingestre estate; and in this village, immediately opposite to the residence of Mr. Heywood, (Palmer's brother-in-law,) lived Mr. Tylecote — a shrewd, intelligent, but not over prosperous country surgeon, to whom was apprenticed William Palmer — a great strong lad, described to have been as tall, though not so stout, as he is now. The first impression that he made upon everybody around was that he was industrious, kind, and not devoid of application; but it was not very long before circumstances transpired that induced a different opinion.

The readiness with which he would (when called up in the middle of the night) put to the horse and accompany his master, was not thought so favourably of when it was

---

[1] The 1861 census records Edward T. Tylecote as born in 1831 and living in Staffordshire.
[2] There are now two villages, Great Haywood and Little Haywood, that are about a mile apart. The area is known as the place where J.R.R. Tolkien spent 1916 recovering from trench fever, and the landscape might have inspired the look for Middle-Earth. The reference to "Shoughborough Park" is probably another misspelling of the Shugbrough Estate referred to earlier.

discovered that swindling and seduction were two of his weaknesses.

Mrs. Hawkins, a widow woman with nine children, who resided at Gayton, but is now living at Grey Friars, Stafford, was tossed by a bull belonging to Mr. Parker, a farmer of the same place, and severely injured. The poor woman, after being carried home, sent for Mr. Tylecote, her "club doctor;"[3] he being very ill at the time, could not attend; Mr. Parker therefore requested the woman to let him call in another surgeon of the name of Masfen, offering at the same time to pay the fee. The widow Hawkins accepted the proposition, and Masfen attended her, Palmer also being sent over by Tylecote for the purpose of making up any medicines which Masfen might prescribe. It was during the progress of this case that Parker, Palmer, and the widow being together alone —

"I say," said Parker, "what's the amount of Masfen's fee?"

"Two guineas," replied Palmer. Whereupon Parker took out his canvass bag, and, extracting there from the required amount, threw it into the widow's lap. In so doing, he dropped some gold.

"By-the-bye!" asked Palmer, suddenly, "can you change me a five-pound note?"

"Certainly," said the farmer, and gave him five sovereigns. Palmer searched his pockets all over without finding what he appeared to be seeking for; but at length seeming to recollect, "Ah!" he ejaculated, "I remember now; I was in such a hurry to meet Masfen to-day, that, in changing my trowsers I left the note in the pocket; but it is of no consequence, I can send it over by the boy when he brings the medicine." But he did not send it over.

Three months after, Parker writes for the money, threatening to prosecute; Palmer's master hears that some money is owing, scolds Palmer, who excuses himself by saying that he has not been able to spare it; his master advises him to ride over to his mother, and get it from her; he does so the next morning; getting back before breakfast. "Now," said his master, "Go, at once, and pay it."

---

[3] An early form of health insurance, in which people would band together to form a "sick club" that would pay a doctor to treat members as needed.

He went, at once, and did not pay it.

Five weeks afterwards, his master, Tylecote, meeting Parker by accident, hears the particulars.

The money was eventually paid by Mrs. Palmer.

During this period of his career Palmer managed to scrape an acquaintance with a footman at "the Abbey," a picturesque old mansion in Haywood, and, before long, he succeeded in inducing him to take his savings (fifteen pounds) out of the bank, under a promise that, on his (Palmer's) coming of age, he would pay him twenty pounds, and the interest; but the money was only recovered after repeated applications to the mother.

It frequently happened that, after dinner, when Tylecote, tired with his morning's round, and anxious for a little rest, was settling himself for a nap, young Palmer would come into the room, and in the blandest tone suggest that a certain patient at some miles distance should be visited; at the same time offering to go. Almost as a matter of course, his master would give his permission, and tell him which horse to take out of the stable. Palmer having harnessed the horse, would ride "up village" in the direction of the patient; go round by the Abbey, through a croft[4] belonging to the Clifford's Arms Inn; enter by the back way into the Clifford's Arms yard; put up his horse, and go off to a young woman in the village, whom it is believed he had seduced, returning in due time to his master, and even making a false entry of a visit paid to the patient in his master's books.

Tylecote had an assistant, a diminutive young man, rather weakly in frame, but affecting a fashionable exterior. He was received in the "society" of the village, and was a most respectable young man. One day he had occasion to scold Palmer very severely for some shortcoming, and it is curious to notice Palmer's revenge. He could have knocked him down with ease, but that was not Palmer's way. He said nothing, but went upstairs into the assistant's bedroom, opened all his drawers, poured a corrosive acid over all his fine clothes and linen, finishing with a new pair of dress boots (which had just come home in time for a ball at the Clifford's Arms), which

---

[4] An enclosed field used for farming or pasture-land that is attached to a house and worked by the occupant.

unfortunate boots he cut and hacked, in every conceivable way, with a penknife.

Although no other person could have done it, he denied it to the last — with tears and protestations.

Early one morning he asked his master to let him go out for a day's rabbit shooting, and having obtained permission, he started off — not to the rabbit warren, but to Walsall — with the girl whom he was said to have seduced. Nothing was heard of him for some days, until a letter came to a Mr. Lomax, of Stafford, asking for money to redeem Palmer from the inn in Walsall, where he lay in pawn for his bill; but this letter was enclosed to Mr. Tylecote, who, in turn, took it over the way to Mr. Heywood, Palmer's brother-in-law; but neither of them feeling justified in advancing money to him, the letter eventually reached his mother, who sent two of his brothers to fetch him home.

They reached the inn at Walsall, where they found him with his bottle of sherry and port, and his dessert before him, quietly cracking his walnuts in company with the girl. At first he attempted to fight his brothers, but after some conversation a reconciliation took place; the bill was paid, and they prepared to return to Rugeley; but in the inn yard Palmer suddenly disappeared, and did not turn up until the next day, when he entered Stafford in a chaise, and after leaving the girl in the town, started off home to his mother.

The girl with whom Palmer went off to Walsall was Jane Widnall, the illegitimate child of Jane Widnall, married to a man of the name of Vickerstaff.

Vickerstaff was an assistant gardener, he worked in Shoughborough gardens, where he had many privileges in the way of perquisites, working over time, &c, and being a careful, plodding sort of fellow, managed through a course of years to save £100.

When Palmer became acquainted with Jane Widnall, his master, Mr. Tylecote, was not in the habit of going to church. Palmer, however, used to go, but invariably bribed a village lad to call him out (as if from his master) about a half an hour after the service commenced; he then went to the girl, who was alone, her father and mother being safe in church; and this, we believe, was carried on for some time.

When Vickerstaff and his wife discovered them, there is no doubt but that Palmer promised to marry the girl; and it was on the strength of this promise that Palmer, hearing from Jane Widnall of her father's savings, managed to borrow of Vickerstaff his £100, the whole of which sum was squandered either in paying his "debts of honour" at Haywood, or in dissipation at Walsall, where many a drunken game is remembered.

This girl, after Palmer deserted her, met with another man, whom she is said to have married; they went out together to Australia, where it seems she died.

CHAPTER IV.

PALMER IS WALKING PUPIL AT THE STAFFORD INFIRMARY — DEATH OF ABLEY AT THE LAMB AND FLAG — PALMER GOES TO LONDON — PASSES HIS EXAMINATION.

MRS. PALMER TRIED VERY HARD to get her son William back to Tylecote's; he would have gone, but the surgeon refused to take him again; and it was now only after a great deal of trouble, and because he did not want to hinder his advancement in life, that Mr. Tylecote consented to procure him admission into the Stafford Infirmary as a walking pupil, and give him a certificate at the end of his term.

A curious circumstance happened at this time, which people now regard as of more importance than, possibly, the facts warrant. Palmer, it seems, had not been long at the Infirmary before his interference with the dispensing of medicines (of what nature the interference was we have failed to discover,) was so strongly objected to by the medical officers, that a rule was expressly passed forbidding pupils to have anything to do with the dispensing of medicines. The medicines are now dispensed by the pupils, there being no paid officer for that purpose; but at that time there was undoubtedly a rule passed, which as far as we can learn, was for the purpose of keeping Palmer out of the Dispensary.

It is somewhat singular, that, immediately after Palmer left the Infirmary, a gentleman (now in India) of the name of William Palmer, was elected to the office of dispenser.

Palmer does not seem to have been either liked or respected at Stafford. It is generally said that he was "advised" to leave the place.

It was at this period of Palmer's life that he was concerned in what people at the time considered to be a medical student's lark, but which was accompanied by such serious results, that Palmer had a narrow escape of proceedings being taken against him — we allude to the death of a man named Abley.

Concerning this there are two accounts, and we give them both, because, although the first mentioned is not the most reliable, it is the most generally received.

One day in the spring of 1816, Palmer invited Abley to the Lamb and Flag,[1] and there gave him brandy and water; ordering the landlady to give him eight pennyworth each time instead of four pennyworth, as the man supposed. He became very intoxicated, and refused to drink any more; but, Palmer offering him half a sovereign to drink another, he tossed it off — vomited directly — staggered out, and died in the stable. At the inquest there was a great deal of talk about Palmer and Abley's wife, which was undoubtedly untrue.

The other and most reliable account is, that a bet was made between William Palmer and another Rugeley man that Abley would drink off two tumblers of brandy. He did it; went out into the stable (it was a cold day) and vomited continually, until they, finding him there and so ill, brought him in, and put him to bed — but it was too late, and he died.

Abley was a thin, pale man, in indifferent health. A *post mortem* examination was made by Mr. Masfen, but the verdict which was found at the inquest, "Died from natural causes," was the only one which, with justice, could have been recorded.

It is a singular fact that the foreman of the jury was strongly opposed to this verdict at the time, and that he has ever since been constantly in the habit of expressing his suspicions that Abley was unfairly dealt with. For years past he has not scrupled to state openly that he thought Palmer had poisoned him — a circumstance on which he prides himself not a little at the present time.

---

[1] This pub in Little Haywood, Staffordshire, still exists. It is one of two around which the social life of the village is centered. The lamb refers to the Lamb of God, the title for Jesus that appears in the Gospel of John ("Behold the Lamb of God who takes away the sin of the world."). The lamb is usually depicted holding a white banner with a red cross on it that resembles the cross of St. George, the patron saint of England.

CHAPTER V.

PALMER COMES TO LONDON — HIS MEDICAL "GRINDER" — PALMER A STUDENT OF ST. BARTHOLOMEW'S — HIS EXTRAVAGANT MODE OF LIFE.

IN THE LATTER PART OF the year 1846, Palmer came to London to complete his medical studies under the direction of Dr. Stegall, a gentleman well known in the profession, with the view of passing his examination. At the time Palmer placed himself under the tuition of the doctor, he was, as may be supposed, very backward in his medical knowledge, a fact of which he was himself perfectly sensible; and he promised to pay the doctor, who was to act as what is familiarly styled his "grinder," [1] the sum of fifty guineas, if he enabled him to pass his examination and escape being plucked.[2] Mrs. Palmer also promised an additional ten guineas, as did also his friend Mr. Jerry Smith.

Dr. Stegall worked hard with his pupil; but Palmer, true to his usual character, never paid him the promised fee, although he passed his examination with credit, and was not plucked as has been reported. Of the many stories told of him, one goes so far as to say that he only got his Diploma by paying somebody to personate him. This, however, is not true. Mr. Jerry Smith declined to pay the ten guineas he had promised; but an action which was brought for the amount went against him. Jerry Smith stated that he had seen Mrs. Palmer pay into the hands of her son the ten guineas she had promised to Dr. Stegall. It is, however, almost needless to say, that it never reached the person for whom it was intended.

Palmer, during this period of his life, did not reside with Dr. Stegall, excepting for a few days. His habits were

---

[1] Someone who helps a student study for an examination. Also called a crammer.
[2] Slang for failing to pass an examination for a degree.

extravagant and irregular in the extreme. He was constantly giving parties, at which large quantities of champagne were consumed. His associates, even at this time, were sporting men, and Palmer was very often the victim of their duplicity. His studies were not pursued with any degree of pleasure on his part; his whole time was taken up with horses and racing matters; which were his favourite topics of conversation. During the time he was in London, Jerry Smith was frequently with him; indeed, they were inseparable companions.

Dr. Stegall, who is an accomplished artist, painted two portraits of Palmer: one was presented to his dear Annie, the lady he was then courting, and who afterwards unfortunately became his wife; the other remains in the possession of Dr. Stegall, and an admirable portrait it is.[3] Since Palmer has been in custody, charged with the Rugeley murder, he has written to Dr. Stegall, requesting that he would let his brother George have this portrait; but as the doctor was never paid for it, and had moreover lost a large sum of money by Palmer, we presume he saw no reason for complying with this request.

It was, of course, necessary, that Palmer should attend lectures at one of the great London hospitals, and Bartholomew's[4] was the one at which he entered himself a student. He lodged with a Mr. Ayres, in Bartholomew-close, and it was during his residence here that he commenced that course of reckless extravagance which first led him into pecuniary difficulties.

The medical student of the present day is still "sad dog"[5] enough, but he was even more so at the time of which we speak. We cannot tell what there is in the study of medicine that produces such results, but we believe that it is a well-

---

[3] Sadly, this portrait has been lost. There is a portrait drawn by Joseph Simpson (1879-1939) taken from Palmer's death-mask and a contemporary sketch.

[4] One of the oldest hospitals in Great Britain, founded in 1123. More popularly known as Barts, it began teaching students officially in 1843. Its most famous fictional alumnus is Dr. John H. Watson, who also met Sherlock Holmes in the chemical laboratory at Barts.

[5] A term of abuse to describe a debauched, wicked fellow. In one magazine, he is defined as "he who loves pleasant things, but wrong ones, and doesn't care if they are wrong, if they seem to him pleasant. Sad-dogs often come to bad ends."

known fact that the majority of medical students have generally, if not always, been, *par excellence*, "fast men." Of course there are exceptions to the rule, as to every other. We have ourselves known one or two most honourable exceptions — men who have taken up the healing art as a profession, and have gone conscientiously to work to learn whatever could be learned during their studentship.[6]

Some few years since, the *summum bonum*[7] of human happiness to the medical student's mind seemed to consist in strolling down the Haymarket or Regent-street, clad in the roughest of all overcoats, smoking the strongest of cigars, and peering under the bonnet of every female passer-by, delighted if he could succeed in staring out of countenance some poor little dressmaker or milliner wending her way homewards all alone, and wearied with the long hours of labour. This he would call a "lark."

Great was he at the bars of public-houses, and copious were his draughts of half-and-half,[8] which he would always take, as he expressed it, "in its native pewter." [9] Boisterous was

---

[6] The archetype for the medical student of the time can be found in this episode from Dickens' *The Pickwick Papers,* when Ben Allen and Bob Sawyer use medical equipment to mix their rum-punch: "After dinner, Mr. Bob Sawyer ordered in the largest mortar in the shop, and proceeded to brew a reeking jorum of rum-punch therein, stirring up and amalgamating the materials with a pestle in a very creditable and apothecary-like manner. Mr. Sawyer, being a bachelor, had only one tumbler in the house, which was assigned to Mr. Winkle as a compliment to the visitor, Mr. Ben Allen being accommodated with a funnel with a cork in the narrow end, and Bob Sawyer contented himself with one of those wide-lipped crystal vessels inscribed with a variety of cabalistic characters, in which chemists are wont to measure out their liquid drugs in compounding prescriptions. These preliminaries adjusted, the punch was tasted, and pronounced excellent; and it having been arranged that Bob Sawyer and Ben Allen should be considered at liberty to fill twice to Mr. Winkle's once, they started fair, with great satisfaction and good-fellowship."

[7] Latin for "the highest good." In Greek philosophy, it is used to define the most worthy purpose a human can pursue.

[8] A drink that combines ale, beer and "two-penny," a "small beer" that contains very little alcohol.

[9] Before bottles and cans were mass-produced, beer was served in pubs

his merriment, too, later in the evening (civilized people call it night), when all the shops were shut up, and he would walk along with three or four companions, all abreast and arm-in-arm, taking up the entire width of pavement, and shouting Lullaliety!" [10] whatever that may have meant, in a voice that would not only wake the slumbering echoes, but the slumbering householders as well, and make them wonder what on earth they paid police-rates for.

Then he was very clever at the extremely fashionable and highly exhilarating amusement of wrenching knockers off street doors (a sport now quite gone out, like cock-fighting and other intellectual pastimes). He would exhibit the trophies of his prowess in this line — which, by-the-bye, the law might look upon as petty larceny — but what cared he for the law? — and would boast of them to his friends, (he called them "chums"), much as a savage might exult over the number of scalps that he had taken from a hostile tribe.

The style of living of those students who had not, like Palmer, an indulgent parent to draw upon, was every bit as singular as their amusements. With them beer was their morning beverage. Tea, coffee, and such like, were scorned as "slops." [11] The breakfast usually consisted of whatever happened to be in the cupboard; cold meat, or bread and cheese, or butter all came alike, provided there was beer to wash it down; or, in default of that, cold gin-and-water. Their appetites were, for the most part, vigorous; and no amount of raking[12] over-night appeared to weaken them; nor would some

---

and ale houses in lidded pewter cups. Pewter is a metal alloy consisting of tin and bits of copper and antimony to harden the metal, and sometimes silver to make it shine, or lead as a cheap filler. It was a mainstay of plates, dishes, cups, steins, and other dinnerware from medieval times until the early 19th century, when ceramics and metals were introduced. Since antique pewter could contain lead, it should never be used for serving food.

[10] A yodel-like cry. A couplet in the burlesque play *The Rise and Fall of Richard III* (1868) shows how to pronounce it: "They're simple folks of scrupulous sobriety, / They live on la la la, and lullaliety."

[11] Any weak or watered-down beverage, such as tea or small beer. Also called swish-swash.

[12] Gardening is a spectator sport in Britain, but not in this case. Raking meant to live a dissolute life, carousing, gambling, drinking,

mouldering human bone (on which the student had been operating, or pretending to do so), lying in the cupboard close beside the loaf, take from the relish with which he attacked his breakfast.

Yet would he get the eating business over in as little time as possible, that he might have his pipe, which he invariably smoked the moment he had finished with the solid portions of his morning meal, and long before the liquids were put by.

He seldom breakfasted alone though. He preferred to drop in on some "chum," or have some "chums" drop in on him, that they might talk over the last night's "larks," whilst they were breakfasting. And though at these gatherings, knives and forks, plates and glasses, might run short, it did not in the least interfere with the meal. The cold meat could be cut with pocket-knives, and eaten in the fingers; the gin-and-water drunk from pickle-jars or gallipots,[13] or even, at a pinch, from the

---

and seducing. They were known as blackguards (pronounced *blaggards*), rakes, or rakehells.

[13] A small pot made of glazed earthenware used by pharmacists to hold medicines or ointments.

ornamental vases on the chimney-piece. The beer was, of course, in the pewter, so with that there could be no sort of difficulty.

Dinner, of this class of student, when he dined at all, was generally taken at a cheap eating house (he called it a "slap-bang" [14]); where he was always on most friendly terms with the waiters — especially the female waiters, whom he invariably called "my dear," and winked at.

Of course he never dreamt of tea. That was a meal no man on town could ever condescend to take. He liked his supper, but it was taken irregularly, and varied according to his pecuniary resources at the moment.

Palmer, however, was not a student of this genus. *He* ate and drank of the best, spent his days and nights in riotous living, and gave but little thought to those severe studies which he was required to surmount to become fitted for his profession.

He would frequently commence the day with the luxury of a champagne breakfast, given for no earthly reason whatever, to some party of fellow students, who, in return for his misjudged prodigality, did him the honour of speaking of him among themselves as stupidly good-natured. Few men would feel an inclination for study after so respectable an orgie, even as the above; consequently the remainder of the day was run through in going the rounds to certain betting-houses, at which William Palmer was better known than in the Lecture Theatre of St. Bartholomew's Hospital, or in an adventure in the pursuit of female beauties of doubtful reputation.

Evening would at length draw on, and then the theatre would perhaps furnish its hour or two of amusement. Then would come the supper at the night-house at some adjacent oyster-shop, where ruddy lobsters and thick-shelled crabs lie in luxuriant profusion over the slabs of slate in the window; where pickled salmon hides in shady groves of fennel; where stout oyster-tubs balance themselves on each other against the

---

[14] Called because money is slapped on the table when the plate of food is banged on the table. It appears in Charles Dickens' *Sketches by "Boz"* (1836): "They lived in the same street, walked to town every morning at the same hour, dined at the same slap-bang every day, and revelled in each other's company every night."

wall, and Finnon haddocks,[15] truly Scotchlike in their hardness and crispness, are ranged in tempting layers; where the gilt placard hanging from the gas jet, invited the passer-by to partake of chops, kidneys or steaks. At the counter are ruffling gallants cooling their parched throats with natives,[16] and swearing at the flannel-aproned attendants; in the inner rooms there are to be seen many rustling silks and satins, many feathers, much ochre and bismuth,[17] technically termed "slap;"

---

[15] Cold-smoked haddock from Scotland. Because it was lightly smoked, it was best eaten within three days. With the introduction of mail coaches cutting transportation time, it became possible for haddocks to be shipped to London where it became a popular delicacy.

[16] Slang for illegally distilled whiskey, possibly from the phrase "native brew."

[17] Minerals used in cosmetics. Ochre came in two colors: yellow to lighten the skin or red to rouge the lips and cheeks. Bismuth lightened the skin, but when exposed to heat, it would turn black. The *Dublin Penny Journal* in 1834 recounted the story of "a lady of fashion, who had incautiously seated herself too near the fire at a quadrille table, that her countenance changed on a sudden from a delicate white to a dark tawny, as though by magic. The surprise and confusion of the whole party had such an effect on the disfigured fair one, that she was actually dying with apprehension; when the physician dispelled their fears, by informing his patient that nothing more was necessary for her than to abstain from the use of mineral

much male mirth, and alas! forced female gaiety. This was the sort of company that William Palmer delighted in. Here he found men who were well-up in the slang of the racing fraternity. Men whom he regularly met on the race-courses, in the neighbourhood of London — flashy in dress — shallow in intellect — and depraved in morals. Or, perhaps, Palmer and his companions would wend their way down Coventry-street and across St. Martin's-lane, entering for a few minutes through the open door of a public-house, where the ex-champion of England,[18] that enormous giant might be seen standing behind his bar, confronted by fighting men, with flattened noses and contused eyes; dog-fanciers, ratting-match concoctors, and the scum of sporting life generally.

They would then turn up quiet Little New-street, even at this hour blocked up by the carts opposite the cheesemonger's; along King-street, past the Garrick Club,[19] through the illumined windows of which late diners might yet be seen congregated round the mahogany; down a steep flight of steps, and into the supper-room at Evans's.[20]

---

cosmetics, and trust in future to those charms which nature had bestowed on her."

[18] Readers then would have recognized Ben Caunt (1815-1861), who at 6 feet 2 inches stood out at a time when a man's average height was 5 feet 5 inches (he also weighed 260 pounds). His stature inspired the nickname "Big Ben" which was given to the Palace of Westminster's clock tower. He retired in 1845 and became landlord of The Coach and Horses pub at St. Martin's Lane.

[19] Named for actor and producer David Garrick (1717-1779) whose realistic acting style changed the theatre and, in the words of his friend Samuel Johnson, "made his profession respectable." As manager of the Drury Lane theatre for 29 years, he changed the way plays were staged and the way audiences acted. His funeral was held in Westminster Abbey, and he was laid to rest in Poets' Corner. The Garrick Club was founded in 1831 on King Street in Covent Garden. In 1864, it was moved around the corner to Garrick Street, where it can be found today.

[20] A forerunner of the music hall, Evans' Music-and-Supper Rooms opened in the early 1840s by comedian W.H. Evans in the former dining room of the Grand Hotel. In 1842, it was taken over by one of the entertainers, John Paddy Green, who added a music hall to the back of the house. A variety of entertainment was offered, including

Far-famed as this supper-room has been for many years, it was destined for its present proprietor to raise it to the reputation it now enjoys — that of being the most excellent place of the kind in the metropolis. Visit it, reader, and judge for yourself.

In the "cafe" part of the establishment, there sit the guests who come simply to get their supper and to enjoy each other's conversation; for in the large hall you are expected, and very properly too, to give your whole attention to the viands and the singing. The walls of the "cafe" are hung round, as you will perceive, with portraits of the most famous theatrical personages of ancient and modern times. The large hall is thronged: there are perhaps six or seven hundred persons seated round the various tables; at the upper end is a platform on which is stationed a grand piano, and on this platform stand the singers. Immediately below the platform is stationed the chairman; you hear his hammer now rapping on the table, while he loudly calls for "Attention to the music from *Macbeth*, No. 63 in the books, gentlemen, if you please." On to the platform come some dozen singers, half of whom are boys, with fresh singing voices, and never did you hear Locke's beautiful melodies[21] more sweetly executed. The most decorous silence reigns throughout the room, broken only at the end by a tumultuous clapping of hands and knocking on the tables. Here, moving quietly through the room, courteously inquiring at every table whether his guests are satisfied, and ever and anon offering his silver snuff-box, is the proprietor of the establishment; then, coming round with a goodly burden of cigars is the old German *siffleur*,[22] who must be associated, O,

---

choirs singing madrigals and glees and performances by comic singers. Admission was for men only.

[21] Matthew Locke (c.1621-1677) composed the music for *Macbeth* (1673), a precursor to opera that combined the play with singing and dancing.

[22] The German word for whistler. In the memoirs of comic writer and longtime *Punch* contributor F. C. Burnand (1836-1917), he recalled the *siffleur* at Evan's: "One Herr von Jöel, 'retained on the establishment on account of his long services' (Heaven knows what they were!), who, in a shabby alpaca coat, very dingy shirt collar and wristbands, used to hand round cigars in a tumbler, and held himself

reader! with your earliest reminiscences of town-life.

At the various tables, you will see some of the principal notabilities of London. Take the party nearest to us. The short, bald-headed man, with the clear blue eye and sharp features, is one of the cleverest comedians in London; that huge massive head and huge beard belong to a man whose name will ever be associated with mountain ascents,[23] strict perseverance, and extraordinary success, while the square-shouldered, broad-built gentleman, with hair fast turning grey, is one of the best antiquarians and finest judges of good living the world can boast. At the next table is seated a party of swells, to whom the gin-and-water, or stout of ordinary life is pollution; they are drinking champagne up as befits such able creatures, and are regarded with intense astonishment and veneration by their neighbours, sometimes provincials from the neighbourhood of Wolverhampton,[24] who are in the greatest state of bewilderment at all they see passing round them. More rapping of the hammer; the great comic singer is about to come forth, but we cannot wait for him.

Evans's, in Palmer's student days, through making less pretensions to the magnificent, was every bit as well frequented as now, and boasted much the same style of entertainment. Palmer and his companions would, doubtless, come to hear the comic song, and, in the small hours of the morning, would be found wending their ways homewards with certain female companions of doubtful reputation.

Strange to say, with nights spent like these, Palmer was, nevertheless, invariably a very early riser. He was particularly nice about his dress, which was neat rather than showy in style. He was quite the gentleman, both in manners and in conversation, when he came in contact with others than his ordinary familiars. His rooms were fitted up in approved medical style; the walls were covered with anatomical

---

always in readiness to take a turn on the stage with his imitations of birds, which he had brought to considerable perfection."

[23] Possibly a reference to William Mathews (1828-1901) who co-founded the Alpine Club, the world's first, in 1857. It could also be Francis Fox Tuckett (1834-1913), or E.S. Kennedy (1817-1898), both of whom sported impressive facial hair.

[24] A city in the West Midlands area of Staffordshire.

preparations and models. It is said that he purchased more of these than any other student, and that the library of medical and other works which he possessed, was not matched by any of his acquaintance. It is said by those who were at Bartholomew's during Palmer's time that he must have spent at least £2,000 while he was in professional parlance "walking"[25] the hospital.

A gentleman who has been connected with the hospital for nearly thirty years, and who well remembers Palmer as a student, gives him the following character:— He says that he was one of the most extravagant fellows he ever knew. The parties at the hospital say that he would give them wine in a tumbler whenever they called on him. Those among his equals who were on friendly terms with him, and perhaps showed him some slight kindness, he would recompense with a most-liberal return, in the shape of hampers of game; bundles of cigars, or bottles of wine. Whether his wine-merchant's and his poulterer's bills were, like his grinder's bill, never paid, we have no means of ascertaining.

It is, moreover, recorded of him, that to the poor patients in the hospital he was very kind; he would frequently get up subscriptions[26] for them, when they were on the point of leaving the hospital.

In his anatomical studies he was very backward. Just before going up to the college for examination, he worked night and day at dissecting subjects. On one occasion, when he had been drinking rather freely, and was in a state of some excitement (although not intoxicated) he became so nervous while at work that he went to one of the porters and asked him to come and keep him company; saying, that he did not feel quite comfortable over such work alone. "It is very stupid," he said, "but one cannot always control one's thoughts."

---

[25] The practice of students walking through the wards and observing how a senior physician treated patients. Medical students still do this today; there's even an amusing manual that can help them become more aware of what they can learn when "walking the wards" (*101 Things to Do with Spare Moments on the Ward*, London: Wiley, 2012).

[26] Collect money to give to the patient. Also commonly known in British offices (such as when soliciting funds to buy a parting gift for a co-worker) as "a whip-around."

One could not desire a better proof of the progress which Palmer had made in his career of vice and profligacy since his sojourn in the metropolis, than is furnished by the following little fact. It seems that Palmer was very partial to one of the hospital officials, and was very anxious to reside with him. He had both female servants and daughters, and although he liked Palmer well enough in most respects, he felt that he was such a reprobates in the matter of female virtue, that it would be dangerous to admit him within his doors!

CHAPTER VI.

COLONEL BROOKES AND MRS. THORNTON. — "GOOD ANNIE BROOKES."

WE NOW COME UPON A Family of Suicides.

Of five brothers who successively and by similar means died by their own hands, Colonel Brookes was the last, and it is of him we are about to speak.

A rather reserved and quiet man, gentle in his manners, considerate, liberal, and wealthy, fond of little children, with few associates, and without a wife, he comes to Stafford from India with a debilitated constitution, bringing with him but few introductions; his reserved habit makes him but few friends, and with nothing to boast of personally but a strong animalism,[1] he settles down in a house in what is called the "Front Street," with a servant maid of the name of Ann Thornton.

Almost his only friends at that time were old Mr. Wright, of Stafford, Edward Knight, M.D., Thomas Davis Weaver, solicitor, and Charles Dawson, Esq., a wealthy druggist, and, as may be supposed, all men with habits totally distinct from those of the quiet, old Indian epicure.[2]

Now, though a gentle-minded elderly man may allow himself to be merely tolerated by his friends, he would rather be devotedly loved by a woman. The Colonel's friends did

---

[1] Reduced to base cravings either through poverty or moral laxity such as those found in ancient Greece and Rome. "If you want to make human animals," the *Western Literary Magazine* warned in 1851, "impoverish the race. There is no surer way to develop animalism. Men will prize that of which they are deprived. A hungry man will ever over eat himself. A man crushed with want will so feel the pressure, that the cravings of the body will exclude all the nobler aspirations of the soul."

[2] A person devoted to sensual pleasures, especially food and wine. From Epicurus (341-270 BC), the Greek philosopher who advocated living a self-sufficient life in peace and ease.

"merely tolerate" him. The housemaid, Ann, professed affection. He rewarded her devotion by making her his mistress; and his friends, although they still held by him, refused to receive him in society.

In a few months after, defying the good advice of his friends and relations, he removed from the "Front Street" to a large house (one of nine that belonged to him) behind St. Mary's church. In this house it was that Ann Thornton (properly known as Mrs. Thornton) gained a complete ascendancy over the old Colonel. He had originally loved her, he now feared her — she had professed affection only that she might tyrannise over him. He had thought her a lovely kind-hearted young girl, and had only refrained from marrying her because of her utter ignorance and want of position; she had soon ceased to be beautiful, and nothing remained of her former self but her ignorance — which was gross, savage, and complete.

The beautiful dream of Ann Thornton, the pretty servant maid, had vanished; and Mrs. Thornton, tall, thin and angular — a drunkard and foul-mouthed, loose in her habits, and not even true to her old Colonel — was all that remained.

It is said that the Colonel's eyes were first opened by finding her dead drunk in bed, shortly before they moved from the "Front Street." Mrs. Thornton, in addition to her drunken habits, was given to wild fits of ungovernable passion. The old Colonel, evidently a man of feeble mind, though strong appetites, would flee from her anger to a neighbouring tavern, and there seek refuge till the storm had blown over. Not unfrequently, however, she would track him to his retreat, and drag him home in ignominious triumph. Indeed, as it is naively remarked in the neighbourhood, "he might as well have been married."

This much is certain, that the poor old Colonel was harassed out of his life by Mrs. Thornton, who was not only an habitual drunkard, and a notoriously bad woman, but was in the habit of chasing him round the room with a knife, swearing she would kill him. So frequent, indeed, were these outbursts, that when at last he was found dead, if it had not been for the Colonel's statements made a day before he committed suicide, she would undoubtedly have been suspected.

It appears, that one afternoon he called upon Mr. Wright, and in the course of conversation told him an anecdote of the Captain of a vessel coming from India, who, being a Freemason, and having inadvertently divulged some of the secrets of his order, was so distressed in mind as to shoot himself in his cabin.

"When he shot himself," said Colonel Brookes, "he was in his dressing gown, his slippers, and his cap."

The next day the Colonel also shot himself, and he was discovered in his dressing gown, his slippers and his cap.

Now, although the Colonel and his mistress were in the habit of living so retired, and although they were not received in society at Stafford, it was not so with their daughter.

Annie Brookes, born in 1827, soon after they moved from the Front Street, was the most engaging little child that can be imagined.

A gentleman who knew her very intimately has given us

the following particulars:—

He informs us that he knew her about twenty years ago, when she was quite a child; that she was proverbial for her simplicity, her kindness, and engaging manners. He tells us that she was the general favourite of the town, and that, as she grew in years, her virtues kept pace. Beloved by all who knew her, she acquired the title of "the Good Annie Brookes." She had not an enemy in all the world.

Over the death-beds of Mr. Charles Dawson's two wives she gave every one an opportunity of testing her intrinsic kindness of heart, and her vigilance not only by day, but by night, was, considering her age, something more than surprising; at all hours she was present not only to administer medicine, and to perform the duty of a nurse, but to give spiritual consolation in the absence of the clergyman.

It was the Rev. Mr. ———, of Stafford, who told her that she occupied the place of three — "the clergyman, the doctor, and the nurse."

As a girl, she was very cheerful and fond of company; she was partial to concerts and balls, and was altogether, a universal favourite.

When Colonel Brookes shot himself in 1834, he had already, by a will dated July 27, 1833, bequeathed the interest of some thirty or forty thousand rupees[3] to his illegitimate daughter, and had also bequeathed to Mrs. Thornton the nine houses in St. Mary's churchyard; but, by a flaw in the will, the property was thrown into Chancery, and Annie Brookes became a ward in Chancery,[4] under the guardianship of

---

[3] The name for India's currency. Comparing the value of money then to now is a tricky business. No answer can be considered authoritative, because values for currency and goods fluctuate wildly. In 1842, the *Times* reported that a rupee shifted in value between 1 shilling, 11 pence and 2 shillings, 2½ pence. Using 1 rupee = 2 shillings, 40,000 rupees equal 80,000 shillings or £4,000, enough for a comfortable life.

[4] The Court of Chancery oversaw equity cases including trusts, land law, estates, and the guardianship of infants. It followed a set of guidelines intended to sidestep the inequity of the common law, but it became so riddled with inefficiencies and corruption — as satirized by Charles Dickens in *Bleak House* (1852) — that several reforms were

Charles Dawson, druggist, of Stafford, and Edward Knight, Esq., M.D., also of Stafford; these gentlemen being the same guardians as were appointed under the will of Colonel Brookes.

They sent her to school at Miss Bond's, at Haywood; and from the fact of Palmer being with Tylecote at the time, and Tylecote being a cousin of Dr. Knight's, it has been rumoured that it was here that William Palmer was introduced to Annie Brookes. But we can venture to say that this is not true. Palmer was introduced to her at Abbot's Bromley (on the Bagot estate), the country residence of Charles Dawson, the wealthy druggist; and; indeed, it is said that T.D. Weaver, Esq., solicitor, of Stafford, was the "go-between."

A conversation is narrated as passing between Weaver and Palmer on the subject. "Do you want a wife?" says Weaver, "for if you do, I can introduce you to a very pretty little girl, who has got a very comfortable fortune." Palmer said it was the very thing he should like; and the introduction took place. Annie Brookes was then eighteen.

attempted before the court was dissolved in 1875.

CHAPTER VII.

PALMER'S COURTSHIP AT ABBOT'S BROMLEY. —

SOME LOVE-LETTERS.

BBOT'S BROMLEY,[1] THE COUNTRY RESIDENCE of Charles Dawson, Esq., to which Annie Brookes was removed when she left Miss Bond's school, is one of the prettiest residences in Staffordshire; it is surrounded by the most lovely and romantic scenery that can well be imagined.

Adjacent to it is Bagot's Park, famous for the largest oaks in the world; and it is within walking distance of Cannock Chase,[2] with its herbage of a thousand tints — of Shoughborough Park, with its beautiful ferns; and it commands a view of Colwich Nunnery,[3] with the river Trent and its magnificent swans.

We wondered, as we drove past all this variety of landscape, amid the bounties of nature which are here so widely spread, whether William Palmer had ever noticed (between the residences of Thomas Salt, the banker, and John Twigg, the millionaire farmer), a place called "Weeping Cross,"[4] where criminals used in times gone by to be executed — whether he had ever pictured to himself the well-tended estate of Thomas Salt, stretching far away, a wild, unreclaimed common, with the old Roman Cross before which the Staffordshire Catholics had knelt, and on to which the Staffordshire clowns had climbed, to see a fellow creature hanged.

---

[1] A village in Staffordshire about 6 miles northeast of Rugeley.
[2] A highly scenic area of countryside in Staffordshire consisting of woods, coniferous plantations, open heath, and the remains of early industries such as coal mining.
[3] Located halfway between Rugeley and Stafford to the northwest, Saint Mary's Abbey in Colwich was founded in 1836 by a group of Benedictine Roman Catholic nuns expelled from France. It is still in use today.
[4] An estate on the east side of Stafford.

Anne Thornton is reported to have been "painfully sensible of her own false position as an illegitimate child, and it is said that she was habituated to look upon herself as an outcast — a being of an inferior order — one who should be deeply grateful to any man who would bestow his name upon a creature unrecognised by the laws, and tainted from her birth. Her first love was unpropitious.

But the fountains of that great deep, a woman's heart, had been broken up. The ark of her existence now drifted to and fro, recklessness at the helm, and hope in the hold, until the waters of disappointment decreased, and the keel grated on the strand. Her mountain of Ararat was destined to be William Palmer." [5]

---

[5] This particularly beautiful description was cribbed from a story in the *Exeter Flying Post*, Jan. 31, 1856.

Palmer is spoken of as displaying, at this period, peculiarly fascinating manners when in the society of women. This is not at all unlikely; for he appears to be one of those individuals who make up for the want of brilliant parts by the assumption of a certain superficial amiability, which causes them to be regarded as universal favourites by their own, as well as by the opposite sex.

It was at Abbot's Bromley, and among the oaks at Bagot's Park, that the plausible, soft-spoken William Palmer, fresh from the embraces of one of his many victims round about Haywood, spoke to the unsophisticated girl in the accents of love; it was here that vows of constancy were sworn; and it was here that Mr. Dawson discovered the lovers, and forbade William Palmer to enter his house.

It is to be supposed that Dawson cautioned his ward, and, in so far as he could, exposed the man who sought her only for her money; for she rejected him about that time (the latter part of 1845); and it only explains the art and dissimulation which he knew so well how to practise, when we narrate that he repeated his offer with such effect as to be this time accepted; and Annie Brookes, notwithstanding the strong and continued opposition of her guardians, became (by an order of the Court of Chancery in 1847), his wife.

During these so-called halcyon days of love, innumerable letters, of course, passed between them. We have been so fortunate as to procure three unpublished specimens, which we here lay before the reader.

The two letters subjoined were written to Palmer by his intended bride — the first has no date, and we are unable to suggest one by internal evidence. We may, however, state, that the "Bath Post" on which it is written, bears the year 1845.

"TUESDAY.

"MY OWN DEAR WILLIAM,

"Why did you sulk when you bade me good-bye in the park this morning. Mr. D. is always very kind to me, and I should ill requite his goodness by acting directly contrary to his wishes. Come, put on one of your best smiles, and write me a real sunshiny note,

for you have made me very unhappy. I shall expect a letter on Thursday. — Ever yours, dearest,

"ANNIE BROOKES."

The next letter bears both date and address:—

"ABBOT'S BROMLEY, SEPTEMBER 13, 1846. — 9. A.M.

DEAREST WILLIAM,

"I think it was your turn to write, and I fancy that if you will only try and recollect, you will think so too. But never mind, although I have not written, you know quite well that I am *always* thinking of you.

"Mr. Dawson went to London on Monday last, and yesterday Miss Salt came over to see us. We gathered ferns together. I hope you will continue your botanical studies, and allow me the opportunity of puzzling you. I have two secrets to tell you, but these I must reserve for Saturday. I don't mind telling you that I think it is your friend M— who is trying to prejudice Dr. Knight. Miss Salt says she knows it is that very crabbed gentleman, whom, of course, you will now love dearer than ever.

"I have got a present for you, but as it is intended as a surprise, I must not spoil it by telling you what it is. Suppose instead that I tell you something you will not care to hear half so well, namely, that I am ever, my very dearest William, your affectionate,

"ANNIE."

The next letter is from Palmer. It has no year affixed to the date; we believe it, however, to have been written in 1847, as the "other four months" spoken of, apparently relates to their anticipated marriage. The "yard" is the name given to old Mrs. Palmer's place:—

"RUGELEY, MAY 16.

"MY DEAR LITTLE ANNIE,

"It was not the rain that prevented me from joining you at Stafford, as you wished. I sprained my foot, and it was so painful that I could not keep it on the ground. I slid off the pathway as I was turning the corner from the "yard," past Bonney's. Now you know the reason, I am sure you will forgive me.

"Oh, Annie! you cannot tell how dull I have found the last few days; I sit and think over my miserable bachelor life, and feel so dull and lonesome, I really cannot explain. I resolved, yesterday, to write again to Mr. D—, but you forbid me doing this, so I must wait the other four months. My dear Annie; I cannot tell you how much I love you, and how I long to call you mine for ever.

"Yours, most affectionately,

"W. P.

"Did Dr. Knight get the game I sent; did he mention

anything about it?"

It must have been rather above a year before his marriage that the letter (which Serjeant Shee read to the jury in his defence, and a copy of which was found in the volume on poisons that formed his favourite book of study) was written by Palmer to his wife. This letter we venture to subjoin:—

> "MY DEAREST ANNIE, — I snatch a moment from my studies to write to your dear, dear, little self. I need scarcely say that the principal inducement I have to work is the desire of getting my studies finished so as to be able to press your dear little form in my arms.
> "With best, best love, believe me, dearest
> Annie, your own,
> "WILLIAM."

It is, perhaps, as well that we should understand Palmer's precise position at the time of his marriage. He had, after the finish of his education at Rugeley, turned out very badly — he had been embezzler, swindler, and seducer by turns. We heard an old man at Haywood count upon his fingers as many as fourteen girls whom Palmer had got in the family-way. He had, by a foolish freak, been concerned in the death of Abley. An illegitimate child, which a woman in Haywood had by him, died suddenly; and he is reported to have been suspected of foul play. He had been to London and led a very indifferent life, and had only just escaped being plucked. He had at last obtained his diploma, and was, at the time of which we now speak, William Palmer, Esq., surgeon, of Rugeley.

Do not forget that, through all this, he was neither addicted to drinking or swearing; but a cool, cautious, sober young rascal.

Perhaps, like many another rake held captive for a while by the novel fascinations of a virtuous and really loveable girl, Palmer seriously thought of reforming; at any rate, Mrs. Remington, the person with whom he lodged at this period of his career, gives him a first-rate character. This is what she says:—

"He was a good young man as ever walked; he was with me

nearly a twelvemonth; he came to me in October, 1846, I think. I remember he asked me when my wedding-day was, and he said, 'Well, then, that shall be mine'; and so it would have been but for the Lord Chancellor. The wedding dinner was provided for forty at Abbot's Bromley. My husband and I were to go.

"I never saw him intoxicated but once, and that was one night when he came back from a party.

"'Mamma,' he said — he always used to call me mamma — 'Mamma, I am very ill; I have been drunk; it is not what I have had, but I have been drugged.' Those were his very words.

"He told me, when he was going away, that he had spent the happiest days of his life in my house. He let my rooms, when he was going away, without my consent; and, as I felt rather hurt, he said, 'Never mind, I have let them to a very respectable man, and I have got you 2s. a-week more rent; but I am sure you deserve it, you are so very kind.'"

CHAPTER VIII.

THE TOWN OF RUGELEY.

EFORE WE PROCEED TO SPEAK of Palmer's career since his return to Rugeley with the intention of settling down as it were, and of abandoning all his former bad courses, let us say something about that dull country town which has recently obtained so large a share of notoriety in connexion with Palmer's fearful crimes.

We will take the picturesque description of it, which we find in the *Illustrated Times* newspaper, penned by a special correspondent on the spot:—[1]

---

[1] Quoted from *The Illustrated London News*, Feb. 2, 1856. However, a *News* reporter took a far harsher view of Rugeley only two weeks before, an account which didn't make it into the book, presumably to keep from outraging local sensibilities:

"No account of the Rugeley tragedies would be complete or quite comprehensible without some slight description of the town of Rugeley itself. If cities have, as has been said, their destinies as men have, then, unquestionably Rugeley was built to be the scene of a tragedy. There are many towns of the kind in Holland like Staffordshire.

"Seated in the centre of the railway system, the county in the beginning made great arrangements to develop itself. Every village made a rapid rush to be a town and stopped half-way; and, at present, Staffordshire has only about two towns, neither of second-class importance, while she is almost totally destitute of that beauty of less energetic shires — a village. Birkenhead has been described as a premature Palmyra, and, in a lesser way, Staffordshire is crowded with Birkenheads: places of pretension incompletely fulfilled, too big for the business, considerably 'to let.'

"Rugeley is the worst of these; for it seems to have fallen back — from the staring red brick, perfectly modern, outworks that can get nothing to do — upon the old village street, which is built of sad, sullen-looking dirty-brown stone, miserable without the once-adjoining fields, and most disheartening to the passenger from the utterly unprosperous look of the place.

RUGELEY FROM THE SOUTH, LOOKING TOWARDS THE RAILWAY.

"Rugeley is a long straggling town of small houses, kept very clean, and occupied by persons extremely well to do in the world. It is about as large as Twickenham, and seems to have been built up without any apparent design beyond the whim of the bricklayer. Commercial travellers say it is a good place for business, and that the accounts 'are particularly safe.' It

---

"You enter Rugeley from the station by a road that winds between two churchyards — an old and a new one — and which seem to compete with one another in dismal suggestiveness. The people are neither country people nor townsfolk, have neither rustic ease nor civic smartness, and the gloom of failure appears to pervade talk and 'trade.'

"An inn in a town is always a representative place. In Rugeley the inns are as miserably inconvenient, insufficient, and as uncomfortable as posthouse inns in Poland. Like the other houses, they are dreary. The principle inn looks like an aged gaol; and the next most melancholy building in Rugeley is that opposite — and that building is the house of William Palmer the surgeon.

"A deserted inn as the Talbot Arms is was not a healthy sight for a surgeon without practice and heavy in debt as Palmer was. 'The Talbot Arms,' a dilapidated sign swings in front, and its creaking at night must have wearied William Palmer's wife when she lay dying. The motto of the Talbot's — "Nihil humani alienum" ["Nothing human is alien" —Ed.] — is emblazoned on the arms — a constant, beneficent suggestion to the eyes of Mr. Palmer but of which he availed himself in the manner sinister."

RUGELEY TOWN HALL.

certainly is a peculiar little place, with its cottage shops and red-brick houses, with large leaden lights and big shutters.

"To those who like bustle and crowded pathways, of course the country quietude of the town would be oppressive and saddening. But to us there is a certain charm in the deserted thoroughfares, when the only persons to be seen are the housewives at the windows, behind the rows of geraniums, plying the needle, whilst the husband is working in the fields. We prefer the noise heard from the other end of the street, of Mr. Wright's hammer, ringing on the anvil, to the rumbling of bus and cab wheels under our windows. The young lady on the hot pony standing on the footway of bricks, close up to the shop-door, and giving her orders to the baker's wife, turns nobody into the road, for nobody is out walking, and yet there are plenty of inhabitants — hard-working people — who are earning their day's hire at Bladen's brass-foundry, or Hatfield's manufactory.

"Rugeley has a Town Hall, which occupies the centre of the Market-place, with its justice-room in the upper story, and a

WILLIAM PALMER'S HOUSE.

literary institution and a savings' bank on the ground-floor. It has three or four London-looking shops, and a hundred countryfied ones. There are butchers with only half a sheep as their stock in trade, and grocers that sell bread, and tailors that keep stays and bonnets for sale. It is a very curious little overgrown village, and too pretty to be abused.

"Soon after you leave the railway station, and have crossed the bridge by the flour mill, and left Mrs. Palmer's house and the two churches in the background, you come to the Talbot Inn; and, at the bend of the road, near the half-timbered cottage, is the shop of the only person who has benefited by Palmer's ill deeds — Mr. Keeyes, the undertaker, for he has had the job of getting up all the funerals.

"You are now in Market-street, where the new post-office is, which two dashing young gentlemen have come down from London to manage, in the stead of Mr. Cheshire.[2] Already you perceive in the distance the sign-board of the Talbot Arms Hotel

---

[2] The town postmaster had been sent to prison for tampering with the mail. A longtime friend of Palmer's, he had kept creditors' dunning letters from reaching Palmer's mother so she wouldn't find out her son had used her name to take out loans. Cheshire also opened Alfred Swain Taylor's letter to the coroner and told Palmer the results of his tests for poison.

swinging over the stone steps before the entrance-door. The Talbot Arms is a bold-faced house, something like a cotton-mill outside, only the windows are too large, with an acre of backyard, surrounded by stables and coach-houses, which no doubt are filled during the horse-fair, but are nearly empty for the remainder of the year. You will most likely see an old gentleman in drab breeches and cut-away coat standing at the door, supporting himself on a stick. That is Mr. Thomas Masters, who has lived in the house for seventy-four years, and rides a brown mare, aged thirty. 'We make a good bit over a hundred together,' he will tell you, if you like to go and chat with him.

"William Palmer's house is in front of the Talbot Arms, that stone-coloured building standing back, as if in shame, a little from the road. It will be a good time before that house lets again. The paper will peel off the damp walls, the tiles will become loose, and the little strip of neatly-kept garden at the back be choked up with weeds before the next tenant takes possession. We should not wonder if that house becomes haunted. However, the property belongs to Lord Lichfield, and he can afford the loss of rent.

"Now the shops become bigger, and the stocks-in-trade more extensive. The bookseller's shop, with its fashionable mahogany front of plate-glass, appears to do a thriving business.

"Down the first turning to the left, where the foundries are, used to be the post-office before Cheshire was found out. It is an ugly street, like a back street in Manchester, where spinners live. The post-office is closed now; the little slit is blocked up in the black band that occupies the under-sash of the window.

"You pass by other shops, and amongst them Mr. Ben Thirlby's, the prisoner's assistant. Here, too, is the crockery shop, where Palmer used to deal; there is the saddler's, where his harness was repaired; there the tailor's, where his clothes were made. Everything in Rugeley is Palmer now. Nothing else is talked of.

"We come to the bank where Palmer kept his flickering account; now immense, from the sudden influx of £13,000;[3] now down to almost nothing from losses on the race-course. They do

---

[3] The proceeds from the life insurance policy he took on his late wife.

not seem to work very hard at country banks, for this one opens at ten and closes at three.

"Now you are in Brook-street, where the horse-fair is held. It is as broad as Smithfield, and as long as Regent-street,[4] with plenty of room for looking at the horses, even though they should chase down the road like a cavalry regiment. The tall pole facing you is called the Maypole, and although it is as high as a three-decker's mast, it is said that boys sometimes climb up it; but it must hurt their legs, for half way is a quantity of iron hooping.

"Now we see Rugeley in its beauty. The houses on both sides are large and comfortable, and country-looking. The trees that line the road give it a country air. The waggon before the miller's door, and the drove of sheep and cows raising the cloud of dust in the distance, are sufficient to destroy the solitude of the landscape. In the far background are the dark hills of Cannock Chase framing-in the view.

"'Rugeley,' observes an inhabitant to us, 'is one of the prettiest places in Europe. The country around is most beautiful for miles. There are nothing else but noblemen's mansions and grounds; and do you think they would come down and live here if it wasn't a pretty spot? There is the Marquis of Anglesey's within four miles — the beautiful desert, as they call it — Beau Desert,[5] with the most lovely scenery, all along the road leading to it, you can imagine. There, in the other direction, is Lord Hatherton's[6] park and woods, from

---

[4] This reference is aimed at Londoners. Smithfield, specifically West Smithfield, was originally a field that became a livestock market up until the present day. Regent Street is one of the major shopping areas in the city's West End.

[5] Beaudesert actually is a rough translation from the French meaning "beautiful wilderness." The estate in the southern part of Cannock Case had been a seat of the Paget family since 1546. The 6th Marquess of Anglesey (1885-1947) ran into financial troubles after World War I, when progressive taxes were passed over the House of Lords' objections to pay for the war. Unable to pay, he sold off the furniture, furnishings, and the land and moved to his other family home at Plas Newydd in Wales. The house was left abandoned until it was partially demolished in 1935, leaving the ruins that can be seen today. Part of the former estate is now the Beau Desert Golf Club.

[6] The first Baron Hatherton, Edward Littleton (1791-1863), was a

which half the navy dock-yards are supplied. Oaks, sir, as big round as cart-wheels. Then there is my Lord Bagot's; the finest woods in Europe Lord Bagot's got. Then there is the Earl Talbot's estate, and Weston Hall, and a hundred such. Bless you, sir, compared to Rugeley, Nottinghamshire[7] is a fool to it. Then there's Hagley Hall, within a hop, skip, stride, and a jump of the town — only a mile, with the finest shrubberies in the world; and the Hon. Mr. Curzon[8] is so kind as to allow the people of Rugeley to enjoy them. It's only this Palmer that has set people against the place, or else everybody would be singing its praises.'"

To the above smart description, we will add a few additional particulars:—

Rugeley contains 7,120 acres, and has a population of 4,500. Its principal fair — the Rugeley Cattle Fair — for which it is so famous, commences on the first of June, and closes on the 6th. The other fairs are the second Tuesday in April, the 21st of October, and the second Tuesday in December.

The Free Grammar School at Rugeley, to which William Palmer went, and which is the only school he ever attended, is supported by endowment from Queen Elizabeth: consisting of land in and about the town, the present annual value of which is about £400. Rugeley has nine schools, all endowed, and belonging to the Established Church. It has one Catholic school, not endowed; and one Wesleyan Methodist, endowed.

The Free Grammar School is a square brick building, surrounded by a high brick wall. Premises have been recently built out from the house, which, being pretentiously Gothic, are peculiarly unlike the plain square houses they are connected with. The scholars' entrance is through an iron gate. There are

---

major landowner and farmer. He held a number of political posts, including Chief Secretary for Ireland, and long stints in both houses of Parliament where he helped oversee a number of major reforms.

[7] A county east of Staffordshire.

[8] Hagley Hall, not to be confused with the one in Hagley, Worcestershire, was at the northeast end of Cannock Chase, a half-mile from Rugeley. It was owned at the time by Robert Curzon, 14th Baron Zouche (1810-1873), who was notable for acquiring Biblical manuscripts from Eastern Orthodox monasteries. Hagley Hall was demolished in the 1980s.

some fine trees round the school-house, and holly has been trained along the top of the wall. Very little of the house can be seen from the road, as the wall is very high, and the trees very luxuriant in growth. It stands immediately opposite the grave of Palmer's former friend — John Parsons Cook.[9]

FREE GRAMMAR SCHOOL.

---

[9] The grave can still be seen today in Rugeley. It sits by itself in front of St. Augustine's, opposite the house formerly occupied by William Palmer's mother.

CHAPTER IX.

PALMER'S MARRIED LIFE — HIS SHOW OF RELIGION.

ALMER, WHEN HE RETURNED TO Rugeley, after obtaining the diploma of the College of Surgeons on the 10th of August, 1846, with the view of practising his profession, found, it seems, that patients were not forthcoming.

There was residing at Rugeley at that time a Mr. Benjamin Thirlby (the same individual to whom allusion will occasionally be made in the course of this narrative), who fulfilled the duties of medical assistant to Mr. Salt, a most respectable surgeon of that place. He was familiarly known throughout the county as "Ben at Salt's." Ben had the reputation of being a capital man of business; and Palmer, thinking that if he secured him, a practice might possibly be got together, made the necessary overtures, and was successful. This act of his, as may be supposed, was not, however, generally admired by his co-professionals.

Palmer's marriage with Ann Brookes took place at Abbot's Bromley, on Thursday, the 7th of October, 1847. She was then under age;[1] was clever, amiable, cheerful, pretty, accomplished, and loveable.

Many now speak of her almost with affection, and the poor of Rugeley still deplore the loss of a most sympathising benefactress. The poor old Rugeley sexton says of her: "Mrs. Palmer was a very nice little woman. She was very good to me. I never bought a sock nor a pair of shoes for any little one after my missus died, nor yet for the girl that was in the house. She gave me all that, and many a thing beside that. Many a time she's given me food for the children."

With such a wife, one would have thought that William Palmer would have lived in contented obscurity in his snug

---

[1] Anne Thornton was born in 1827, which would make her 20 on her wedding day.

two-storeyed cottage, standing a little off the street, with its three square windows above, and one on either side of the door. At that time he was following his profession with steadiness and the prospect of success. His house was furnished with some degree of elegance; he had a handsome carriage, and was not troubled in pecuniary matters. Moreover, he had no connexion with the turf; and, altogether, his former moral delinquencies set aside, was somewhat of a "catch" in this dull neighborhood.

In a year and a few days after the marriage of William Palmer and Ann Brookes, viz., on October 11th 1848, their eldest child was born. Three months afterwards he was christened, as will be seen by the following extract from the entry in the church books:—

"BAPTISM.
"*January 3rd*, 1849 — WILLIAM BROOKES, son of WILLIAM and ANN PALMER, RUGELEY *Surgeon*.
"T. D. ATKINSON, *Vicar*."

"The above is a true Copy, taken from the Parish Register, this 9th day of June, 1856;
"T. D. ATKINSON, *Vicar*."

Willie, the child referred to above, is still living, and people speak of him as being remarkably intelligent.[2] Four other children, the issue of this marriage, all died in infancy. Three died at a fortnight old, and one at three weeks. They all died in convulsions; and the nurse, Ann Bradshaw, is said to have run into a well-known public-house in Rugeley when the fourth child died, exclaiming, "I'll never go back to that wretch Palmer's house again."[3]

---

[2] William Brookes Palmer became a solicitor and lived in London. He died in 1926 at the age of 76 after the gas had been left on in his flat. An inquest ruled that it was "death by misadventure." He never publicly wrote or spoke about his life and the tragedies that surrounded it.

[3] Bradshaw had plenty to say about Palmer after the trial. She quoted him saying that he would not blame God for his babies' deaths since they would impose a financial burden on him. She also would claim that he killed them by dipping his finger in poison then sugar or

"The poor dear child was as well and as hearty as possible, when Palmer comes upstairs and says to me, 'You can go down, Bradshaw; I'll nurse the child for a few minutes.' But in a few minutes the poor child's screams made me run up again, when I found the poor baby had just died in violent convulsions."

There are two things in Palmer's career that would be extremely difficult to reconcile with the rest of his life, were it not for the known hypocrisy of the man.

He was an indulgent husband, and a man who always attended Divine service.

As a husband, he was not attentive, still he was not unkind; so long as no questions were asked as to his goings and comings, his wife might have what she liked, and do what she pleased. He bought her a handsome chaise and a beautiful pair of ponies, which she used to drive about the country with; and if his conduct (other than his long absences) ever gave her cause to complain, it must have been in some way that did not meet the public eye.

We had it from the lips of a female friend of Mrs. Palmer's, that Mrs. Palmer had told her that "she was very happy indeed; she had everything her heart could wish for, or that money could purchase."

Beyond this, we subjoin a couple of well-authenticated anecdotes in exemplification of Palmer's excessive fondness for his wife:—

Mrs. Palmer, and an intimate acquaintance, went (some little time before Mrs. Palmer's death) to London, and from thence to Ramsgate; after stopping a fortnight, they came back. The young lady, Mrs. Palmer's companion, asked Palmer whether they had not stopped too long?

"No, indeed," replied Palmer, "I do not think you have stopped half long enough; if you had stopped another fortnight, it would have done Mrs. Palmer a great deal more good."

Palmer went up to London and came back the same day, bringing with him a present for his wife, in the shape of a wicker chaise. Mrs. Palmer was delighted; and said she should certainly ride out in it the next morning.

---

honey and let them suck on it. When pressed for proof, she would admit she never saw him do it, "but I know it in my heart to be true."

At this, Palmer was very angry indeed. "How can you think of such a thing?" said he; "the horse is not used to the wicker-work, he might run away and you be thrown out — why, you might be brought home a corpse, and then what should I do?"

Palmer made a great show of religion: he would travel as much as fifty miles[4] on a Saturday to reach Rugeley in time for Divine service on Sunday; and in his pew he would read the responses louder than anybody else in the church. He was exceedingly attentive; was the only person in Rugeley who took notes of the sermons, which he almost invariably did. In short, if his attendance at church would have gained him a good name, he might be said to have done every thing in his power to obtain it.

Rugeley, though a small place, has yet two churches — the one a "handsome fabric," kept like best clothes, to be used only on Sundays, and the other an old neglected ruin, a kind of every-day building, very picturesque and interesting — that, like an old servant, is allowed to keep its "place" because of past services.

The handsome fabric cost a great deal of money, and is kept up in style, with gravelled walks leading to its oaken doors, and the turf about it well swept and trimmed. The deserted ruin is now nothing more than an old square tower, with empty holes for windows, that look deathly as the hollow eyes of a skull, and a large patch of ivy clinging like rags and

---

[4] This meant something in a time when train travel was the fastest way to get somewhere. Assuming a well-maintained train and track, a locomotive could reach speeds of 40-45 mph. Otherwise, a person had to walk or drive a carriage.

tatters to its bleak grey sides. What remains of its chancel has been roofed in with boards, and turned into a Sunday-school, where the children sit in rows beneath and around the old tombs, and read hymns when the mistress is looking, and when her eye is turned away, amuse themselves by watching the flies crawling over the quaint marble tablet of Ralph Weston, or the curiously-carved monument of Johannes Weston, "Senior de Rugeley."

The new church has an insulting air of prosperity about it, and holds its tall turret high in the air, as if it knew it owned more tombstones than its neighbour on the other side of the road. The windows are glazed with diamond panes, all free from cracks, and sparkling in the sun, and its inner doors are of red cloth, new and bright as a postman's coat in May.

The interior of the church is clean, and varnished, with the brown oaken pews ranged against the white-washed walls, and the narrow strip of matting leading to the altar. A long red curtain hangs before the huge window, and casts a warm glow upon the polished sides of the goblet-shaped pulpit.

Palmer's pew has a row of dark-covered prayer-books and bibles resting on the ledge in front. On the fly-leaf of one of the books is written, in ink, "William Palmer, Rugeley, August 28th, 1837; the gift of his mother, Mrs. Sarah Palmer, Rugeley." Just nineteen years since he received the present! His father was living then, and the timber-yard was well stocked, and the business going on prosperously. What would the criminal give to call back those years?

In the bible are some pencil-notes taken during sermon time. The following are some of them:— "He was a teacher come from God." "Means — Prayer. God's word all the means of grace. Particular means — Faith in Christ. Faith has an heavenly influence."

Wretched man! Was he acting to the crowd around, when, pencil in hand, he took down these words? Was he hoping that it would be whispered after service, how attentive William Palmer had been to the sermon? Was he using religion that it might turn suspicion from him, and ward off the punishment due to the murderer? Or did he, in the desperation of fear, sincerely pray, hoping by three hours' worship to atone for a poisoned wife and brother? Or was he speculating upon "the

forgiveness of sins?"

Palmer was a regular subscriber to the Stafford Church Missionary Association, and in the last report his name thus makes its appearance:—

  W. Palmer, Esq. £1 0 0

We feel quite satisfied that William Palmer was a thorough hypocrite in religion, and we much question whether he was even a kind father. He would have wished to have appeared so, but he could not.

We subjoin a copy of a letter from Palmer to little Willie, which is peculiar for two or three things. In the first place, it is written as if to a grown person; in the second place, it does not (excepting the conventional commencement and termination) contain a single term of endearment; thirdly, the commencement is written carefully (almost as if printed) — in fact, as if for a child; but after the first line, it is evidently hurried over — words illegible, and, indeed, not nearly so plain as his usual hand:—

"Rugeley.

"My dearest Willie,

"As your birthday is Thursday, I shall send for you home to-morrow, and shall be glad if you will ask Mrs. Salt to be good enough to have you ready for the 12 o'clock train to-morrow, and I will send Henry for you by the first train from here in the morning, and

"I am, my dearest Willie,

"Ever yours, most sincerely and affectionately,
"Oct. 9, 1855.   "Wm. Palmer.

"Please present my kind regards to Mrs. Salt."

"Ever yours, most sincerely and affectionately." What an unfatherly ending — how differently do the letters of Mrs. Palmer read! Here is one; it is undated, and is surmounted by a copper-plate view of the Crystal Palace[5] in Hyde Park, executed by Arthur Walkley, Brompton, Nov. 9th, 1850. There is an engraved inscription under the view, viz. —

"PALACE OF GLASS FOR THE INDUSTRIAL EXHIBITION, HYDE PARK,
"Designed by Joseph Paxton, Esq., F.L.S.[6]
"This magnificent structure is 1848 ft. long, 408 ft. wide, and 66 ft. high, and is built entirely of glass and iron."

"My dearest Willie,

"I hope you are very happy, and also very good — Mamma has been to purchase this little picture for you: I was sorry not to get a coloured one. I shall hear from Papa all about you, so let him have to tell me that you are a Dear Good Boy. I shall not forget, all being well, some pretty toy for you. Give Papa twenty kisses for Mamma, and twenty for yourself,

---

[5] An massive exhibition hall built for the Great Exhibition of 1851. Made of wood, glass and iron, the structure took advantage of the latest developments in modular construction and mass production that enabled it to be built in under a year and at a relatively low cost. It was destroyed in a fire in 1936.

[6] Fellow of the Linnean Society of London, a group devoted to the study of taxonomy and natural history. Joseph Paxton (1803-1865) was a gardener in addition to being an architect.

and with love ever —

"Your affectionate Mamma,

"A. PALMER.

"LONDON, THURSDAY.

"Tell Papa I will write to him to-morrow from Ramsgate."

What a tender mother's letter this is — how it breathes affection in every word!

Palmer does not seem to have practised much as a surgeon. It is true that the confusion of names between William Palmer, of Rugeley, and William Palmer, the dispenser at the Stafford Infirmary, has helped him to some reputation that way; but the fact is, that his antecedents were too well known round about Rugeley for people to have much faith in his medical skill.

CRYSTAL PALACE.

CHAPTER X.

PALMER QUITS PHYSIC FOR THE TURF — HIS RACING ESTABLISHMENT.

HE NEWLY MARRIED SURGEON EITHER had not the application necessary to succeed in his profession, or else his antecedents were so much in his disfavour, that patients fought shy of employing him. Either his indolence, or the force of circumstance, inclined him towards turf pursuits; and from this time forward he indulged his passion for horses and horse-racing without restraint.

Accustomed from his earliest infancy to live among horses — for Rugeley fair is famous throughout the midland counties — he was not long in acquiring the expensive habits and unscrupulous practices of the horse-dealing fraternity. He eventually became an owner and breeder of race-horses, and betted freely and largely.

Among the horses known to have been owned in part or whole by Palmer, the following are the most important:— "Goldfinder," "Doubt," "Mermaid," "Rip Van Winkle," "Polestar," "Chicken," and "Nettle." It is a great mistake to suppose that he had only one trainer, as has been represented; he had two or three.

The stables which Palmer had for his brood mares are in the outskirts of the town of Rugeley. They present the appearance of a long well-built shed; the roof is thatched, and inside they appear to have been carefully fitted up with iron troughs, &c. In addition to the paddock where the stables are, several fields adjacent used to belong to Palmer, and were used for his horses.

The groom who showed us over the premises, informed us that Palmer never bred any horses to ran that he knew of.

"I know," he continued, that "he bought a good many, and gave very large prices for them; he had about three or four brood mares, but there was generally a good many young things about.

"He used to sell them for most curious prices. He sold two for £10. He wanted money, I suppose; but they were worth a great deal more than that, you may depend. He bred some good horses, I can assure you, sir.

"He always seemed to sell his horses for a great deal less, and buy them for a great deal more than they were worth. I don't think he betted well; he lost large sums of money.

"He was a very singular man. He never changed countenance whatever happened. We used to notice it as he passed by. We never could tell whether he had won or lost.

"Palmer's horses were not all at Rugeley; he had some at Hednesford, at Saunder's, the trainers. He would have three mares at a time with colts at Rugeley.

"He did bred some horses, but he bought many. His race-horses were all purchases."

Those who know nothing about horse-racing except from what they see when the running actually takes place; who go to the Derby[1] as they would to the first night of a new play, and criticise the performances of the different horses as they would those of the actors, without having any knowledge of the difficulties that have taken place at the rehearsals, or ever having been "behind the scenes" in either case, can form but a faint notion of the extraordinary preparations, the cares, the anxieties, the schemes, the tricks, the "dodges," which accompany the racer's career, from the moment of his birth until he starts for his great race.

The colt — the offspring of some celebrated winner — is, of course, the object of the most intense interest to his owner, who, it may be, has been heavily involved by previous losses, and who looks to this new comer as a drowning man would look

---

[1] The Epsom Derby in Surrey, the most prestigious race in Britain. Inaugurated in 1780, it now forms the second leg of Britain's Triple Crown, between the 2,000 Guineas in Suffolk and the St. Leger in Yorkshire. The race is named for its planner, the 12th Earl of Derby. Those who want to get a feeling for what the race was like in Victoria's day can consult William Powell Frith's painting "The Derby Day." Exhibited at the Royal Academy in 1858, the 40 by 88-inch painting of the massive crowd attending the race is considered a masterful portrayal of Victorian society.

to the rope thrown out to save him from the sea of difficulties, the waves of which are closing over him. With breathless anxiety he watches every movement of the colt; eagerly consults the groom upon the chances of success that this new adventure may present; and listens with delight to the flattering prophecies that the High Priest of the stable utters. The groom is satisfied — there never was a colt like this colt — he has known many, and may be allowed to judge. And if the master will but take his advice and put the "pot on pretty strong," not only will all past disasters be remedied, but —

The picture that he draws of wealth and prosperity to come, is almost too dazzling a one for us to follow. What, though his master has already sunk some thousands, the money is not lost, but invested; and, with a colt like this in his possession, must come back again a hundred fold.

Well may the youthful aspirant for racing honours proudly toss his head as he gallops round the paddock in which his early days are spent. Such interests, such hopes depending on him, who shall dare blame him if, in the pride of conscious importance, he is a little wild, and now and then kicks out playfully and breaks the arms or legs of one or two plebian stable boys. What are their vulgar anatomies compared with his importance? His mighty spirit must not be controlled; his high mettle spoiled by contradictions. Send the wounded stable-boys to hospitals, and rub the colt down carefully, and cover him up well at night, lest he catch cold after the exertions that attend the kicking exercise he has just been indulging in.

A name is next bestowed upon him — not, it is true, with any sacred rites, such as attend the christening of human juveniles — but still with solemnity and due deliberation. It is a matter of some slight importance certainly to choose a name, which it is fondly hoped will make a noise in sporting circles, and some day figure at the very head of the betting list. The colt is named, and becomes at once an individual member of society.

We cannot look upon him as such before this period: the preliminary description of him by a reference to his projenitors is nothing. Our next door neighbour's little boy, till yesterday, could not be said to possess any individual rights of citizenship, or any personal existence. Yesterday morning he became, for the first time, "little Johnny," and acquired personal standing in society; before then he was only "Mrs. Jones's baby," just as the goods and chattles that surrounded him were Mrs. Jones's chairs and tables.

But we are wandering from the subject of the colt — the future race-horse. The time has come when something must be attempted towards his education. Although, as we have said, his haughty spirit must not be subdued, his juvenile inexperience and childish eccentricities must still be accommodated to the usages of equine society.

He must be taught, in the first place, to carry riders on his back. Accordingly, as human bone and sinew, although held cheap enough in all conscience, still costs more than timber, a wooden substitute for a jockey is strapped upon his back. It is, of course, immediately flung off by the indignant thorough-bred. But the "dumb-jockey" as the log is called, being only wood, not flesh and blood, is not much hurt in falling; and is picked up again and once more strapped on, to be again and yet again flung off, until the colt becomes in some degree accustomed to it.

Then, when the horse does not rear up, and plunge, or throw, or kick up quite so often, the log of wood is laid aside, and a cheap stable boy placed on his back instead.

About the same time the operation known as "Ringing" is commenced; a bridle is put on the colt's head with a long rein affixed, and the head groom holding the end of this long rein, forms the centre of a circle, round the circumference of which, the colt, with the "dumb-jockey" before-named on his back, is made to run, to gallop, jump, kick, dance, or plunge, or get round any way he chooses, incited thereto by the occasional application of the groom's long whip.

The groom still stands, his eye fixed on the colt, as the late Mr. Widdicomb was wont to stand at Astley's,[2] (only that in this place the "ringing" is performed without the rein, except when very young children ride, and have to be tied on with cords, as nearly invisible as possible, so as not to take off any of the spectators' pleasure at the fancied danger). The head groom is usually accompanied by one or more inferior stable-boys, who watch the operation with the same breathless interest that is invariably displayed by Mr. Merriman in the Astley's "ringing" before alluded to.

The colt is now sent to the "trainers," an establishment which may be regarded as a kind of college, for which the practice already gone through has served as a preparatory school. Here, as befits his high position amongst the aristocracy of horse-flesh, the future racer has a private footman or groom attached to his own person, whose duty it is to see to his food, to rub him down, sponge him well, and generally polish him off whenever necessary.

---

[2] Astley's Amphitheatre was the brainchild of Philip Astley (1742-1814), an able trick rider who also had military experience serving as a sergeant-major in the light dragoons. He started his post-military career in London teaching horseback riding at a school that also held performances of acrobatic riding. By holding his performances in a ring, and hiring clowns and other performers, he became the founder of the modern circus. John *Widdicomb* (1787-1854) worked with Astley for 34 years as riding-master and conductor of the circus. *Merriman* was not a person, but the standard name for a clown (alongside Merry Andrew), whose job was to trade quips with the riding-master. As circuses grew to encompass two and even three rings, clowns had to fall silent and resort to pantomime, creating the circus clowns we know and, some of us, loathe today.

We have likened the trainers' establishment to a college. In one important particular, however, the routine of the two establishments varies materially; for whereas in colleges for the human race, the inmates lead a life that may be called, in some degree, irregular — not to say dissipated, do now and then drink rather too much wine, and smoke more cigars than is quite good for their juvenile constitution; at the trainer's, the quantity of food given to the horse at this point of his education is calculated to the grain of corn, the thread of hay, not one atom being given more or less, than is just suited to produce the finest possible state of health. His drink too, is, if possible, more closely looked to than his eating, and the allowance of water reckoned to the gulp, or "go-down," as it is technically called.

When the colt has been for some time in training, he is  taken out for his first run to try his paces. He is led out with several others, who are formed into a line — or rather let us be technical and say, are put "into the string" — and conducted to the exercise-ground to try a gentle gallop; or, in the language of the training stable, "a pipe-opeace."

The trainer accompanies them, riding on one side and about the middle of "the string" so as to be able to observe each individual horse's doings. The colts are ridden by their own particular grooms, the trainer sitting calmly by as umpire of the race.

The greatest care is taken of the horses after the "pipe-opeace." Their legs and feet are carefully examined to see if any injury has been sustained, or any swelling brought on. They are bathed with hot-water, and then bandaged; and, instead of water, the horse frequently has gruel given him to drink, and a bran mash in lieu of corn to eat.

They could not have more care bestowed upon them, even were they reasoning human beings in a workhouse.

But it will often happen that they — we mean the horses in training, not the paupers in the workhouse, by any means — gain too much flesh. This must be brought down by a course of perspiration; we will not use the stable term for it on this occasion, for the word is not a pretty one (it rhymes with "betting.")[3]

The horses' allowance of hay is lessened, and extra cloths are put upon such portions of his body (when practicable) as require bringing down. Thus he starts off to the exercise-ground, at a good canter, accompanied by two or three other horses, and, on the word being given, away they start at the top of their speed, as though running a real race.

When, in the trainer's opinion, they have galloped long enough, the horse is taken to the "rubbing-house," where more clothing is piled on him, until the perspiration runs from his limbs in streams. Then the smallest possible quantity of water is given him — from a bottle — just as a refresher from his exertions; his nostrils, lips and face are well sponged, his body scraped all over, wiped down with wisps of straw, and subsequently rubbed until there is not a damp hair left upon it. A fresh, dry suit is then put on, hood, cloths, and all; another sparing draught of water given from the bottle, and the horse conducted back cool and comfortable to his stable.

During the greater portion of the period that a colt remains in training, his ordinary time of exercise is, on an average, about three hours daily. The exercise, like the food and everything else, is varied according to the individual temperament of the horse; the whole object of the training process being, of course, to get the animal into the best physical condition possible.

But we will suppose the training over, and the horse in the

---

[3] The vulgar word is most likely "sweating," which is described in detail in several manuals from the era such as *Stable Practice, or, Hints on training for the turf, the chase, and the road* (1852).

prime of strength and beauty, entered for some great race — we will say the Derby. Now there may be innocent and unsuspecting persons who conceive that after all this trouble and expense in preparation for the great event, there can be nothing but the obvious fact of meeting a superior animal that can prevent the horse from winning. The owner may think, having gone to so great an outlay, in order to get his horse into first-rate racing order, having, too, such a prize before him as the Derby stakes, must at least *wish* his horse to win. To such unsophisticated minds, the statement, that it is not always absolutely sure that the best horse will win, might seem ridiculous.

And yet, if they would bear in mind that large though the Derby Stakes may be, it is still possible to make the betting  considerably larger, and that, by judicious book-making, and extensive wagers *against* his own horse, (layed by friends for him, of course; were he to do it *in propria persona*, the trick would be expounded at once,)[4] the owner's interest may not always point to his horse's coming first in for the Derby — and it may turn out far more profitable — paradoxical though it may sound — for him to lose than win. Why all this trouble and expense then in the horses' training? To make him look as much like a winning-horse as possible, and lead those not in the secret to lay wagers on him.

And yet, to see the admiring glance his owner casts upon the noble animal — whose impatience to be off almost prevents his jockey mounting him, you could not in your heart believe but that that owner's whole delight was in his horse's powers, his every hope wrapped up in his success.

You are not, of course, aware that the jockey, now

---

[4] Explained. *In propria persona* is Latin meaning "For one's self." Why the author used a legal term in this non-legal sense remains a mystery, unless it was to show off his legal learning.

struggling into the saddle, has had instructions given him beforehand, to "rope" the favorite — or, in other words, to pull him short up in the middle of the race, and thus ensure his losing.

But even if the owner "runs his horse to win," has backed him heavily and may perchance be ruined if he lose the race; even though, as far as he is concerned, everything has been conducted "on the square," there are a score of dangers that the race-horse has to run before the eventful day arrives.

Though men are paid to watch and guard him night and day with the most jealous care, to keep off everything that could by any possibility injure him; though his health and safety are, to all appearance, more vigilantly cared for than that of the infant heir to kingdoms. What if these guardians should themselves find it their interest that their precious charge should lose the coming race? Such things may have occurred ere now.

We have heard of a stable keeper coming like a thief in the night, and when all was still, no eye upon him to detect his doings, administering deadly drugs — not in such quantities as to kill; that would spoil half the chances — but in sufficient doses to remove all possibility of the favourite winning. This is the operation technically known as "making a horse safe," although we must confess we do not see the "safety," at least as the poor horse is concerned.

But there are other ways of making horses "safe" — even supposing that his guards are faithful, and no drugger can approach to tamper with his food.

One plan, a most effective one, insomuch as the horse comes even on to the course in full health and vigour, and is more largely backed in consequence — is the so-called "painted bit." Instead of the poison being given in the horse's food, it is smeared on the bit; so when the horse is saddled for the start, and every body looks with pride and hope upon him, the bridle is put on, the "painted bit" is placed within his mouth, and instantly the drug exerts its power. The horse starts, then suddenly foams at the mouth, staggers, turns sick, and — loses.

One highly effective method of preventing the best horse from winning, formerly much in vogue, has, we believe, been put an end to by an alteration of the laws of racing. This was

PALMER AND PARTY IN A FI[X]

RETURNING FROM THE DERBY.

the "false start." The same proprietor entered two horses for the race. One of these was intended, if it were possible, to win;  the other was to "make the running" against the rival horse.

Accordingly, when all were stationed at the starting-post, and the word to "go" was given, the horse that it was meant to win with stood quite still, the other starting off at a good speed. It was a "false start," the whole not having gone off at the same time. They were called back, and again, and yet again the word to start was given. The horse, that might have won, got thus fatigued and irritated by these constant pullings up, while the one who had not yet left the starting-post was fresh as when he left the stable; and so, when he thought his rival had been sufficiently fatigued by the false starts, he went off boldly, with all this advantage in his favour.

But to enumerate a tenth part of the tricks of horse-racing would be an endless task. Nor is it an agreeable theme to dwell upon. We will suppose the start has taken place.

"They're off!" sounds on the course, the same two syllables  cried simultaneously by thousands of voices, while the crowds that press against the ropes so closely that it seems impossible for them to move an inch, yet do accomplish the seeming impossibility, and are compressed into one-half the space, as every eye is strained and every neck out-stretched to catch a glimpse of the flying steeds.

On — on! Like arrows from a bow; on, on! Like the rushing whirlwind. But all these similes are trite. On come the horses, through a long living lane of intently gazing eyes — of wildly-cheering throats — of frantically gesticulating arms — of madly waving hats! On, on! While, amongst all those thousands of spectators, every one screams out encouragingly

the horse's name, on whose success his gains depend, or yells indignantly if he beholds his horse behind the rest.

On, on! while every faculty is absorbed in the intense excitement, every nerve strung up to the extreme point of tension! for something like two minutes and a-half, and then the race is won — and lost!

Oh! how the winning horse is idolised by his backers! How they flock round and cheer him! With what pride, what joy, they gaze upon him, as he walks slowly past towards the scales.

And what of those who are *not* winners? Poor wretches! It may be they have risked their all — nay, more; they may have risked that which was not their own upon this race. How sound these shouts of triumph in their ears? With what feelings do they look upon this splendid animal, now walking proudly along in the midst of his exulting admirers. What does his victory portend to them? Ruin, despair, disgrace! Well, let us drop the curtain — and, if we do hear of distressing suicides following the great race so nobly won, let us say nothing. Call

in the coroner — swear in the jury. Verdict, "Temporary Insanity," and there's an end!

The race is won and lost. The idol of the hour is conducted back in triumph to his stable. Fresh victories are in store for him. He wins another race, and yet another. He carries all before him. And, for a time, is the theme of universal conversation, of universal adulation!

But for a time. Another horse comes out and wins his races in his turn. Brief popularity! A few years and the former favourite is entirely forgotten. Or, if remembered at all, when a poor worn out shadow of his former glorious self, turned loose to spend the brief remainder of his days in ignoble ease after his mighty triumphs — he is but pointed at, half pityingly, half decisively as the once celebrated So-and-So that won the Derby such a year.

Well, well; would we could all of us with any reason hope that after we had done our work in life, and done it well as has that race-horse, we might rest calmly, peacefully, and have as comfortable an asylum found us by the world, that we have done our best to benefit, as has the superannuated[5] race-horse.

---

[5] Retired because of age or infirmity.

CHAPTER XI.

PALMER AS A RACING AND BETTING MAN.

AVING INITIATED THE READER INTO the mysteries pertaining to the breeding and training of race-horses, we now return to our narrative of Palmer's career.

A gentleman, whose name we are not at liberty to mention, but who is well acquainted with the circumstances, furnished us with the following information:—

"Palmer, in the first place, has been on the turf for six years; he was a defaulter five years ago, and it is in consequence of that, that he is not admitted a member of Tattersall's.[1] He was a defaulter again, I don't recollect in what year; but I do know, that, shortly after, he could not run 'Goldfinder' in consequence. Buxton, of Stafford, and Ashton, of Birmingham, lent him money to pay his bets. He ran 'Goldfinder' for the Chester Cup, and, with the money he won, bought 'The Hawthornes,' at Stafford, just over the railway bridge, close to Painter's. 'The Hawthornes' is a very pretty place, and formerly belonged to a clergyman of the name of Anglesark. Palmer gave £2,520; he might have bought it the night before for £1,800, but he waited for the public sale; told his agent to bid as long as he kept his hand in his waistcoat; when he took his hand out he was the last bidder, and the price was, as I have said, £2,520. He mortgaged it, the very next day, to Cooper, of Newcastle, for £1,600. Palmer let it to Green, all except the land, and that Painter had."

"The Hawthornes" was lately sold to George Spilsbury, Esq., Solicitor, of Stafford, and Clerk to the County Magistrates, for £1,820.

---

[1] An auction house that specializes in race horses, founded in 1766 by Richard Tattersall (1724-1795). It was located until 1865 near Hyde Park Corner, then on the edge of the city. The business's willingness to transact bets attracted sporting men and gamblers from all classes. It is still in business in Newmarket, Suffolk.

Another gentleman spoke of Palmer as follows:—

"I knew him, sir — I have done business with him — I had a great difficulty in getting my money — he was bad pay, sir — he was not admitted as a member at Tattersall's, nor was he received by the first-class betting men. I've seen him over and over again take his place in a sort of corner immediately under the grand stand just with two or three — and, amongst them, a little dwarf of a man, name of Dyke, who used to stick pretty close to him — but none of the nobs[2] went anear him."

When Palmer ran Nettle for the Oaks,[3] he stood to win a matter of about £10,000. At starting, the betting was 2 to 1 against her. Nettle, while second, just after passing the milestone on the brow of the hill, bolted to the left, fell over the chains, and afterwards made her way down among the furze bushes. Marlow, the jockey, was thrown, and unfortunately fractured his thigh.

Had Palmer won this race, the amount of his gains would have been nearly sufficient to have extricated him from his embarrassments. George Bates[4] dates Palmer's ruin from this untoward accident. And yet when Mr. Dorling at the time commiserated him on his misfortune, Palmer, who seemed almost indifferent to it, merely remarked, "It is a bore though isn't it?"

Among the more disreputable portion of the racing fraternity, there is a practice which is more general than at first sight would be imagined, which goes by the name of "nobbling,"

---

[2] Slang for nobleman, as in the aristocracy. From the early 19th century. Hence, the nobs' houses referred to the Houses of Parliament, with the Lords called the upper nobs' house and the Commons the lower nobs. (Knowing this reveals the joke in Terry Pratchett's Discworld series, where a lowly policeman of uncertain species is named Nobby Nobs). The word also jumped the Atlantic to San Francisco, which has Nob Hill, where the mansions were built.

[3] The Oaks Stakes has been held at Epsom Downs every June since 1779. It is the middle leg of the Fillies' Triple Crown, after the 1,000 Guineas and before the St. Leger.

[4] Palmer's hired hand. After Walter's death, Palmer tried to insure his life, representing him as a well-to-do man with his own wine cellar. The proposal was rejected after the insurance company sent Inspector Charles Field to Rugeley and found Bates hoeing turnips in a field.

and, means, in plain English, the doctoring of horses. Scarcely a race is run at which some cases or other does not occur. Of course the wealthy and unscrupulous betting man, who is the most interested in it, is not at all seen in the matter — he neither brings the poison nor administers it; in fact, he generally contrives to be fifty miles away, while the nobbler, who has quietly bought his favorite drug (possibly strychnia), waits about for days, until an opportunity occurring, the horse is found prostrate in his stable. It is more frequently noticed that the horses are "doctored" rather than poisoned, the object being not so much to kill as to disable.

It is said that Palmer was his own "nobbler," and this, if true, will at once account for nine grains of strychnia known to have been purchased at Apothecaries' Hall fifteen months ago by Palmer and Cook, under a certificate from a London surgeon.

"Nobbling" is a crime necessarily so mysterious, that but few records of it are obtainable; but the following is reliable:—

Mr. John Scott, the trainer, has extensive training stables at Malton, in Yorkshire, and also a farm adjacent. At the farm, on the 26th of last December, a hack of the name of AURIFFER was poisoned under very curious circumstances. It seems that a portion of the farm stables abutted upon the road, and through a hole in the end wall a carrot was thrown, which had previously been scooped out and filled with arsenic. This being eaten by the horse, a violent death immediately ensued. Proceedings were taken to investigate the affair, and a poster, of which the following is a copy, was extensively distributed through the kingdom:—

£200 REWARD.

Whereas, on 26th day of December last, a RACE HORSE in the stables of Mr. John Scott, at Whitewall-house, near Malton, in the East Riding of the county of York, was wilfully and maliciously POISONED by the administration of arsenic.

A reward of £200 will be paid by Mr. Scott to any person or persons who shall discover the guilty parties; or, if the party who actually administered the poison, will furnish Mr. Scott with such information as shall lead to the apprehension of the persons who incited or procured him to administer the poison, the reward shall be paid to him, and an application will be made to the Secretary of State, to obtain her Majesty's pardon for any person giving such information.

Whitehall House, Malton, February 14th, 1856.

This, however, proved of no avail; an anonymous letter was received, suggesting that another £100 should be offered — which was accordingly done — but without success.

The detective skill of Mr. Field — the judgment and experience of Mr. Peart, John Scott's "right hand man," were, all alike, insufficient to discover the perpetrator — and we have heard that a reward of £1,000 would have had no more effect, such was the wealth of those who were parties to the crime.

A stranger unprovided with an introduction, and that of the very highest order, to be procured from a racing-man whose character was above all suspicion, might as soon attempt to walk into the Queen's boudoir as into a racing stable-yard.

Indeed, as soon as it is known that any stranger has arrived in the neighbourhood of a training establishment, the precaution of delusiveness,[5] which are always excessive, are re-doubled.

We have heard from a reliable and perfectly authentic source, the following story of the "nobbling" of the favourite for a very heavy stake. The details were procured from the confession of the "nobbler" himself, who was afterwards transported for another crime.

One evening in June, a tall, thin, spare-looking man arrived at the only inn in the village of ———, situated between Epsom and Ascot. He engaged a private room, and desired that any one asking for the name of Raven, should at once be shown up to him.

Soon after dusk, a broad, thick-set man, dressed in a heavy overcoat, long leather leggings, and a wide-brimmed countryman's hat enquired for Mr. Raven and was accordingly shown up to the stranger's room. They were closeted for upwards of one hour; the countryman then retired, and the stranger retired to rest. From his subsequent confession, it transpired that, rising at about 2 a.m., he made his way to the stable in which he knew that the favourite, whom we shall call Blueskin, was installed. With the exercise of much natural agility, he climbed to the top of the stable, removed the slates, cut asunder the battens,[6] and made a passage wide enough to admit his body. Creeping through this aperture he found himself in the loft over the stable, into which latter, he finally descended, sawing through two bars of the rack, through which he dropped on to the straw.

His course was now tolerably clear; enticing the horse to him with a handful of oats, he slipped off its muzzle, and instantly pulled forth a twitch, *i.e.*, a short thick stick about two feet long, terminated by a loop of stout whipcord, into which the upper lip of the horse was at once inserted. A twist of the stick then produced such excruciating pain, that Blueskin opened his mouth in agony, and at that instant, Mr. Raven's hand containing the drugged ball, went halfway down the horse's throat and returned empty.

---

[5] Taking steps to deceive an unwanted visitor.

[6] Thin strips of wood laid horizontally across a roof. They are used to provide a nailing surface for tiles or shingles.

Returning, by the same way that he had come, and replacing everything, even to the slates and rackbars, Raven made the best of his way to town, and told his employer of his success. In the race Blueskin was "no-where;" an immense amount of money changed hands, and the secret was never discovered until several years had elapsed.

Some years ago, and before the railroad was in use, Palmer was in the habit of attending the Derby with a friend, whom we shall call Watkins, and an uproarious party, and their return by the road was always made the scene for riot and row. We have heard the particulars of one such return.

The fun commenced at the very edge of the race-course, where a solemn-looking old gentleman driving quietly home in his four-wheeler was hit on the head by a pincushion thrown by a moustached swell on a drag,[7] and, becoming indignant, was

---

[7] A four-wheeled wagon used for pleasure drives. It is usually pulled by four horses.

immediately assailed with a very frail storm of musical pears,[8] snuff-boxes, pincushions, dolls, and all the variety of "knock-'em-down" prizes.[9] There was a van filled with cheap crockery,

---

[8] A pear-shaped whistle.

[9] A booth at a fair where boys could throw coins to knock down prizes. In *The Boy's Autumn Book*, Thomas Miller (1807-1874) recalled one such booth:

"What things were to be won, if we could but knock them off the sticks, — and so cheap! six things for a penny — musical pears, and a nice little box; such a handsome pin-cushion! and a knife that, to look at, any boy would have given a shilling for it. Then, the boy that belonged to the man who owned all these treasures would try for nothing, to let us see how easy it was; and down he would knock the knife, and the box, and the musical pear, without one of them dropping into the hole, where, if they fell, they were claimed by the owner. Oh, it looked so easy, that we must try; so we did; and, alas! all the prizes invariably fell into the hole, as we shied away our pence and got nothing, so hurried off again to see the shows."

Apparently this kind of law-breaking was common on the race courses, fueled by a combination of alcohol and a lack of law-enforcement. In *The Pottleton Legacy* (1854) by Albert Richard Smith (1816-1860), a mixed group of swells attended the Derby in their drag. After consuming a lot of champagne, losing money at the races, and attempting to woo the women in their party, they joined the massive crowd trying to leave:

"At length the time came to be off. Amidst the confusion attendant upon the breaking up of this mighty assembly — the people looking after their carriages, and the carriages looking after their company; with post-boys franticly persisting in trying to get through impossible places, believing that where their horses' heads could go the rest of the equipage could easily follow — amidst one thousand post-horns blowing at once, to the utter bewilderment of those to whom the note of some particular one was to be a signal — amidst jibbing cattle and tipsy whips, and the roar of the brass orchestra on the large show, combined with the score of smaller bands about the Course; with splitting panels and shivering poles, locked wheels, unworthy linch-pins, red-hot axles, imbecile spokes, and dissipated fellows — amidst all this whirl of wild recklessness did the journey home commence.

"They were ready for anything, and the larking began at the very edge of the race-course. There were two large vans there, advertising some cheap crockeryware, with specimens of the dishes and basins affixed, and placards of 'Halloo! look here! here's a dinner-set for ten

a bad investment to bring to the Derby, and that is, of course, immediately stormed. Every carriage, cab, or omnibus that passed was assailed with chaff, mild in the first instance, but growing stormy and abusive under provocation; long peashooters were produced, and volleys of missiles blown against the windows of the houses in Cheam and Sutton;[10] post-horns,[11] which during the day had, by the simple insertion of a cork in the mouth-piece, been turned into drinking goblets, now once more become post-horns, and blow defiant, sentimental, and drunken notes.

Palmer's party were more uproarious than any on the road; and when they pulled up at the Cock, at Sutton,[12] so much

---

shillings!!' or, 'What! only a pound for that service? it's impossible!' This was too tempting a mark to be overlooked; and as the landau came near, Mr. Spooner, who felt that it was time he did something to keep up his reputation of being a fast man before Mrs. Wracketts, took aim at it with a musical pear, which he had brought down from one of the sticks, and knocked off a devoted milk jug. Philip was not in the humour to be behind him in anything, and threw a shell at the sugar basin. The first blows had been struck, and the war against china was determined on. From the masked batteries of the carriages near them there came such a shower of toys — such money-boxes, wooden apples and snakes — such Jacks, pincushions, and lemons, that in two minutes every vestige of the crockery was cleared away, a shout of triumph shaking the air as each cheese-plate, pie-dish, and slop-basin fell smashed upon the turn. In vain did the proprietor, mad with rage, remonstrate — he was driven back by a discharge of grape from a pea-shooter, at least a yard long; and, when the ruin of his citadel was completed, he remained, as Mr. Spooner observed, 'Marius-like, amid the ruins.'

The Marius quotation, by the way, refers to the painting by American John Vanderlyn (1775-1852). Based on a story by Plutarch, it shows the Roman general, who had been banished from Rome during a political power struggle, sitting amid the fallen columns and rubble of Carthage.

[10] Villages in northeast Surrey within a few miles of Epsom.

[11] A cylindrical brass or copper instrument without valves and a cupped mouthpiece, used to signal the arrival or departure of a mail coach or post rider. Because the wagons operated on a tight schedule and were pulled at high speeds, the horns were blown to warn people to get out of the way.

[12] The Cock Inn was a roadside business that catered to the wagons

additional liquor was imbibed, that even the driver lost his head; and, just before they reached Kennington-gate, ran into a gig,[13] in which a stout old gentleman was quietly driving home with his wife, and, to use Mr. Watkins's elegant expression, "upset the whole biling of 'em." [14] Such an accident as this, however, was but little thought of on the Derby-day, and, after a few minutes, Palmer and his friends were again on their way to town, to wind up a day of excitement with a night of debauchery.

THE DEAD HEAT BETWEEN 'ST GATIEN' AND 'HARVESTER' IN THE 1884 DERBY.

---

hauling goods across the country. Situated at the crossroads at the top end of High Street, it saw a huge amount of traffic on Derby Day. The building was demolished in 1961.

[13] *Kennington-gate* was a turnpike gate in the London borough of Lambeth, near Vauxhall Pleasure Gardens. *Gig:* A two-wheeled cart with a front-facing bench.

[14] Biling is short for "boiling lot." The identity of Watkins was not discovered.

CHAPTER XII.

SOME SUSPECTED CASES OF POISONING — AN ILLEGITIMATE CHILD — MRS. THORNTON (PALMER'S MOTHER-IN-LAW) — BLADON, THE SPORTING BAGMAN — BEAU BENTLEY — THE CHICKENS AND THE PILLS — THE YOUNG MAN NAMED BLY.

OME TIME AFTER HIS MARRIAGE, William Palmer had an illegitimate child by a Rugeley woman, of the name of Jane Mumford, and he had, in consequence, to pay for its keep. It is related that this child, a little girl, was brought to him that he might satisfy himself that it was still alive; he saw the child, and sent her home again. Shortly afterwards she died.

The case of Mrs. Thornton, Palmer's mother-in-law, is pregnant with suspicion. She resided, as we have before stated, behind St. Mary's church, Stafford, and was a person of rather eccentric habits, not keeping any servants, although possessed of considerable property. Palmer, it seems, came to see her for the purpose of borrowing money; he was in great difficulties from the want of a little ready cash, and it is fair to suppose that he had already tried to obtain some from his own mother; however, he came to Mrs. Thornton, and not only asked her to lend it him, but to come and live with him. She said she had a great objection to lending him the required amount, but a still greater one to living with him. He went away very angry, and the old lady, fearing that her daughter might probably be ill-used, sent him a cheque for £20, drawn on Salt and Webb's bank, the corner-house in the Market-square; but Palmer, not satisfied with £20, again and again urged her to come and live with him; and at last, over-persuaded, she went, using these remarkable words previous to her departure, — "I know I shall not live a fortnight!"

Nor did she.

By her death Palmer became possessed of the nine houses behind St. Mary's church; but recently, by an order of the Court

of Chancery, he has been obliged to disgorge them in favour of a Mr. Shallcross, proved to be Colonel Brookes's next heir.

Another suspicious case is that of Bladon, who came down to receive some money, £400, it is understood, and never went back.

"Come down," Palmer is reported to have written, "and you shall have some sport. I will pay you before you go back."

Mr. Bladon was a native of Ashby-de-la-Zouch,[1] and a brother of his still resides there. It was in May, 1850, that he visited Palmer at Rugeley; and, while there, was driven over from that place to Ashby by Jeremiah Smith. They spent the day with a Mr. Bostock and returned to Rugeley the same evening.

Bladon was at that time in good health, though not quite recovered from the effects of an accident he had met with. He had more than £100 on his person, and also a betting-book.[2] In

---

[1] A small market town in northwest Leicestershire, England. It is about 20 miles east of Rugeley.
[2] Betting was not the organized activity it is today, but conducted person-to-person with much faith needed that the bookie will pay winners and losers will cover their losses. An earlier attempt in the 1840s to offer printed odds on races in working-class businesses led to worries over promoting the evil of gambling. It was suppressed by Parliament in 1853, but this only pushed gambling out of the pubs, billiard saloons, and tobacconists into the streets.

At the track, bookmakers would stand near the course, shout the odds and negotiate with punters willing to place a bet. Everyone would record their wagers in their betting-books and settle up after the race. Those higher up the social scale could buy a subscription at

less than a week he fell desperately sick, and after William Palmer and his assistant, and subsequent partner, Mr. Benjamin Thirlby, had exhausted their skill, old Dr. Bamford was called in to "prescribe a mixture." Palmer never sent to Mrs. Bladon to acquaint her of her husband's illness; but a friend of Bladon's, named Merritt, on his return from Chester races, called to see him at Rugeley, and found him in so fearful a state of illness, that he thought it right instantly to proceed to London by the express train, and send her down.

She arrived there to find him on the point of death and speechless, and having expressed a wish that her husband's friend, Mr. Bostock, or her husband's brother, should be sent for, Palmer made the excuse that Ashby was a long way off, across country roads, and would take two or three days for the journey, although he knew very well that Bladon had only a very short time before been driven to Ashby by Jeremiah Smith, spent the day there, and returned to Rugeley the same day. There were other suspicious circumstances: for instance, she was only allowed to see her husband for a very short space of time and was then hurried out of the room and was not allowed to see him again, neither whilst living nor after death. The reason assigned by Palmer after Bladon's death was that his body was fast decomposing and not fit to be seen. He was also buried with indecent haste.

Tattersall's, the horse market in London. For two guineas a year (42 shillings), they could bet on credit and Tattersall's would act as banker. Palmer had been a member but was ejected after failing to pay his losses.

Upon Mrs. Bladon expressing her surprise that so little money was found upon her husband's person (namely £15) as she knew that he had a considerable sum with him, Palmer said that Bladon had been to Ashby and paid away a good deal of money there — the contrary being the fact as he had money to receive in Ashby and none to pay. Another circumstance was that his pockets had been rummaged, his papers all turned over, and some abstracted; his betting-book, too, was missing. His death occurred immediately after Chester races, and there were strong reasons for believing that Palmer had lost considerably to him.

A very suspicious circumstance connected with the affair was this: Palmer used very great exertions to induce Mrs. Bladon to sign a certain document which set forth that Bladon was indebted to him in the amount of £59, whereas the fact was the very reverse. This she would have done in a moment had her affairs not been embarrassed, and had Palmer not said he had never borrowed a farthing from her husband in his life.

The end of the matter was that although Bladon's brother and several of his friends entertained very grave suspicions of unfair proceedings, and one went to the extent of writing to the police at Rugeley on the subject, yet Mrs. Bladon was disposed to feel pleased with such treatment she thought her husband and herself had received and was opposed without some proof more than mere suspicion to accusing any one of so foul a crime. She counselled Mr. Bostock, the friend who had shewn himself most active in the matter, if his mind was not easy to go over himself and make inquiries, but to pause ere he did anything to render Mrs. Palmer so uneasy as so dreadful a suspicion must make her and exhorted him to think, in such a case, what the feelings of his own wife would be and to consider hers.

The following is the letter written by Mrs. Bladon to her friend, Mr. Bostock, at the time:—

"June 14, 1850.

"DEAR SIR, — I am exceedingly obliged to you and Mrs. Bostock for the kind interest you take in my affairs, and have no doubt, from the respect you bore my late husband, you would have done what you say; but if you take into consideration the afflicting circumstances I was placed in, with no one of my own friends round me to advise or counsel me, ignorant of the distance (which I considered much further,) bowed down by grief as I was, that I did not act with the coolness of after-reflection.

"In the midst of my trouble Mr. Palmer insisted on my signing a paper for £59, £50 of which he said Mr. Bladon borrowed of him, and the £9 he said he had paid him for twenty gallons of gin, which he had not received.

"The gratitude I felt for the kind treatment Bladon had, I thought, received from them, would have induced me to have signed it in a moment, could I have done so without distressing myself; but knowing the embarrassed state of my affairs, which I candidly informed them of, still Mr. Palmer insisted on my signing the paper, urging, if it was not in my power to pay, he would not compel me to do so; and I think I should have been induced to have done so had he not said he had never borrowed a farthing of Mr. Bladon in his life. I knew in that he told a falsehood, as I had seen a letter in which he acknowledged £100, and told him so. From that moment he ceased to insist on my signing the paper, telling me he would make me a present of it; and on Mrs. Palmer coming into the room, from which she had been absent a short time, he told her to throw the paper (which was lying on the table) into the fire.

"Now, as regards the notions that William and you seem to entertain of his brother's death, I entertained no suspicions. I felt, and still feel, extremely obliged to Mrs. Palmer for her kindness to me, which could not be greater if I had been a relative of her own. Consider how shocking it would appear, without some proof more than mere surmises, to accuse any one of a foul crime, which your letter more than hints at. If your mind is not easy, go over yourself and make inquiries; but pause ere you do anything to render Mrs. Palmer so uneasy as so dreadful a suspicion must make her. Think in such a case what the feelings of your own wife would be, and consider mine.

"That Mr. Palmer has acted unjustly in money matters I have good reason to believe; his letters I have placed in the hands of the Brewery firm, and if they think proper, and that there are sufficient grounds, they will, no doubt, investigate the matter. Thanking you and Mrs. Bostock for your kind invitation, of which I shall be happy to avail myself, allow me to subscribe myself your sincere friend,

"E. J. BLADON."

We can readily sympathize in Mrs. Bladon's anxiety with respect to Mrs. Palmer. She, poor lady, was dreadfully agitated when she heard of Bladon's death, and exclaimed, "My poor mother died when on a visit here last year — and now this man. What will people say?"

What will people say, indeed! Beyond these deaths, there were also other grounds for suspicion, and rumour, with its thousand tongues was soon at work. People called to mind Abley's case, and then the sudden death of one of Palmer's uncles on the mother's side, under circumstances of grave suspicion. This uncle was one of the Bentley family, and brother to Mrs. Palmer, the old lady, and was known everywhere by the nick-name of Beau Bentley[3] — for he was a great fop, and continued so to the time of his death. His real name was Joseph Bentley. He lived at Longdon Green, near Lichfield. All the Bentleys were well off.

This man's first wife was a woman of property; she died, and he inherited it. He married again; and his second wife died very strangely. After the death of his second wife, he lived with a woman as his mistress, and by her he had a daughter. Horrible to tell, his own illegitimate daughter fathered a child upon him. From Longdon Green this Beau Bentley moved to Dodsley, near Uttoxeter; and, whilst there, married a third wife. She was a widow at the time, and very badly off, and there is no doubt she took him to get a home.

Whilst Beau Bentley was living at Dodsley,[4] William Palmer went to see him. It is the general opinion that Palmer wanted his uncle out of the way, and it is reported that they drank some brandy and water together, and that next morning Bentley was taken ill and three days afterwards died.

Palmer has another uncle who is possessed of a good property and considerably advanced in life. He is a cripple and consequently confined to the house. Mrs. Bentley, his wife, has always exhibited such care and affection for her lame husband, that her father-in-law, on dying, left her, in case of her husband's death, the property — so Mr. Bentley has no power of willing the estate away so long as she lives.

One day, when the old lady was in town at William Palmer's, she complained of not being very well. He mixed her up a couple of pills, telling her to take them that night at bedtime. She, however, feeling better, and disliking pills, determined on "cheating the doctor," and not taking them.

Early the next morning came a message from Mr. Wm. Palmer to inquire how the old lady was. The messenger appeared very much disconcerted that she had not taken this medicine, and said Mr. William felt very anxious about her health, and that she was to be sure and take the pills the next

---

[3] The nickname is a reference to "Beau" Brummell (1778-1840), a leading figure in Regency England whose fashion sense, favoring dark coats, full-length trousers, and shirts with knotted cravats, moved men's clothing toward the modern suit.

[4] A small village about 11 miles north of Rugeley.

night. Instead of that, however, the old lady thought it better to throw them out at the window. Unfortunately, she chose the window looking into the poultry yard and the chickens, eating the pills, died after their meal.

Here is another case, which is put forward on the authority of the *Norfolk Chronicle*:—

"It seems that a few years ago a young man named Bly, residing near Beccles, had formed an unfortunate connection with the turf, chanced to be professionally attended by William Palmer, either at Rugeley, or at some town adjacent to a race-course, by many said to be Leicester. Bly had, singularly enough, won largely of Palmer, when he was thus taken dangerously ill.

"His wife, on hearing from him, immediately hurried to his bed-side. On her arrival, Palmer tried to persuade her not to see her husband. She succeeded, however, in having an interview with him, and he told her he believed he was dying, and after expressing contrition for his ill-spent life, stated, that in the event of his death she was to apply to Palmer for £800 which he owed him.

"He died shortly afterwards, and after his funeral Mrs. Bly related to Palmer the conversation. Palmer replied that it was only a proof of the state of mind in which the deceased had died, for instead of his owing him £800, it was just the reverse, the money being due from the deceased to him. He added that he should never have applied to Mrs. Bly for it, if she had not mentioned the subject to him."[5]

Beyond the above rumours of deaths by poison, it came to be noted as a singular circumstance, that Palmer's children, with the exception of the eldest, all died in earliest infancy. The last of these died in January, 1854. Ere, too, a few short months had gone by, it was destined to be the poor mother's turn.

---

[5] Stephen Bates brings up this case in *The Poisoner* (2014) as an example of the way newspapers tied any suspicious death to the doctor. In this case, important details that could confirm or refute the rumor were missing, such as Bly's Christian name, the date of his death, where it happened, and how Palmer could have treated the man, or even knew him, when they lived 180 miles apart.

CHAPTER XIII.

THE ILLNESS AND DEATH OF PALMER'S WIFE. — £13,000 NETTED BY THE TRANSACTION.

IT WAS DISCOVERED BY THE legal fraternity some years since that the language of Colonel Brookes's will, conveying the bequest to Anne Thornton, was not sufficiently forcible to convey it to her absolutely, but only to give her a life interest in it; consequently, at her decease it was liable to be claimed by the heir-at-law to Colonel Brookes.

Under these circumstances, there would be nothing unusual in Palmer's insuring his wife's life in order to protect himself from the loss which would ensue in case of her decease. And since her property consisted of seventeen acres of land, valued at between three and four hundred pounds per acre, besides nine houses, and the interest of the sicca rupees[1] — upon however, which he had borrowed largely from his mother — there could be no doubt of his having such an interest in his wife's life as would justify insurance, though certainly not to the amount eventually effected.

In January, 1854, Palmer seems to have insured her life for £3,000 in the Norwich Union, and during the following March, in the Sun for £5,000; an insurance was also effected in the Scottish Equitable for £5,000.[2] It is a remarkable fact, that the annual premium on the policies exceeded in amount the

---

[1] A rupee is the basic unit of currency in India and other Asian countries. The British East India Company issued its own rupees and because of its soundness was called "sicca," which translates loosely as "widely accepted."

[2] The author got the figures right, but the insurance companies wrong. The Prince of Wales insured Anne Palmer for £13,000, but got the Scottish Equitable and The Sun to each cover £3,000, reducing its liability to £7,000. Plus, Palmer sought another £12,000 in insurance, not the £15,000 mentioned below.

income which William Palmer's wife enjoyed in her own right. Supposing her to have died, the greater portion of her income descended to her son. Palmer, therefore, could have had no interest in her life which could have warranted an assurance to the extent of £13,000, though that was only half the amount he endeavoured to effect. In fact, the proposals declined by other offices amounted to more than £15,000.

On Monday, the 18th of September, 1854, Mrs. Palmer accompanied her sister-in-law, Miss Sarah Palmer, to a concert at St. George's Hall,[3] Liverpool. The lady ventured there in light summer costume, and fancied she took what is commonly called a chill. She slept at Liverpool that evening, and spent the following morning there.

After partaking of a luncheon of cold roast beef, she started with Miss Palmer in the train for Rugeley, and on her arrival there appeared to be very unwell and went to bed. Next

---

[3] Built in 1841 and still standing, the neoclassical-style building is one of Liverpool's landmarks. When architect Harvey Elmes (1814-1847) won two competitions, one to design the hall and one to build the assize courts, he suggested combining the two to cut costs. The result is a huge complex that has seen notorious murder trials (Florence Maybrick in 1889 and William Herbert Wallace in 1931), public performances (Ringo Starr performed from its roof in 2008 marking the city's yearlong tenure as a European Capital of Culture), and rallies celebrating football cup finals and agitating for socialism.

morning her husband took up to her room a cup of tea with sugar in it, but no milk, and some dry toast. Soon afterwards vomiting commenced. Whatever substance she received, tea, gruel, and once a little arrowroot, was prepared by the servant girl Eliza Tharm, but administered only by Mr. Palmer, or Ann Bradshaw, a deaf old nurse subsequently called in.

On Sunday, Dr. Bamford (aged 82, be it remembered) was sent for, and being given to understand that the case was one of English cholera, though the patient was then suffering from constipation, he prescribed some pills containing calomel and colocynth, and an opening draught.[4] On Tuesday evening he again called, and found that only one pill had been taken, and that the bowels were still unmoved. This was the last time he saw her.

She died on the following Friday; and at her husband's

---

[4] A laxative, the inspiration for which I'll leave to your imaginations. *Calomel:* Mercury chloride, a chemical compound used as a laxative and purgative as well as a treatment for syphilis. *Colocynth:* A plant from the Mediterranean, particularly Turkey. It has a number of uses in folk medicine, but in this case it was probably used as a purgative, where it provokes a violent reaction.

Colocynth and calomel were used so much that Gilbert & Sullivan parodied their use in *Patience* (1881):

What time the poet hath hymned
The writhing maid, lithe-limbed,
Quivering on amaranthine asphodel,
How can he paint her woes,
Knowing, as well he knows,
When from the poet's plinth
The amorous colocynth
Yearns for the aloe, faint with rapturous thrills,
How can he hymn their throes
Knowing, as well he knows,
That they are only uncompounded pills?
Is it, and can it be,
Nature hath this decree,
Nothing poetic in the world shall dwell?
Or that in all her works
Something poetic lurks,
Even in colocynth and calomel?
I cannot tell.

request, he, without a moment's hesitation, signed a certificate that she died of English cholera.

Another medical gentleman, Dr. Knight — one of the antiquities of Stafford, he being also above 80 years of age — the deceased's very deaf guardian — also signed the certificate with equal facility. He saw the patient twice on Monday, when she was too much reduced to hold any conversation with him. However, her husband supplied the deficiency, and described all the usual symptoms of English cholera. It does not appear that he ordered anything but a small dose of diluted prussic acid[5] to relieve the retching, nor is there any reason to believe that he made any further inquiries on the subject till Saturday, when he heard that the poor lady had expired on the previous day.

A third medical man, Benjamin Thirlby, Palmer's partner, likewise saw the sick woman. It was on the day she died, and when she was so completely prostrated as to be unable to answer any questions. Thirlby recommended some arrowroot and brandy,[6] which the nurse promised to give her.

In addition to the medicines prescribed by the doctors, it appears that Mrs. Palmer frequently took effervescing draughts,[7] which were given to her by her husband. "They were given in my presence," said the nurse, "in this way:— He brought some clean water in a glass, and a spoon with some powder in it. He put the mixture into the water, and when he stirred it with the spoon it

---

[5] A poisonous liquid containing hydrogen cyanide. Today, it is called hydrocyanic acid. Diluting poisons to use in a treatment is not uncommon. Strychnine was used as a stimulant up until the 1940s.

[6] A starch obtained from one of several tropical plants. The resulting powder was nutritious and safe, so it was used in biscuits, cakes, puddings, and jellies. It was boiled with flavoring and used to feed children and invalids with dietary problems. It could even be served in beef tea or milk. *Brandy* was valued as a medicine and a stimulant, although alcohol was later discovered to work as a depressive. The *British Pharmacopoeia* of 1907 said a dose of alcohol "increases the output of blood from the heart, and slightly raises blood pressure. ... Its action may be due either to a direct stimulant effect on cardiac muscle, or to the fact that it affords a readily assimilable source of energy." Brandy could also be given by injection, intravenously or rectally.

[7] A bubbling or foaming mixture. From the Latin *ex* plus *fervescere* for "to begin to boil."

effervesced. It looked like the ordinary effervescing draughts, and Mrs. Palmer used to say that they were very refreshing, and did her more good than anything else. She took these draughts two or three times in the course of the day."

During the illness of the poor woman, her chief, and indeed only anxiety appears to have been for her little boy. When the clergyman came to visit her and to pray with her, she asked his prayers on her dear child's behalf. Of five children, the fruits of her marriage, he, the eldest born, was the only one that survived, and he had ever been to her a source of deep anxiety. Whether or not any dark suspicions ever crossed her mind as to the cause of death of her other dear babes, it is impossible to say. One lady, however, relates that while staying with Mrs. Palmer at the sea-side, whither she had gone for the benefit of her health, speaking of her child, she one day said, "My dear boy — I hope he is *safe*!" and then, quickly recalling her words, she exclaimed, "I mean, I hope he is *well*."

Shortly after the poor mother's death, Palmer placed the little fellow, then between six and seven years of age, under the care of Mrs. Salt. When he brought the child to her, he appeared greatly affected, and, with tears in his eyes, said, "I have brought dear little Willie to you. It was Annie's desire, and I wish to carry out my dear wife's last injunction, which was to place him under your care."[8]

The nurse tells us that when poor Mrs. Palmer was at her last gasp she rang the bell, and Mr. Palmer came up. "He did not quite come round the bed. I said to him, 'I fear Mrs. Palmer is dying.' He appeared very much hurt, and went out into the next room, and returned again directly. I think that then she was gone. After she was dead, I stayed with her twenty minutes. I went into the next room to Mr. Palmer. He appeared quite unconscious of what had taken place. I asked him to take a little brandy. Upon this he looked at me, and said, he thought that he had been asleep, rubbed his hands, and he appeared a little better."

Palmer chronicles his wife's death in his diary in this

---

[8] William Palmer Jr. grew up to become a London solicitor. He lived by himself till his seventies when he died in 1925 when a gas tap in his office fire was left on. The inquest ruled death by misadventure. If he discussed his father, and the fate of his infant brothers and sisters, it has not been discovered.

wise:— "Sept. 29th, (1854) Friday — My poor dear Anne expired at 10 past 1." Nine days after he writes — "Oct. 8th, Sunday — At church. Sacrament." The mortal remains of his dead wife were laid beside those of her mother and the sporting bagman, in the family vault of the Palmer's in Rugeley churchyard. According to all accounts, at his wife's funeral, Palmer appeared to be greatly distressed. The first time too that he saw Mr. Dawson, after his wife's death, he seemed very much depressed in spirits, and said, crying, "My poor Annie is dead; I shall not stop long after her!"

Nine months subsequently, however, when his maid-servant, Eliza Tharm,[9] gave birth to an illegitimate child in his own house, and of which there is little doubt he was the father, people naturally enough thought this grief had been assumed for the nonce.

We have heard it stated by people who knew William Palmer well that although he most probably murdered his wife, he was nevertheless undoubtedly fond of her; but his aims and desires were so low and debased that he could not afford to let her live.

Mrs. Palmer being dead, application was made to the various insurance offices, who paid the amounts without a murmur, though not, it appears, without some suspicion; for it has since come out that the London manager of the Norwich Union communicated with the Sun Office, and suggested withholding payment until a full inquiry had been made into the circumstances attending the death of the deceased.

The directors of the Sun Office, however, thought that as three medical men had signed the certificate, pronouncing Mrs. Palmer to have died of diarrhea, they would not be justified in postponing payment. Acting upon this impression, the Norwich Union and the Scottish Equitable thereupon paid the money.

---

[9] Little is known of Tharm; she disappeared after the trial and vanished from history. Questioned after Palmer's arrest, she admitted he tried to seduce her before his wife's death. She stood by Palmer to the despair of prosecutors. As someone wrote in the margin of a legal opinion considering whether she should be called to the stand, "This woman is a very unwilling witness. She cohabitated with the prisoner and had a child by him nine months and 14 days after his wife's death. Nothing further can be learnt from her."

Nevertheless, suspicion was rife in the town, and the matter was even hinted at by sporting men far away from the county of Stafford. One old Yorkshire trainer was heard to observe at the following Epsom meeting: "Hoi's noa going to win Oakes as hoi poison'd woife."

Shortly afterwards, at Newmarket, too, where Palmer, as a betting man, was well known, an old man, in answer to an inquiry about Palmer, observed: "What, do you mean Palmer of Rugeley? Oh, yes, I know him; the man whom the little boys in Rugeley say poisoned his wife. Mind, it's only the *little boys* in Rugeley say so; *I* don't."

Many people who knew Mrs. Palmer well thought that for some time preceding her death she had become rather proud. They now believe that it was melancholy that made her so reserved; she had seen her children die, one after the other; and, after the death of Bladon and her mother, she instinctively seemed to dread the fate, seemingly reserved for herself and her boy.

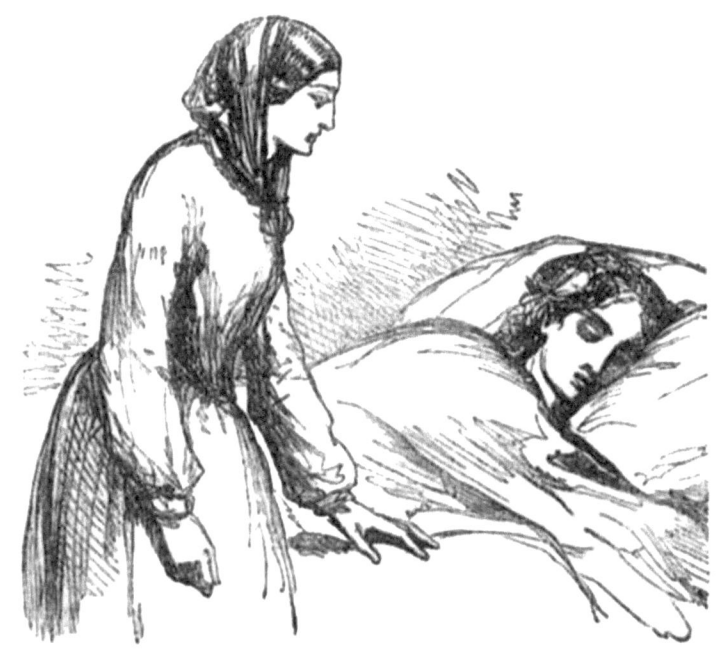

CHAPTER XIV.

PALMER FREED FROM HIS PECUNIARY DIFFICULTIES — HIS MAID-SERVANT ELIZA THARM — A FASHIONABLE "HELL" AND CASINO.

THE MONEY RECEIVED FROM THE Insurance Offices was soon swallowed up in the discharge of pressing liabilities; the larger portion of the amount going into the hands of Mr. Pratt, a West End lawyer and bill-discounter, who had been advancing Palmer money from time to time, at ruinous rates of interest, on bills presumed to be accepted by Mrs. Palmer, sen. The death of the wife relieved him, therefore, from a load of pecuniary embarrassment, and, what was of equal consequence, it left him at full liberty to gratify his sensual appetites perfectly uncontrolled.

Eliza Tharm, the maid-servant, openly stated several months since that she was certain Palmer would have taken improper liberties with her before his wife's death, if she had only given him encouragement. Whatever may have been the relations existing between the parties during the life-time of Mrs. William Palmer, Palmer's diary leaves us in no doubt as to the nature of their relations subsequent to this event. Whether or not he spent the night following his wife's decease in the guilty embraces of his servant-maid, is known, of course, only to themselves; but it is certainly pregnant with suspicion that nine months afterwards Eliza Tharm gave birth to an illegitimate child in Palmer's own house.

Eliza Tharm was a pretty-looking girl when she first went into service at Palmer's. She was good-tempered, quiet, and unassuming, and was at all times doatingly fond of little Willie, never even checking him for things for which, in the words of our informant, "anybody else would have even shaken him well."

Palmer's racing pursuits, of course, continually carried him

away from home, and much of his time was necessarily spent in London in reference to his betting transactions, and to procure the discount of "Sarah Palmer's" bills. It is not to be supposed that when a man of Palmer's temperament arrived in the metropolis on occasional excursions for betting purposes, that he remained quietly in the coffee-room of his hotel until eleven o'clock, and then retired to bed, or that he favoured Exeter Hall[1] or the British Museum with much of his company. On the contrary, though a small drinker, he liked good living, and had a taste for all those *quasi* loose places of resort which, although there is really nothing particularly objectionable in most of them, are seldom, if ever, hinted at before the female members of those families by whose sons and brothers the establishments in question are principally supported.

Palmer, however, we are informed, did not confine himself to frequenting merely those places of public resort which most provincials, during a trip to London, seldom fail to visit. He

---

[1] A building erected between 1829 and 1831 on The Strand near Savoy Hall. In its two auditoriums, people would gather for religious and philanthropic meetings, such as the Anti-Slavery Society, the Royal Humane Society and the Sacred Harmonic Society. It was torn down in 1907.

required the excitement of the gambling-table or the equally vicious betting-room. With the first of these phases of London life we have the best of grounds for stating him to have been familiar, and he is well-remembered, as an occasional visitor, at certainly one first-class "hell," in the aristocratic neighbourhood of St. James's-street,[2] the characteristic features of which we will attempt to describe.

It is a house with the usual bright fan-light over the door, with a couple of police constables generally standing in front of it, one on either side of the doorway. Some years ago the son of an eminent statesman, recently deceased, lost a very large sum of money in one of those places, and, since that time, the doors of all suspected gaming-houses have been watched by the police. They are supposed to take an accurate account of the number of persons who enter, their style of dress, and apparent position in life.

The chances are that one or both the peelers[3] will wish a quiet "good-night" to those who pull the ivory knob communicating with a spring bell that does not make the usual clatter, but sounds only once; and for that "good-night," should the visitor win, he will perhaps tip the peeler half-a-crown as he emerges into the cold grey light of morning. The sergeant passing on his rounds will, perhaps, see the coin slipped into the hand of his subordinate, and, in return for his "good-morning," will, in all probability, be paid with a cigar. On the gay spirits of the metropolis do the proprietors of houses of this stamp mainly depend, and many little perquisites like these

---

[2] The main street in central London, running from Piccadilly to St. James's Palace and Pall Mall. It is the home of gentlemen's clubs such as Brooks's, Carlton, and White's, none of which would ever consider accepting a country doctor and betting defaulter such as Palmer.

[3] An early nickname for the police, after Sir Robert Peel (1788-1850) who as Home Secretary established the Metropolitan Police Force at Scotland Yard in 1829. By 1857, all cities were required to create their own police force. Peel's name is also the source for the contemporary nickname "bobbies" for the police. (Terry Pratchett echoed this use in Discworld. The policemen in Ankh-Morpork are nicknamed "Sammys," after Samuel Vimes, the Night Watch boss who revived the force.)

solace the arduous duties of the west-end night-policemen.

No sooner has the bell sounded, than, as in the story of the White Cat, the door is opened by an unseen hand;[4] and, on the entry of the visitor, it is immediately closed behind him. He finds himself faced by a second door, panelled with iron, and covered with green baize,[5] with a small square aperture in the centre, at which a gleaming eye appears; he is recognised — an iron bar is swung back, two bolts withdrawn, and, having ascended a flight of most softly-carpeted stairs, he finds himself face to face with the mysteries of a London gambling-house.

The first floor is generally the portion of the house in which play is carried on. The basement may be a tailor's or bootmaker's

---

[4] *The White Cat* was a German fairy tale collected by the Brothers Grimm. A young prince competing with his brothers to fulfill three quests for his father's throne comes upon a castle. When he pulls the bell, the gateway opens and a pair of beautiful disembodied white hands conduct him through the castle and toward an encounter with its owner, a White Cat in a long black veil.

[5] A coarse woolen cloth. It is traditionally used in wealthier homes to indicate that you're about to enter the back rooms where the servants live and work.

shop; the mysteries of the upper regions have never been penetrated, but the drawing rooms contain the real Lares and Penates[6] of the proprietors: and very handsome rooms they are; brilliantly lighted, warmly curtained, and plentifully mirrored. The table spread out in the back-room is covered with cold fowl, ham, tongue, beef, and salads: these, with wines, spirits, and cigars, are provided gratuitously; indeed, the more a visitor drinks, the better pleased are his hospitable entertainers.

He will generally find a knot of men lounging in the doorway, and discussing racing matters — (what an odd thing it is that your horsy-doggy-kind of men always congregate in doorways!) this he will break through to make his way to the play-table, which is an ordinary billiard-table, furnished with pockets, cushions, &c.; and yonder, in the corner, stands a rack of cues — an arrangement which has been adopted recently, in consequence of the frequent visits of the police. And now let the visitor look round at the company.

That tall, dark man, standing at the centre of the table, is one of the proprietors of the house, and a handsome, dashing Israelite he is. He is very rich, always dresses to perfection, and, besides being the owner of two or three racers, keeps a cabriolet and a mail phaeton;[7] in one or the other of which you

---

[6] Guardian deities in the Roman religion. Lares typically appeared in households, but they also were called upon to protect domains outside the home, such as crossroads, fields, and even the nation. Penates were responsible for protecting the home's food, wine, and other supplies. To cover all their bases, many households would install statues of both, a practice so common that "Lares and Penates" entered the language.

[7] Victorian England had as many models of carriages as we have motor vehicles. A mail phaeton was a four-wheeled open carriage drawn by one or two horses that carried passengers and luggage. It was called a mail because it used a spring — basically a curved piece of metal, as opposed to the screw-type — designed for mail coaches. Phaetons (pronounced fay-tons) also came in a sporty high-flyer model that had larger wheels and were impressively taller. *Cabriolet:* A light, one-horse vehicle with two wheels and a folding hood to protect the occupants from the elements. The groom would accompany the driver by standing at the back of the carriage, even in the wet. In the tradition of assigning sports car dangerous names — Cobra, Jaguar, Pinto — Phaeton came from a doomed character in

may see him nearly every afternoon in the Park;[8] and you seldom go down to dine, either at the Crown and Sceptre[9] at Greenwich, or the Star and Garter[10] at Richmond, on a Sunday, without finding his "trap" at the door during some portion of the evening. Idiotic guardsmen, would-be-aristocratic stockbrokers, green hands from the universities, and fast youths about town have paid for that vehicle, and honest Moss[11] gives them a subdued, but intelligent, nod of recognition as he drives in it.

The sharp-looking, wiry little man, opposite to him, is the croupier. He calls the odds and never makes the slightest miscalculation; sees that the proper sums are staked at a single glance; and helps his principal to pay the winners and sweep up the stakes of the losers. For this latter purpose they do not use rakes, such as you may have seen at Wiesbaden or Aix,[12]

Greek mythology. Phaeton, the son of Helios (a.k.a. Apollo), asked dad if he could drive the sun chariot for a day. He lost control of the horses and was about to flash-fry the Earth when Zeus killed him with a thunderbolt.

[8] A reference to Hyde Park, one of the Royal Parks near Buckingham Palace and the place for the aristocracy to see and be seen.

[9] An inn in East Greenwich, noted for the exceptional quality of its dishes, especially the locally caught whitebait. The tavern was built with weather-board fronts and bow windows that commanded a view of the Thames. The fish was so popular that playwright John Maddison Morton (1811-1891) featured the inn in his one-act farce *Whitebait at Greenwich* (1853).

[10] A hotel in the then-rural Richmond Hill area. Starting as an inn in 1738, it grew and expanded over time until it became a large hotel that contained a concert hall, banquet hall, and gardens. It reached the height of its popularity from the 1830s to 1890s when it hosted visitors such as Charles Dickens and the crowned heads of Europe. The spread of train and automotive travel threw the hotel into a decline, and the buildings were demolished in 1919.

[11] As with "handsome, dashing Israelite," the writer is implying that the owner is Jewish. "Honest Moss" could not be traced; it might be a misspelling of "honest Moses."

[12] *Wiesbaden* is a city in southwest Germany famous for its hot springs. Gambling had been allowed in the city since 1771. *Aix* is Aix-la-Chapelle, now known as Aachen in Germany. This spa town near the Belgian border also drew tourists to its thriving sex trade, much like Bangkok today.

but small hooked sticks. The rakes would be too *prononces*[13] in the event of any magisterial interruption; and, moreover, from the size of the table, they are not required.

"Seven's the main!" shouts that tall, blond moustached, handsome man taking up the box.

"Seven's the main!" repeats the croupier; "make your game please; the castor's backing in at seven, gentlemen!" Down comes the box, out roll the dice: "Eleven's the nick," says the croupier; and stakes are swept up, winners paid, and a fresh main called with inconceivable rapidity.

That man with the dice-box in his hand is the type of a certain class. He is of excellent family, holds a commission in the Household Brigade,[14] and is one of those fellows you see everywhere. Driving a drag full of other solemn and moustached Heavies[15] to the Derby; leaning against the orchestra at the Opera, and examining the house by the aid of his enormous *lorgnette*;[16] bestriding a beautiful horse in the park, or ponderously waltzing at Almack's;[17] he is always "about." He

---

[13] Strictly speaking, strongly marked, but more likely in this case obvious. Police officers not on the take would enter gambling hells in search of illegal gaming, only to be thwarted with well-rehearsed displays of innocent behavior. In one trial, a police sergeant testified that "he had entered the Berkeley two or three times, to arrest any one found gaming. There were two doors of unusual strength in the passage leading up-stairs. One was watched by a doorkeeper. In the room was a large table covered with green baize; but by the time he got up, all the gentlemen present were 'idle and smoking.'"

[14] Elite infantry and cavalry units charged with protecting the royal family and participating in public ceremonies for the crown such as coronations and royal marriages and funerals.

[15] A member of a heavy cavalry regiment. They wore heavier armor than the light cavalry, requiring heavier, stronger horses. In battle, they were used as shock troops, thrown at the line to break up and demoralize enemy units.

[16] A pair of eyeglasses or a monocle with a handle. From the French *lorgner* for "to take a sidelong look" or *lorgne* for "squinting."

[17] A casino called Almack's Assembly Rooms opened in 1765 by William Almack (whose last name was Macall; he reversed the syllables to hide his unfashionable Scots heritage). It was unusual for its time because it admitted women as members. By 1800, it had gained the reputation of being *the* place to see and be seen by high

does not come here for the purpose of increasing his income, or even for the sake of excitement; he has to pass the house on his way home from his club, and having a horror of going to bed, looks in merely to pass another hour.

Of a very different stamp is the man next to him, the old *militaire*,[18] with the tightly-buttoned frock coat,[19] well-clipped grey whiskers, and carefully brushed hat. They call him "the General," for he is an old Indian officer[20] with a small annuity, to which he largely adds, by a systematic method of play. He is a regular attendant here; is never ruffled or put out; and is reckoned to win on an average three sovereigns a night.

That heavy-eyed, dissipated-looking man in the brown great-coat was once one of the gayest spirits at Cambridge. Brought up to the church, he conceived a violent disgust for a quiet life, and determined on entering the army. Play, that dreadful demon, which had cast a cloud over his otherwise brilliant college career, pursued him still; he became irretrievably involved, and was at length compelled to sell his commission.[21] Since then he has existed, one can scarcely tell how; but, from the terms on which he appears to live with the proprietors, and from the fact that he is always seen here — the first to risk his few shillings at the commencement of the evening — he is believed to be an *employé*, or, what is commonly termed, a "bonnet"[22] of the establishment.

---

society.
[18] Soldier.
[19] A man's knee-length coat.
[20] By 1765, the British East India Company had control of India's Bengal region, and its army subdued most of India by the 1820s. By 1856, there were plenty of men who had served their entire career in India and were pensioned off as "old India officers." One of them, coincidentally, was Col. Brookes, whose "natural daughter" (the common term for a child born outside of wedlock) married William Palmer.
[21] Beginning with the reign of Charles II (1630-1685), it was possible to buy an officer's commission from ensign to lieutenant colonel in the cavalry and infantry regiments. The price varied by rank and regiment, with higher prices charged to get into more prestigious units. There was also an unofficial "over-regulation price" which might double the cost.
[22] A gambler hired by the house to pose as a regular customer. The

This is a fair description of one of those particular night-houses in which we *know* that Palmer occasionally passed his time when in London.

If the reader is desirous of being introduced to another favourite place of resort where Palmer, while in London, was frequently met with, we will give him the opportunity of visiting it under our guidance. It is in the height of the London season[23] — the time is between nine and ten o'clock at night,

---

bonnet would win frequently to lure unsuspecting players to the game, then return his winnings to the house at the end of the night. The word is of unknown origin.

[23] The time of year when the roughly 10,000 members of the ton congregated in London to meet, mingle, gossip, court, gamble, and scandalize. Women who reached the age of eighteen were eligible to attend. They could "come out" into society, were introduced to the Queen in court, and attended the whirl of balls, parties, and dinners in an attempt to find a husband. It was an exciting, exhausting time. One lady recorded in her memoir that she attended during her first season "50 balls, 60 parties, 30 dinners, and 25 breakfasts."

In general, the season ran from after Easter until the end of August (although many considered August 12 the "official" end date). The actual length varied depending on which sports and hunting pastimes were popular with the aristocracy at the moment. That, in turn, affected when Parliament met, as many peers sat in the House

and the streets are thronged. Clerks returning homeward, after a long detention at their places of business; men about town, who, having dined at Simpson's[24] or the Wellington,[25] have turned out to begin the pleasures of the evening; thrifty matrons bent on making cheap purchases before the final closing of the shops; milliner[26] girls toiling under heavy oil-skin-covered wicker baskets; young gents and 'prentices released from behind the counters of the neighbouring shops, dressed in excruciatingly bad taste, and smoking cigars, the odour of which would cause Messrs. Hudson, Benson, or Bryant, to faint; stout, broad-built, florid-faced men from the country, in wondrous-cut clothes, and hats, the long nap[27] of which is all ruffled and awry; pale, roughish-looking men with sunken eyes; sharpers from the neighbouring billiard-rooms; shining beggars, male and female; dirty, shoeless boys, with brooms, with which they make vast pretence of sweeping nothing, at the same time imploring a trifle for "poor Jack" — all these fill the streets, and go eastward and westward in two overflowing streams.

Let us enter at this large door, and paying our shilling

---

of Lords. As *Harper's* put it in 1886: "The season depends on Parliament, and Parliament depends on sport."

The height of the season was in May, when several major events were held: The Derby and The Ascot horseraces; the Royal Academy of Art's official exhibition; the May Presentations to the Queen at Court; and the first of the gala balls and concerts.

[24] One of London's oldest restaurants, founded in 1828 as a smoking room and later a coffee house. By 1850, it was famous for its traditional English food. One man-about-town in his memoirs remembered the "large tables and comfortable chairs in place of the boxes and benches; abundance of clean linen table-cloths and napkins; plated forks and spoons; electro-plated tankards instead of pewter pots; finger-glasses; the joint wheeled to your side, and carved by a being in white cap and jacket; a choice of cheeses, pulled bread, and a properly made-out bill; all these were wondrous and acceptable innovations."

[25] A restaurant founded on the Simpson's model. It was located on St. James's Street.

[26] A person, typically a woman, who designs, makes, trims or sells hats.

[27] The hairy side of the leather or fabric covering the hat.

each to the money-taker, proceed into the vast hall. How warmly it strikes! What a crowd there is! and what a dust arises! For an extra sixpence we can ascend into the reserved seats, and the money will not be ill-expended in escaping all the warmth and the crowding.

Now let us look around us. At the farther end of the gallery, and built across the hall, you see the orchestra. In it there are fifty performers, and the gentleman conducting it, in the white choker, standing upright in the midst of them, is M. Henri Laurent,[28] the lessee of the establishment. The band is judged by *connoisseurs* to be the best in London for dancers, and is highly patronised too; for not only are its strains devoted to the enlivenment of the shilling public who frequent the

---

[28] A musician and conductor of the band (died 1861) at the Argyll Rooms. He was quite the entrepreneur. He composed and published musical pieces, including the music for a now-forgotten opera *(Quentin Durward)* and organized grand balls for which tickets were sold. He died when he was 26, according to *The Players* magazine "and had gained a reputation, which few could hope for at so early an age."

The *Argyll Rooms* opened in 1851 by wine merchant Robert Bignell and quickly became notorious for its masquerade balls as much as a meeting place for the nobility and the demi-monde. One attempt to close the Rooms in 1853 failed when the prostitutes moved their business to the neighboring streets. As the *Saturday Review* observed: "It is better that some hundred females of loose life should be entertained for a few hours in a single room, than that they should be encouraged to prowl about the streets."

An American visitor, Daniel J. Kirwan, visited the Argyll in 1870 and described how he "paid a shilling to enter the Argyle Rooms, and received a tin check, which was given up at the door, as in the Alhambra. The Argyle has not such high architectural pretensions as the Alhambra, but the class of visitors are better in the sense of dress and position. I entered through a side door, and found myself in a carpeted room, handsomely and tastefully furnished and decorated.

"...Women, dressed in costly silks and satins and velvets, the majority of them wearing rich jewels and gold ornaments, are lounging on the plush sofas in a free and easy way, conversing with men whose dress betoken that they are in respectable society. A number of these are in full evening dress, wearing their overcoats, and a few of them have come from the clubs, a few from dinner parties, and a greater number from the theatres or opera."

Argyll Rooms (for it is to that locality, indeed, reader, that we have introduced you), but Her Majesty herself condescends to trip it to tunes composed by M. Laurent, and at every ball at Buckingham Palace his band is stationed in one of the principal rooms.

A polka is going on, and looking over the balcony, you will perceive that nine-tenths of the mass let in the hall below is in motion. In capital tune, in the most decorous manner, the dance is carried on.

You, gentle reader, from Bolton-le-Moors,[29] might find it difficult to perform many terpsichorean[30] feats with your hat on, and with your hand clasping the knob of a thick walking-stick, as well as your partner's digits; but the *habitue* of the Argyll scorns such slight matters, and can perform his favourite steps even when encumbered with the thickest poncho or the stoutest umbrella.

You will perceive that there are several masters of the ceremonies, distinguishable by their levee evening dress, and by the gaudy rosettes on their coats, and that the slightest impropriety is instantly repressed — to the great astonishment of M. Cabriole[31] from Paris, the rival of Brididi or the Count Chicard,[32] whose agile jumps and explanatory gesticulations

---

[29] A parish in the county of Lancashire, near Manchester, that was later absorbed into the Borough of Bolton.

[30] A synonym for dance, derived from the Greek Muse who was the goddess of dance and chorus.

[31] Possibly Emma Cabriole — Cabriole means "caper" — one of many dancers who popularized the can-can, a risqué high-kicking dance that could be unintentionally revealing at a time when women wore pantalettes which were open at the hips.

[32] Notable dancers of the era. Little is known about them, but a vivid description of their talents can be found in Jessica Kerwin Jenkins' *Encyclopedia of the Exquisite: An Anecdotal History of Elegant Delights* (2010). In the early 1840s, a wild version of the quadrille scandalized Paris where dandies mingled with lower-class waiters and shopgirls in the pleasure gardens of the Bal Mabille:

"Crowds thronged to watch as dancing partners faced off in a square, the men scrunching their top hats securely on the backs of their heads. The orchestra started in with Offenbach's jaunty 'Galope Infernale,' and *infernale* it was. Instead of prancing sedately in time to the music, as in the regular quadrille, the dancers cut loose,

are immediately cut short by the authorities.

Here, in the corner of the gallery, you perceive a buffet for refreshments, but if you are not particularly thirsty, we would caution you to wait until you retire, as cheapness is not an item that has been overlooked by the proprietor in his catering.

And now for the company: Here, in this gallery, where the more select are supposed to congregate, we have seen Peers of the realm, Officers of the highest rank in the army and navy, leading Members of the House of Commons; aye, and Judges of the land! This young man, lounging idly on the velvet-covered seat, and apparently absorbed in the conversation of his companion in the drawn bonnet,[33] though in reality settling the curl of his moustache in the gilded looking glass; opposite to him is an earl and an officer in the Household Brigade. He has dined late, as usual, and has just come in here to kill an hour or two. He is utterly stupid, but perfectly good-natured, and is regarding with much more astonishment than disgust the costume of his neighbour — one of Swan and Edgar's[34] young men, who talks much louder, gives himself a great many more airs, and is altogether much more haughty and imperious than the peer.

Mark those three men standing together in the corner of the gallery, heeding neither the dancing nor the crowd, but deeply engaged in their conversation. These are the men with whom Palmer associated while in town; turf-men, gamblers, legs, set forth in every line of those deeply-marked faces, every leer of those deep-set eyes — set forth in their cutaway coats,

---

improvising and gyrating themselves into a mad frenzy. The Mabille's beloved dancing queens Le Reine Pomare and Celeste Mogador — Parisian every-girls who became famous for their audacious moves — frisked their long skirts and kicked up their boots . . . Their partners were just as fevered. The double-jointed Brididi spun his arms like a windmill. Eccentric Chicard did a convulsive parody of the ballet, leaping, screeching, and contorting across the hall. Each dancer moved 'like a worm on a hook,' one mesmerized English observer noted, 'shaking so much that their clothes, if not their muscles would burst.'"

[33] A bonnet in which the fabric is gathered into small ridges, creating a rippled effect.

[34] A store on Piccadilly Circus that catered to its high-end clientele with high-quality goods and prices to match.

and trousers fitting tightly to the leg; in their bell-shaped hats, their blue and white neck-ties, their queer jargon, their muttered oaths.

CHAPTER XV.

PALMER'S BROTHER WALTER — HIS HABITS — HIS ILLNESS — THE INSURANCES ON HIS LIFE — THE BOTTLES OF POISON IN THE STABLES OF THE JUNCTION INN — WALTER PALMER'S DEATH.

IVING AT STAFFORD WAS A brother of Palmer's, named Walter, who was possessed of his own unhappy taste for racing and betting. He was a great heavy drunken man, and seemingly very simple-hearted. He selected for his occupation that of corn-merchant; and, when about sixteen, was placed with Messrs. Procter and Co., of Brunswick-street, Liverpool; and, after remaining with that firm for some years, he left Liverpool for Stafford, and entered into business in the latter town as corn-factor. He was at this time a great favourite amongst the members of the trade in both Stafford and Liverpool. He visited Liverpool on business weekly, and was well-known on the Corn Exchange amongst the merchants generally.

He married, in Liverpool, Miss Milcrest, a lady-like and accomplished person, still most pre-possessing in appearance, the daughter of a Liverpool ship-builder, and possessed of an income of £450 a year. Her sister had married Mr. Joseph Palmer, and strongly dissuaded her from entering such a family; of course, in vain.

Devoting more time to his betting-book than to his ledger, he became bankrupt in 1849. But beyond his betting propensities, he was the slave of the most intemperate habits, and it cannot be a matter of surprise that under these circumstances the union proved an unhappy one.

While residing in the Isle of Man he had an attack of

delirium tremens,[1] during which he attempted to cut his throat. With great reluctance Mrs. Walter was compelled to separate from him, for, in spite of the unpleasantnesses resulting from his habits of indulgence, they seem to have been attached to one another.

Stafford, we have said, was Walter Palmer's place of residence. This ancient town, which has since obtained a painful notoriety in connection with his suspicious death, appears, when first seen from the railway, to be built of red bricks, with slate roofs, and a tall, square, white church tower standing up in the midst of them. Around it are flat meadows, covered with water, for the farmers are just flooding their fields to manure them. This takes away from the liveliness of the landscape, for the big patches of shining water give it a greasy look. The river has divided itself into about twenty rivers, making each ditch a stream, and it rushes tearing along with its yellow water as if it were mad, and in a hurry to throw itself into the Trent below.

Stafford is an ancient borough and market town, celebrated for its red bricks and for its shoes. It has about 13,000 inhabitants. It is a very ancient city, and used to be called Betheney; it was built in the year 219, by Ethelfleda, "the heroic widow of Ethelred, Earl of Mercia."[2]

The town of Stafford contains some of the oldest and newest houses in the county. The new ones are in red brick, and hurt the eyes, like staring at a fire; but once cross the long wooden bridge, with the white railings (built by the railway), turn round by the flour mill, and follow the lane until you come into Greengate-street, and there you will find all the old houses standing on a row on both sides of the street, jumbled together, "the tall ones next the small ones," of all manner of different heights — some four, some two storeys — and with all manner of shaped roofs — some high and pointed, others broad and

---

[1] Latin for a "shaking frenzy" caused by a withdrawal from alcohol.
[2] The author was off by a few centuries. Stafford was founded about 700 by Bertelin, a Mercian prince, who it is also believed founded a hermitage nearby called Betheney. In 913, Aethelflaed, the widow of Aethelred (and daughter of King Alfred the Great) seized Stafford as part of her attempt to unify England after the death of her father. Her quest ended with her death five years later.

sloping, with heavy carved gables. To be sure, the jeweller's house has been "repaired" in stucco, and adorned with wreaths over the windows and doors. The Dolphin Inn[3] has also been newly done up and beautified: and they both look like bold-faced upstarts beside their ancient, respectable brethren, and seem cold and miserable in their coats of white paint, next to the rich brown wood-work and warm-coloured plaister of the half-timbered houses.

There is a house next to the market-place, with a big forehead, that hangs half-way over the pavement, with large bay windows, like four-post bedsteads let into the wall. The yellow oaken beams that show through the plaster work are arranged in all manner of lines, tattooing the body of the house with a half-savage grace. The firm of Jenkinson and Co., large linendrapers, occupy the premises now, and the shop window is decked out with every article "that fashion can require, or beauty desire," as the advertisement says. Festoons of pink and blue riband hang elegantly from side to side, and yellow driving-gloves are ranged in straight lines across the panes. At the entrance door is placed, like a stand of arms, a bundle of umbrellas; whilst, through those immense bay windows on the first and second floor, you can see piles of blue hat boxes, tall slabs of linens, and square canvas blocks of unpacked goods, bound round with bands of iron, as if to keep their figures in.

The Town Hall is a big Portland-stone building, situated far in the square, with a clock stuck up against it like a target. It is not a pretty building, for it has no more ornament upon it than a sheet of writing paper — indeed, the windows are more like holes than anything else. But then it has old houses, in their cocked-hat roofs, on each side of it, all half-timbered, till their fronts seem slashed like a soldier's uniform: and they impart to the square and the pale stucco dead-wall of the Town Hall a kind of dignity as if you could judge a house by the company it keeps.

Walter Palmer was, during his residence in Stafford, in the habit of frequenting the Bowling-green.[4] Like the general run

---

[3] As we'll see later, this is where Bates delivered Palmer's first note to coroner William Webb Ward.

[4] A field of close-cropped grass used for playing lawn bowls. Players roll a series of slightly irregular balls (so they wouldn't roll straight)

of drunkards, he had become very reserved in his habits, and would walk up and down for hours without speaking, except to his most intimate friends. That the reader may see what manner of man he was, we may mention that he one night took Mr. Tates and another friend home with him, and after dinner produced champagne and made them dead drunk. He had a very thick glass for himself that held scarcely anything, while they were treated to glasses so thin as to hold twice the quantity.

In December, 1854, less than three months after his wife's death, William Palmer appears to have entertained the design of insuring Walter Palmer's life for no less a sum than £82,000.[5] Proposals were made to six offices with this view, as follows:—

The Solicitors' and General	£13,000
The Prince of Wales	13,000
The Universal	13,000
The Indisputable	14,000
The Athenaeum	14,000
The Gresham	15,000
Total	£82,000

Of the six proposals above-mentioned, there is evidence that four of them, at least, namely, the Solicitors' and General, the Prince of Wales, the Universal, and the Indisputable, were introduced directly or indirectly by a Mayfair solicitor named Pratt.[6]

---

toward a target ball with the objective of getting as close as possible.

[5] The equivalent of £6.7 million or nearly $11 million today.

[6] Thomas Pratt was one of three men who loaned Palmer thousands of pounds, most at 60 percent interest. His letters threatening legal action would cast him as a major villain at Palmer's trial. Palmer's dangerous relationship with the bill discounter is explained further in chapter 17.

Like the villain of a Victorian penny dreadful, Pratt suffered for his sins. Pressured about his role in the insurance scheme at the Walter Palmer inquest, he screamed from the stand "How can you ask such questions of a man with three young children and a wife

The Prince of Wales office accepted, and he gave his cheque for £710 13s. 4d., receiving back £106 12s., as commuted commission.

A Mr. Greville, a solicitor in St. Swithin's-lane, brought the proposal to the Universal Office, and told the Secretary (Mr. Impey) to send the acceptance paper to him, and the policy and the renewal notices to Mr. Pratt. Mr. Greville also requested Mr. Impey to allow him to withdraw the proposal if the directors of the Universal resolved to decline it. The proposal referred to Mr. , surgeon, of Stafford, as medical referee, and to Mr. Cheshire, the postmaster of Rugeley, as a friend who had known him for some years. Mr. Waddell reported Walter Palmer to have been, on the 5th of April, "healthy, robust, and temperate;" but added in a note under the head of "Opinion on the Life" — "Most confidential. His life has been rejected in two offices. I am told he drinks. His brother insured his late wife's life for many thousands, and after first payment she died. So cautious."

The proposal to the Indisputable Office originally came through a Mr. Webb, who said that a friend of his, a solicitor in Old Boswell-court, was requested by Pratt to get an insurance effected somewhere for about £14,000. Mr. Robertson, the secretary of the office, said he would make inquiry; and inquiry having been made, the proposal was declined. The united premiums upon the six policies, taking them all round at £5 9s. per cent., the per centage charged by the Prince of Wales Office, would amount to £4,469 per annum, a sum which it was very improbable that William Palmer could have paid, considering that he had to get a bill for £1,500 discounted by Pratt, to enable him to pay the premium on the Prince of Wales policy.

On the 31st of January Pratt wrote to William Palmer, stating that he had got the £13,000 policy from the Prince of

---

who will probably be ruined by this affair?" Testifying at William Palmer's trial probably finished him off. The press savaged him for his behavior and appearance. One reporter described him as "a sinister figure, tall and big, trying to be fashionable in his style of dress, enormous brown whiskers almost meeting at the chin, the face that of a small boy, the low, weak voice of a retiring female." It is believed that he went mad and died in an asylum within a year.

Wales, and that it was now all right. In other letters to Palmer he cautions him against pressing on the other insurances too fast, adding, "What would the Sun or Norwich Union say (these offices had not then paid the claims made upon them in respect of the death of Mrs. Palmer) of your speculations, if the Solicitors' and General Office were to offer them any of the risk?"

The proposal was made to the Gresham on the 28th of July, 1855; but the office refused to accept it, unless upon the condition that no claim should be made, under any circumstances, for five years.

Walter Palmer was very anxious to have his life insured, as his brother William had promised to lend him a sum of money as soon as the insurance was effected. He had no idea, however, of the amount of the proposals that had been sent in. Mr. Waddell, the surgeon, who very properly gave the confidential caution to the Universal Office, says — "I met him out walking about the middle of July, when, in a conversation I had with him on the Castle-knoll, he stated that he owed his brother William £400, and he wished to repay it; that I had prevented him insuring his life several times; that I must be aware his habits were entirely altered; that he then only drank three glasses of bitter beer in the day and that he eat like a 'thresher.'"[7]

Walter Palmer was not long, however, in relapsing into his usual drunken habits. Dr. Waddell again met him:—

"Well, Walter," said Dr. Waddell, "how are you now?"

"Why, lad, I'm very bad indeed," replied Walter; "I shall never get over it; I'm a very wretched man."

"Nonsense! nonsense!" said Dr. Waddell, "I'll guarantee your cure, if you will only obey my instructions."

"Well, I think not," continued Walter, shaking his head; "but my brother William is going to bring me over some pills tomorrow."

"Then," said Dr. Waddell, decisively, "if you take medicine from any body else, even your own brother, I give you up. Good morning."

Immediately after which his brother William removed him away from his lodgings in Earl-street, close to Dr. Waddell's, to

---

[7] A farm worker who rakes up the grain and throws it into the air to separate the seeds from the stalks.

DR. CORNELIUS WADDELL.

a house beyond the railway station.

Walter is not seen for some time, till Waddell runs against Walkenden, who has a mourning band round his hat. Says Dr. Waddell —

"Good morning, Walkenden; and pray who have you been putting under ground?"

"Poor Watty," replies Walkenden.

"Poor who?" returns Waddell.

"Walter Palmer; I have just come from the funeral."

We can imagine the astonishment of the medical man, when he heard of the death of the patient whose health he had only the other day guaranteed. He was terribly shocked and cried out, "I will let the Assurance Office know of this," for the doctor had a presentiment that there had been foul play.

How the matter came about was in this wise:— It was in April, 1855, while these assurance proposals were flying about like hail, that Walter Palmer was removed from Earl-street, Stafford, to Castle-terrace, close by the railway station. A man named Thomas Walkenden, a broad-faced, powerful-looking man, with a singularly flat countenance and coarse features, received some 30s. a week to live with him.

THOMAS WALKENDEN, WALTER PALMER'S BOTTLE-HOLDER.

Walkenden's chief business seems to have consisted in supplying his friend and master with gin. Sometimes there was a cask in the house, but more frequently a bottle was procured as required. The average consumption exceeded a quart per diem, and a bottle, perhaps, three-quarters full, was placed by his bed-side every night, with a water-jug and a glass. Not unfrequently the wretched man would toss off half a tumbler of raw spirits at a gulp, and then turn quite black in the face.

At an early hour of the morning Walkenden took him a cup of coffee, which he would swallow and cast up again. Then he would "set himself up" by drinking three or four glasses of gin and water. He was constantly complaining of pain all over him, but particularly under the shoulder-blade; he also coughed every morning very severely, and expectorated a great deal.

The following statement respecting Walter Palmer was taken down from Walkenden's own lips:—

"As Mr. Walter Palmer felt he was falling ill, he repeatedly begged of me, in case I saw he was likely to have another attack of *delirium tremens* again, not to take his gin from him, as I did at my own house; for he said, 'If I had only had my gin then when I wanted it, as I had before, I should not have been half so bad as I was.'

"When he had the delirium, I would not give him any gin, because Dr. Waddell said he was only to have two or three small glasses a day. But I used to see that he was sinking, and perhaps I would give him a glass or two more than Dr. Waddell directed, when I saw there was any necessity. But what was I to do? the poor fellow used to beg and cry for it as if it was his life.

"He used to do all he could, and be cunning to get gin. One morning, after I had been sitting up with him all night, I thought he was so ill that he could not possibly leave his bed, and we went down stairs to the kitchen, which was under his bed-room. Whilst I was eating a little breakfast, I heard a noise overhead. 'Why,' I said, 'that sounds as if he was out of bed; but it's hardly possible.' I ran up stairs, and I found him crawling on his hands and knees, and searching for something under the dressing-table, in the same place where formerly he used to hide his gin, to prevent us taking it away from him.

'Halloa, sir,' I said, 'what are you doing there?'

'I cannot find it,' he answered.

'No,' I replied, and never will;' and I lifted him up in my arms and placed him again in bed. He used to hide his gin bottle in all sorts of places — under his bed-head or under his mattress, or in his boots, or anywhere."

Mr. John Burgess, innkeeper and spirit-merchant, residing at Dudley Port, supplied spirits for the use of Walter Palmer, and also wine and porter. He commenced supplying him on the 13th of February, 1855, and continued till the end of July. He supplied nineteen gallons of spirits in that interval! The orders were given by Walkenden, and he was paid partly by Walter, and partly by William Palmer.

On the 3rd of August, Walter Palmer went to Liverpool and saw his wife, and remained with her for five days, keeping perfectly sober while his bottle-holder was no longer at his elbow. He returned on the 9th, and went to Rugeley, and spent the day with William Palmer. It must have been on this very day, or, at any rate, about this time, that he wrote the accompanying letter to his wife:—

"CASTLE-TERRACE.

MY DEAREST AGNES, — I left you last evening, and did feel I possessed a light heart; but on my arrival at Warrington I found the South Express was three-quarters of an hour late, owing to the flood washing away arches, &c. I was lonely — only myself in the carriage. The rain on my arrival was incessant. Thanks to God I had not very far to go. I have been home to-day; am truly sorry to say mother has been very unwell, but is better. I told Sarah you was going to the concert on the 27th, and she wishes to go. Please to write to her, and she can come with me. If I should bring little Miss Barber, you won't be jealous, dear, will you? But I don't know whether we shall meet or not. I should like you to know one steady and sensible creature upon earth, but not a teetotaler on principle. She says, 'I never drink one glass of wine in twelvemonths, and have, therefore, no occasion to be a teetotaller!' I will write you to-morrow, and explain a few little secrets. Good night, God bless you, and ever believe in the affection of
"WALTER PALMER."

On Sunday, the 12th, Mr. Bay, the surgeon, called at Castle Terrace, and found William Palmer there and Walter Palmer intoxicated. He called again in the afternoon of the same day, when the door was opened by William Palmer, who said that his brother was so noisy and intoxicated there was no use in seeing him.

On the following day, William Palmer went to the Wolverhampton races. On the Tuesday, Walter also went to Wolverhampton, accompanied by his evil genius Walkenden, and met his brother on the race-course. William Palmer has the following entry in his diary:— "14th August — Went by Stafford to see Walter; came home by gig from Wolverhampton."

George Whyman, assistant to Mander and Co., wholesale chemists of Wolverhampton corroborated on a subsequent day this entry in the diary, but suggested this little unpleasant addition to it, viz.: that William Palmer came to their shop on that day, between a quarter past twelve and a quarter to one o'clock, and purchased an ounce of prussic acid and some other articles of him. This statement Palmer firmly denied.

Strange, however, to say, Tom Myatt, the "boots" at the Junction Hotel,[8] Stafford, who knew Palmer well from his constantly calling at the house on the occasion of his frequent journeys to and from Stafford, was confident that it was on this day that Palmer gave him two bottles, wrapped up in white paper.

"I could tell from the feel that they were bottles. They were about four inches long. He told me to keep them till he asked for them again, and not to expose them to the air. He came afterwards, on the same day, and fetched them away. He was away about an hour, and when he came back he told me again to take care of them. He said nothing more that day.

"He called the next morning and asked me for them again. I brought them down to the stable to him. He took one of the bottles out of my hand, and, taking a very small bottle, about one and a-half inches high, he poured a little of what was in it into the larger bottle, and then back into the smaller bottle. Mr. Lloyd, the landlord, came in when we were there, and I walked out of the stable door and left them together. Mr. Palmer only took the very small bottle with him, and left me the others to keep for him. In the evening he came again, and told me to put the bottles in his gig."

The landlord of the "Junction," Mr. Lloyd, happened, by the merest chance, to go into his stables just at the moment

---

[8] "Boots" was a nickname for a hotel servant responsible for cleaning the guests' boots and running odd jobs. It was used both as a noun and a proper name, as "send the boots on an errand" or "send Boots on an errand."

The *Junction Hotel* was the Grand Junction, named for the railway line that opened nearby in 1837. (Its landlord, Thomas Lloyd, will reappear in Chapter XXVII during a discussion of Palmer's character.) Built in 1838, The Junction served both railway passengers and commercial travellers. It continued to operate as a hotel, passing through several hands until 1965 when it was purchased by Mobil and closed. Part of it was demolished in 1967 and the rest used by the Staffordshire County Council for storage until the 1990s. It became a homeless shelter until it was burned in an arson attack in 2005. Left to rot, it was demolished five years later, and a new hostel was built on the site.

Palmer was engaged in his mixing operations. His account of the affair is this:—

> "I was coming out of the garden and up the stable-yard, when I saw Palmer standing in the stable, near the door. He must have heard me coming, but he did not look surprised or flurried; not in the least. He was dropping it very carefully out of the one bottle into the other.
>
> "I bid, 'Good morning, Mr. Palmer; how is your brother this morning?' and he says, 'He's very ill, very low; I'm going to see him, to take him something more stimulating. Dr. Day is attending him, but he is not so well acquainted with his habits as I am, and taking his drink away from him and giving him medicine will not do for a person who has been in the habit of drinking, and I hope this will do him good.' He also said, 'He went, very foolishly, to the races yesterday, and it might have been the death of him, from the state he was in.' He continued to say, what a sad thing it was that people would injure themselves by drinking themselves to death.
>
> "He'd got the little bottle in his left hand, and he kept on dropping it all the time he was speaking. It was white, and, as I thought, sal volatile.[9] I did not take the least notice of the other bottle.
>
> "On the Saturday previous, William Palmer came to me, and asked me for a bottle of the very best old brandy for his brother. He took it away with him, telling me that if his brother wanted any more, I was to let him have it, and he would pay for it."

The stable at the "Junction" is situated in the courtyard of the hotel. It is a low roofed, white-washed stable, with stalls for five horses. On one side is a ladder flat against the wall, leading up to the hay-loft. Palmer is said to have stood close to the stable door in the most open manner so that all might see

---

[9] Smelling salts, used to revive a person who has fainted. Sal volatile is from the Latin, meaning "volatile salts." Volatile in this context means easily vaporizable, necessary for an inhalant.

him, and to have held the bottles up in the air a little above his eyes, whilst he slowly dropped the contents of the small phial into the other and bigger bottle.

This scene with the bottles, it must be recollected, transpired on the Wednesday. Now let us see how Walter Palmer was going on in the meantime. On his return home from the races on the day before, he was quite drunk, but Walkenden did not the less supply him with gin to drink in the night.

All next day, Wednesday, he was in liquor. Dr. Day called to see him, but was told by Walkenden that Walter was at the races. Walkenden has subsequently admitted that Walter Palmer was not at Wolverhampton races, but was at home, and did not go out all day. As regards William Palmer, he slept at Rugeley on the night of the 15th, and left home the following morning, stating that he was going to Ludlow races. He did not, however, go to the races, but went to Walter Palmer's house, at Stafford, where he received in the course of the day, a telegraphic message from Mr. Jeremiah Smith, solicitor, of Rugeley, his very intimate friend, stating that a horse of his (Palmer's) was likely to win the Ludlow stakes.[10] This message, directed to Palmer at the Stafford station, showed that Smith was cognisant of his movements throughout the day.

It was exactly thirty-two minutes past two o'clock when this message arrived. At that very moment Walter Palmer, who had been drinking hard for the previous six-and-thirty hours, drew his last breath, his brother William and Walkenden being at his side. Twenty minutes previously he had been suddenly seized with an attack of apoplexy.

Ere his brother's corpse was cold, William Palmer commissions the "boots" at the Junction Hotel to take a message to the Stafford railway station to be telegraphed to London requesting a friend to lay £50 on a particular horse — most probably his own horse entered at Ludlow; for, at a quarter-past four, despite the melancholy event that had transpired so recently before his eyes, his anxiety as to the results of the race is such that he must needs send this message to the clerk of the course — "Pray, Mr. Frail, send me

---

[10] Palmer had bet £50 on his horse Lurley. He lost.

word who has won the Ludlow Stakes."

The instant the breath was out of Walter Palmer's body, an undertaker was sent for, who assisted to take the body upstairs and place it on the bed. William Palmer said to him, "Poor fellow! Walkenden has suggested that you should make the coffin; make it, and make it quick." The shell was sent home that very night.

He went to the house again on the Friday night, and on the Saturday night — when the shell was sealed up, and also the lead coffin — and again on the Monday, when the shell and the lead coffin were placed in the oak coffin. Nevertheless, the undertaker could not tell what the object was of having the shell made in such haste, for the body was not at all decomposed; even when the coffins were closed.

STABLES OF THE GRAND JUNCTION.

CHAPTER XVI.

WILLIAM PALMER VISITS WALTER'S WIFE — SENDS THE INSURANCE POLICY TO PRATT — THE OFFICES REFUSE PAYMENT — MAKES A DEMAND ON WALTER'S WIFE — PROPOSES TO INSURE THE LIFE OF GEORGE BATES, ESQ. — MORE "HOT" BRANDY.

AUGUST 16TH, 1855, WAS THE date of Walter Palmer's death. The next day his brother William proceeded to Liverpool to make the wife of the deceased acquainted with the melancholy event. She naturally asked him why he had not written or telegraphed to her, for up to this time she had been in ignorance of her husband's illness even.

To this Palmer replied that Walter told him he could write himself if he wanted her. Mrs. Palmer proposed to go off to Stafford instantly to see her poor husband before he was buried, but William Palmer observed that they had been obliged to close him up in lead, and that her going would be of no use for she could not see him.

Under the head of the 27th of August is the following entry in Palmer's diary:— "Went to Stafford with George and Tom to follow Walter to his grave at Rugeley." Walter Palmer was buried in the same grave with Mrs. William Palmer, Palmer, senior, Mrs. Thornton, William's four children, and Bladon.

Now that the brother, hermetically closed in lead, was under the green turf of Rugeley churchyard, it was time to see about the £13,000 due from the Prince of Wales Life Insurance Office. The necessary papers were accordingly despatched to Mr. Pratt; Dr. Day, who had attended Walter Palmer a short time previous to his death, but who had been refused access to him by the officious Walkenden the day before it took place, certified that his patient died of apoplexy.

This time the Offices not merely hesitated, but positively withheld payment. They had been told that the insurance was intended to cover an advance made by Mrs. Palmer; but it now transpired that the assignment had been made in favour of William, in consideration of an assumed loan of £400, though the deceased had received no more than £60. Other circumstances occurred to excite suspicion, and the result was that the different Offices combined for their mutual defence, and refer Mr. Pratt to their solicitors.

Pratt upon this lays a case before Sir Fitzroy Kelly,[1] who

SIR FITZROY KELLY.

---

[1] Tory politician, commercial lawyer, and judge (1796-1880). He was nicknamed "Apple-pip" after a trial in which, defending a man accused of poisoning his mistress, he contended that she fell ill on prussic acid from eating the pips from too many apples. In Pratt's case, he was acting in his capacity as a solicitor.

gives it as his opinion that William Palmer did not recover on the ground of want of consideration,[2] but advises that some member of the family should take out administration[3] to the estate of Walter Palmer. The first person entitled to take out administration was Mrs. Walter Palmer, the widow, but as it was known that she would not take out administration, and as it was necessary to obtain her formal renunciation, Mr. Pratt procured two copies of renunciation from Doctors' Commons,[4] and forwarded them to Palmer, one to be signed by Mrs. Walter Palmer and the other by Mrs. Sarah Palmer, the prisoner's mother, who by law was next entitled to take out letters of administration.

Baulked at the unexpected turn affairs had taken, Palmer, who was dreadfully pressed for money, knew not which way to turn. He, first of all, writes to Walter's wife, asking her to pay him sundry sums, which he stated he had advanced to his brother. First of all, "£85 lent on the drawing-room furniture;" then a mysterious £40, which "you know all about;" next, bills amounting to £200.

"I feel certain poor Walter must have told you how very, very often, and on very many occasions, I had stood his friend, and I believe I and his dear mother (except yourself) were the only friends he had on earth. I only wish his career through life had been a different one. He might have been alive, but, poor fellow, he is dead and buried."

But we will give the letter in *extenso*:—

---

[2] A legal term applied to a transaction where no money, property, or goods were intended to pass from one party to another. In this case, since William Palmer did not loan his brother £400 in return for agreeing to be insured, no legal contract existed so he should not benefit from it.

[3] Apply to a court for the right to act as executor of the estate. When a person dies without a will, a close relative becomes administrator of the estate. If that person declines to do so, the court can appoint anyone as administrator.

[4] A society of lawyers, formed in 1511, charged with working on civil law cases, including those involving wills. The society's building was also the location of civil law courts. By this time, the institution was seen as old-fashioned, and over the next decade it would lose its legal monopoly and fade away as its members died.

"RUGELEY, SEPT. 27, 1855.

"Dear Agnes, — I hope the change of air and scenery has, by this time, done you good, and that you are more quiet and reconciled than when I communicated to you the painful, the sorrowful, news of the death of poor dear Walter. Ah, poor fellow, I often think of him, and only wish I could have done now for him than I did while he was alive; and, I assure you, I did a very, very great deal for him — perhaps, a great deal more than you are aware of.

"I know not whether Walter told you that I had advanced him on the drawing (room) furniture £85 — of course, I was aware that some of it belonged to you, but he, poor fellow, told me that you would repay me the money — which I feel sure you will after I have told you — and I shall have much pleasure in sending it to your orders. There was also one other item you must, if you please, assist me to — viz., £40 for a bill, which you knew well of the circumstance, and I must be excused going into particulars. This amount I should not ask you for, but Walter said if I would only take up the bill you would pay me, and I feel sure you will after all the money I have before paid. I have received bills amounting to £200; which, I suppose, must be paid by some one. What say you to this? You cannot for one single moment think but that I ought to have assistance from some one, and I crave yours, because I feel certain that poor Walter must have told you how very, very often, and on very many occasions, I had stood his friend; and, I believe, I and his dear mother (except yourself) were the only friends he had on earth. I only wish his career through life had been a different one; he might have been alive; but, poor fellow, he is dead and buried, and I hope and trust he is gone to heaven. — With kind regards, yours ever truly,

"WM. PALMER.

"MRS. WALTER PALMER, EDITH LODGE, GRAHAM-ROAD, GREAT MALVERN, WORCESTERSHIRE."

To this letter Mrs. Walter Palmer replies in the following terms:—

"EDITH LODGE, GREAT MALVERN,[5] SEPT. 28, 1855.

"Dear William, — I have just received your note, and must say I am *much surprised* at its contents. What right had you to lend your money, supposing that I would repay it, without consulting me on the subject?. Poor Walter's explanation to me *over and over* again, was that you had insured his life for, I think he said, £1,000; and that you had promised to advance him £500 of the money, but that you had put him off from time to time, and were just giving him a few pounds now and then to go on with, until you could find means to pay him the whole. Now, if that is true, and I am much disposed to believe it, you are the proper person to pay all that he owes; but if you make that out to be incorrect, and I have no way, I am very sorry to say, of proving it, I still should not consider that I am the person to be looked to to pay his debts, never having received a farthing from him, or being kept by him, in the whole course of our married life. I should not think your mother can be aware that you are applying to me for payment of her son's debts, and I will not have it for a moment supposed that I am the responsible person. In conclusion, I beg of you to remember, and beware how you belie the dead.[6] — I am, truly yours,

"A. A. PALMER.
"MR. WILLIAM PALMER, RUGELEY, STAFFORDSHIRE."

From the above, it is very evident that neither husband nor wife knew that the life had been insured for £13,000, or that proposals had been sent to different offices for as large a sum as £82,000.

It was now that Palmer sent his friend, Jerry Smith, to

---

[5] The historical center of Malvern, a town in Worcestershire, about 60 miles south of Rugeley.
[6] Give a false impression of.

Mrs. Walter, to get her to sign a surrender of her interest, as Walter Palmer's wife, in the policy. She, however, prefers that her solicitor should see it, to which Jerry Smith replies, "by all means;" nevertheless, he takes the paper away with him.

As Palmer gained nothing by this move, and liabilities were pressing on, he casts about for another life, and fixes on that of George Bates, a decayed farmer, employed by him as a kind of farm-bailiff on a small scale, but whom Palmer describes in his proposal papers as a gentleman and an esquire, desirous of insuring his life for £25,000. John Parsons Cook, and Cheshire the postmaster, were the two referees, and his friend Jerry Smith, was to have the solicitor's commission of five per cent, usually allowed by the offices, and not Mr. Thomas Pratt, of Queen Street, May Fair.

Smith writes up to the "Midland," and gets appointed its agent, and it is reported that he then submitted the name of William Palmer as the medical referee. This being approved of, Mr. Jerry Smith, very soon afterwards, forwards to this office a proposal for an insurance on the life of "George Bates, Esq." for £10,000, being, of course, merely a part of the aggregate sum of £25,000, which it was intended to raise, but which was probably considered as much as any one office would be likely to take on the life of a gentleman in the position of Mr. Bates.[7]

According to the account which Bates himself gives of how the affair came about, Palmer was very friendly towards him, and the reason why he wanted to insure his life was this:— "He wanted," said Bates, "to better my position, and to do something for me, and he proposed to insure my life, and advance me some money; but, candidly, if I had known that he was going to insure my life for £25,000, I would never have had anything to do with the matter. I think Palmer was a friend of mine, and as he never did me an injury, but rather tried to do

---

[7] One wonders: What did Jere Smith and John Parsons Cook think they were doing? Didn't it seem odd to them that Palmer was showing an inordinate interest in insurance, a gamble that could only pay off in the victim's death? Did their suspicions grow after his insured wife died, followed by his insured brother, and then he turned to Bates? Was this what Cook was thinking, as recounted in Chapter 18, when he was asked why he stayed friends with Palmer, and he replied "Ah! you don't know all"?

me a service when he could, I cannot imagine that he would have served me badly; but yet circumstances are so strange, that I am grateful that the assurances were never effected.

"When I signed the application-paper, Cook was present, and witnessed the signature. On that day, I, and Cook, and Jerry Smith, and Saunders (the trainer), dined with Palmer at his house. We didn't talk about it during dinner. A week before, he had talked to me about assuring my life, and I said something joking about my life not being worth much; and then, after dinner, Jerry Smith and Saunders went out shooting, and Cook says, 'Palmer, I think George had better sign that paper,' and I signed it; but then the amount was not filled up, you see — that was the grand secret. I never asked him what amount he had filled up; for to tell the truth, I didn't see him for several days after, for he and Cook went off to some race meeting or other."

The insurance offices were by this time thoroughly well up to the class of customers they had to deal with, and they therefore engaged a detective to visit Rugeley, and to make some inquiries.

"Inspector Field, of the Detective Force,"[8] as he is generally called, though he is not only not an inspector, but also not a detective, according to the meaning attached to that word was the individual fixed upon. It seems that Mr. Field, since his retirement from the police force, has been in the habit of undertaking confidential inquiries of almost every description; and the insurance company, to which the life of Bates had been proposed by William Palmer, thought Field would be the proper person to carry out the investigation.

At this period every one in Rugeley appeared to be a friend

---

[8] Charles Frederick Field (1805-1874) had a long career in London's Metropolitan Police. He joined when it was formed in 1829, rose to inspector and moved to the Detective Branch in 1846, retiring as its chief in 1852. He was friends with Charles Dickens, who wrote about Field in the essay "On Duty with Inspector Field" and modeled Inspector Bucket in *Bleak House* on him. He described Field as "a middle-aged man of a portly presence, with a large, moist, knowing eye, a husky voice, and a habit of emphasising his conversation by the air of a corpulent fore-finger, which is constantly in juxtaposition with his eyes or nose."

of Palmer's. The postmaster, Cheshire, was, as we have already mentioned, one of the referees for Bates. Of him, Mr. Field first made inquiries, and, in answer to questions put to him, Cheshire stated Bates to be possessed of an income of three or four hundred a-year, free from debts and all incumbrances, and that he was leading the life of an independent gentleman. Particular attention was called by Cheshire to Mr. Bates's fine cellar of wine. Field, who would appear to have a slight weakness for port — or, at all events, to have affected it on this particular occasion — inquired whether the bins containing the wine in question could be specially recommended. Cheshire assured him that they were celebrated in Rugeley; at which Inspector Field expressed his gratification, adding, that that was the hour at which he usually took a glass.

The individual known as "G. Bates, Esq.," was next visited, and found hoeing turnips in a field, and the misrepresentations which had been forwarded to the insurance office were at once made evident. Bates was living in a farm-house, occupying a room for which he paid a few shillings a week — or rather for which he owed them — for, at the time of the inquiries being made, there was six months' rent unpaid.

In answer to Field's questions, as to the amount to which his life was to be insured, Bates said for £6,000. Of this sum, he stated that he himself was to have £2,000; and asked Mr. Field whether he considered that a fair share. "G. Bates, Esq.," we need scarcely add, was entirely ignorant of the nature of life insurance, and hardly understood the meaning of the word. The real sum for which William Palmer was endeavouring to insure Bates's life was £25,000, but Bates was ignorant of this, and indeed, knew so little about the matter, that he could not tell the inspector whether he himself or Palmer had signed the letter of application. The people in the neighbourhood seemed to fancy that Bates was about to become a very important person, and Field had been asked whether he would be entitled to a vote for the county.[9]

After Field had called on Bates, Bates told Palmer of it; and he said if they came again, he was to say he should not

---

[9] The right to vote was limited to men who paid rent or held property above a certain value.

proceed any further with the assurance, but let the matter drop.

Palmer did not seem at all put out, or angry, or disappointed. "He was a man" says Bates, "of such a kind that I never saw his nerves shook."

Whilst the detectives were on the spot, they thought it advisable to investigate the circumstances under which Walter Palmer departed this life. The inference they arrived at was that he had been made away with, and they communicated as much to their employers. It seems that when they called on William Palmer and told him of the suspicions that Walter had not been fairly dealt with, and that they were going to make inquiries, Palmer replied "Quite right" and never even changed colour. Then they thought they would try him further and said they also had their doubts about his wife's death; but he never said anything beyond "Very right and proper."

Simpson, one of the detectives in question, is reported to have said that he never witnessed such an impassibility in all his life. He expected Palmer would have jumped up and knocked them down, but he never even stirred, but went on sipping his wine and cracking his walnuts as unconcerned as possible.

Among the other individuals whom Simpson and Field questioned on the subject was Tom Myatt, "boots" at the Junction Hotel, Stafford. Palmer, who, of course, knew these gentlemen again, could not see them engaged in deep conversation with Myatt without feeling somewhat curious on the subject. When the officers had left, he asked Myatt therefore what they had been saying to him; and as Myatt hesitated — not being quite so ready with a cool answer as Mr. William Palmer would have been under similar circumstances — Palmer, with a view, we will suppose, of unloosing his tongue, asked "boots" what he would take to drink. "Boots's" favourite liquor being brandy, Palmer brought him a glass, which "boots" swallowed, and quickly threw up again; nevertheless, he was ill for some time afterwards, and now protests that he is certain he was poisoned.

This is what he himself says on the subject.

"Now, Tom, tell us all about Palmer poisoning you."

Tom therefore rubs his hair as if he were shining up his

thoughts, and then, whilst he is speaking, picks his nails, or hugs his boots — which latter articles, for a "boots's" boots, are singularly devoid of blacking.

"It was some time about October that Palmer met me on the road; 'twixt here and the station, and he says, 'Tom, what'll you have?' I says, 'A drop of brandy, if anything.'

"Then we came back here and had it. He mixed the brandy-and-water. 'Have it here?' he says. To which I said, 'Well, I'd rather have it outside!' 'No! have it here,' he says; and I had it. It didn't taste queer, but was just like common brandy-and-water, as is made hot, with sugar. I shouldn't have drunk it if it hadn't tasted all right.

"After I'd drunk it, I went into the yard, and then I was took bad. I felt drunk, like. I didn't know where I was, like. I certainly had some recollection, but very little; my senses were gone, like. Directly I'd drunk it, I knew there

THE "BOOTS" AT THE GRAND JUNCTION HOTEL, STAFFORD.

was something queer in it. I clapped my hand over my mouth, and run out that way into the yard, when I threw it up. I never was took that way before after drinking brandy. I don't drink so much of it. I generally drinks brandy neat. At one time I used to drink a good deal of brandy, all day, like. I used to begin in the morning and carry it on till night, and I kept this game up for pretty near eight year. I was never sick in my life afore, after drinking.

"I went and lay me down in the kitchen, I think, and the missus says, 'Good God! Why, what's the matter, Tom?' and I says, 'Well, I think I'm poisoned.'

"'Why, what have you been having?'

"'Some brandy-and-water along with Palmer,' says I, and then something was said, I think, about having a doctor; but I hadn't no doctor. I went and lay me down in one of the stalls of the stable. I felt queer for three or four days afterwards. I remember very little about when I awoke, nor how long I lay there. The ostler come and look at me, and covered me up with rugs. I was 'as black as soot in the face,' he said, and he couldn't hear me breathe no how nor nothing, so he thought I was dead.

"I never named it to Palmer. I couldn't positive swear that he gave me anything, you see."

GRAND JUNCTION RAILWAY TRAIN TICKET, 1842.

CHAPTER XVII.

PALMER'S CONNEXION WITH MR. PRATT, THE WEST-END BILL DISCOUNTER AND SOLICITOR.

THE REFUSAL, ON THE PART of the Insurance Office, to pay the £13,000 claimed on the policy on the life of Walter Palmer, and the further refusal of other offices to bite at new proposals on the life of Bates, placed Palmer in a position of extreme embarrassment. He had found it extremely difficult for some months past to make his accounts square. The money that came to him on the wife's death had made matters comfortable for a time, but Palmer was pursuing a reckless downward course of speculation, and a few months sufficed to bring on the same extreme degree of pecuniary pressure as that from which he had so recently escaped. He was borrowing money from Pratt, a west-end bill discounter and solicitor, at the ruinous rate of sixty per cent, per annum. It certainly requires no great arithmetical genius to calculate what £1,000 at sixty per cent, payable monthly, will amount to in a given term of years, nor is there much forethought necessary to show a man that, with the most unceasing and fortunate exertions, he is hardly likely to extricate himself from debt which increases with such terrible rapidity.

Palmer's connexion with Pratt is an old tale, and often told, — the first small loan duly repaid, then a larger sum, then the borrower's acceptances, then those presumed to be his mother's, bills renewed, interest payable monthly, threatening letters, entreaties for delay, falsehood, forgery, appropriation of another man's money, and then the final crash. It is worthy of attention in all its naked simplicity.

About two years and a half since, the acquaintance between Palmer and Pratt began. Mr. Pratt, we should mention, is a tall, large man, rather fashionable in his style of dress, with an enormous pair of brown whiskers, and having the face of a small London boy, and the low voice of a retiring female. The first transaction he had with Palmer was the loan to him of £1,000, which was, of course, duly repaid. More seems to have been borrowed during the ensuing year from Pratt or other persons, for when Anne Palmer died; and Mr. Pratt received £8,000 from the offices on account of the policies on her life, £6,500 was at once applied in payment of bills due.

In April, 1855, Mr. Pratt was again applied to for a loan of £2,000, on a bill purporting to be accepted by Mrs. Sarah Palmer, and by November, 1855, there were eight bills held by Mr. Pratt or his clients, the total amount being £12,500. Some portion of this amount had been advanced to enable Palmer to purchase two race horses — "Nettle" and the "Chicken."

The interest was paid monthly. With two exceptions, these bills were discounted at the rate of sixty per cent. Thus the interest to be paid by Palmer for money borrowed within seven months was probably upwards of £6,000 a-year, the income of a leading barrister or physician. If Palmer had become possessed of an annuity equal to the salary of a Judge or a Minister of State, it must have been swept away yearly during his whole life in merely paying the interest of this temporary "accommodation."

And yet Pratt, when questioned by the coroner at the inquest on the body of Walter Palmer, with regard to any loss he would sustain, makes the following reply:— "Oh, do not ask me that question, I am a young professional man, with a wife and three children, and I have been nearly ruined by this man. How can you ask me such a question?"

Mr. Pratt, nevertheless, looked sharp enough after his money, if we are to judge by the urgent letters he wrote; and to which evasive answers were returned by his client. Walter Palmer is dead, but, even if the Prince of Wales Insurance-office will pay the £13,000, it cannot be received directly; so Pratt writes, "Do pray think about your three bills so shortly becoming due. If I do not get a positive appointment from the office to pay, which I do not expect, you must be prepared to meet them, as agreed. You told me your mother was coming up this month, and would settle them."

Again, on the 2d of October, "bear in mind that you must be prepared to cover your mother's acceptances due at the end of the month."

On the 18th, "I send copies of two letters I have received.

As regards the first, it shows how important it is that you or your mother should prepare for the payment of the £4,000 due in a few days."

What is the position, then, of Palmer? He has £4,000 to pay, and can only pay £250, and promise £250 more.

It is on the 28th October that Palmer, in answer to a letter of Pratt's, threatening proceedings, writes thus anxiously:—

"I will send you the £250 from Worcester on Tuesday, as arranged. For goodness's sake do not think of writs; only let me know that such steps are going to be taken and I will get you the money, even if I pay £1,000 for it; only give me a fair chance, and you shall be paid the whole of the money,"

On the 31st of October Pratt wrote to Palmer:—

"The £250 in registered letter duly received to-day. With it I have been enabled to obtain consent to the following:— That, with the exception of issuing the writs against your mother, no proceeding as to service shall be made until the morning of Saturday, the 10th, when you are to send up the £1,000 or £1,500. You will be debited with a month's interest on the whole of £4,000 out of the money sent up. I impress upon you the necessity of your being punctual as to the bills. You will not forget also the £1,500 due on the 9th of November."

On the 6th of November Pratt issued writs against Palmer and his mother for £4,000. He sent them to Mr. Crabbe, a solicitor at Rugeley. On the 10th of November Palmer called on Pratt and paid him £300, which, with the two sums he had before received, made up £800. £200 was deducted for interest, leaving £600. Palmer was to endeavour to let Pratt have a further remittance. It is possible, Pratt states, "that writs were mentioned, but I have no recollection of it. No doubt Palmer knew of them."

Let us now quit for a while Mr. Pratt's office on the ground-floor of a smart house in Queen-street, May-fair, and betake ourselves to the Shrewsbury race-course.

CHAPTER XVIII.

SHREWSBURY RACES — POLESTAR, THE WINNING HORSE — "BURNING" BRANDY AND WATER.

AMONG THE STRANGE ADMIXTURE OF company that thronged the Shrewsbury race-course on the morning of the 18th of last November were two individuals, both of whom appeared to be deeply interested in the results of the forthcoming race.

One of these had more the cut of the gentleman about him than the other; in fact, he was what is commonly styled aristocratic looking; and, had the reader seen him, he would have guessed him to have been much the younger of the two, although there was only a few years' difference between their respective ages. He was rather tall and slim — his face was thin and pale, his complexion dark. His hair was long, and he wore a slight whisker, and a small moustache. He wore a loose overcoat with large sleeves. A gold cable guard chain dangled from his watch, and two or three rings might be noticed on his fingers. He resided at Lutterworth, in Leicestershire; was supposed to be possessed of some little property, and kept a few race-horses. He had been brought up as a solicitor, and at one time had offices at Watling. It is very certain, however, that he was a constant frequenter of the various race-courses in the Midland districts, both in term and out of term, and that he was not unknown at the different sporting taverns in the metropolis.

Among his tolerably large circle of friends he was a universal favourite, for his easy good nature and the mildness of his disposition.

The companion of this gentlemanly-looking young man, was an individual some thirty years of age, but appearing several years older. He was of a largeish build, though not more than five feet seven inches in height, very broad about the shoulders, and with rather a thick bull-neck. His complexion, which was florid, gave to his features a slight expression of coarseness; his scanty hair was of a lightish-brown, and was worn brushed back; his whiskers inclined to red. The top of his head was almost bald. His style of dress was not remarkable further than that he was in mourning, and his hat was encircled with a deep black band.

There was a something about the heavy figure of this individual which gave him, perhaps, more the appearance of a gentlemanly farmer than of a practitioner of the science of medicine which he really was. He had a pleasant nod and an agreeable smile for almost every one; and yet, despite this apparent cheerfulness, he must have been sadly wretched at heart, for he was at that moment involved in deep pecuniary difficulties, which threatened, unless his "book" on the forthcoming race turned out well, to deprive him of house and home, and banish him for a time from the society of his fellow turfites, of which he seems to have been passionately fond — oh! far worse than this — to place him in the felon's dock.

Need the reader be told that the younger of the two individuals, whose portraits we have attempted to sketch, was John Parsons Cook, and that his friend was William Palmer, the sporting surgeon of Rugeley.

Cook and Palmer were on what may be styled intimate terms. Cook had lost a small independence on the turf, and he looked to the turf to restore him what it had deprived him of. He and Palmer indulged their dreams of success together. They owned race-horses in conjunction; occasionally betted for each other; and raised money on joint accommodation bills. They were at this time both in embarrassed circumstances; nevertheless, the liabilities of Cook were trivial in the extreme compared to the heavy burthen of difficulties that Palmer was ordained to bear. During their racing trips they invariably frequented the same hotel and would occupy the same sitting-room.

Cook's horse, named Polestar, was entered for the Shrewsbury Handicap. The race was run somewhere about two o'clock and Polestar won. The owner was naturally enough elated with his triumph, for, as happens at all races, a good deal of money changed hands, and Cook's pocket-book was crammed full of bank-notes. It is said that for two or three minutes he could not speak. Good fellow as he was, to

commemorate his luck, he gave a dinner at the Raven,[1] at Shrewsbury and treated his guests to foaming beakers of provincial champagne.

The same evening he accompanied Mr. Jones, the friend with whom he usually resided when at Lutterworth, to see him off by the last train. The next day he was on the course, as usual, and, apparently in perfect health. After the race he returned to the Raven Hotel where he dined.

A singular incident transpired at the Raven about eleven o'clock that evening. It seems that a person of the name of Mrs. Brooks[2] had occasion to see Palmer at the Hotel. She, though a female, was connected with the turf, and betted on commission. She had at her disposal an establishment of jockeys, for whom she acted as a sort of register and for whom she made engagements.

Palmer's horse was to run the next day; and she came to speak to him about a jockey whom he wanted to employ; and having ascended the staircase, turned into a lobby into which

---

[1] The Raven Hotel on Castle Street was one of Shrewsbury's principal inns for more than 200 years. The elegant three-story building was demolished in 1960.

[2] The testimony of Ann Brooks, as well as the rest of the witnesses in this chapter, can be found in *The Times Report of the Trial of William Palmer* (Peschel Press, 2015).

Palmer's room opened. As she turned into the lobby she saw Palmer, whom she knew perfectly well, holding up a tumbler to the light of the gas which was burning in the passage, and looking at it with the caution of a man who was watching to see what was the condition of the liquid. Having looked at it through the gaslight, he withdrew to his own room, and presently returned with the glass in his hand, and then went into the apartment where his friend Cook was sitting.

Later in the evening, Mr. Fisher, who went in the room in which Palmer and Cook were and found them sitting in conversation at a table, Cook having a tumbler, half-full of brandy-and-water before him. Fisher went in and sat down, and Cook invited him to have something to drink; at the same time saying to Palmer, "You will have some more."

"No," says Palmer, "not unless you finish your glass." On which Cook said, "That is soon done." He took up his glass, half-full of brandy-and-water, and tossed it off at one gulp, leaving a tea-spoonful at the bottom of the tumbler. He had scarcely swallowed it when he said, "Good God! there is something in it that burns my throat."

Palmer took up the glass and drank what remained and said, "Cook fancies there is something in the brandy-and-water; taste it." On which they said, "It is very easy to say taste it; but you have left none."

Within a few minutes Cook suddenly left the room. He returned after a few minutes and called Fisher out and told him he had been violently ill! adding that he thought "that damned Palmer had dosed him." He then gave Fisher the money he had about him, between seven and eight hundred pounds, to take care of. He was then taken with violent vomitings.

After a little while he was so bad that it was necessary to take him to bed, where he vomited again and again in the most violent way. It became necessary to send for a medical man. These vomitings continued for a couple of hours, the man retching with the greatest violence; the medical gentlemen proposed an emetic,[3] which Palmer would not hear of. They got him warm water, put a tooth-brush to his throat to make him

---

[3] A drug or an object, such as a toothbrush, used to induce vomiting.

eject what he had taken. However, there was no occasion for that, for the vomiting went on. After that, some stimulants were given to him, some comforting matter, and, then a pill and a purgative dose. After two or three hours he became more tranquil, and about two or three o'clock he fell asleep and slept till the next morning.

"On Thursday morning, the 15th," says Mr. G. Herring,[4] (another friend of Cook's) — "Mr. Cook came to my room while we were waiting for breakfast. He drew me to the window, and began speaking to me about money and racing matters. During the conversation, the name of Palmer was mentioned, but I cannot recollect by which of us.

"I remarked, 'how about that brandy-and-water you had?' And he replied, 'Oh! that villain did me.' From the previous conversation I remarked, 'You mean Palmer?' and he said 'Yes;' I then observed, 'It's a very serious thing to accuse a gentleman of such a thing; what could be his motive?' and he replied in a sorrowful tone, 'You don't know all.'

"He then continued talking about racing matters, and I interrupted him by saying, 'Good God, if you suspect this man of such a thing, how can you go back and breakfast with him?' He again replied, in an absent manner, as he was walking towards the door, 'Ah! you don't know all.'"

---

[4] George Herring testified about his conversation with Cook at the inquest. As he explained at Palmer's trial, Cook showed him a thick wad of money he had won at Shrewsbury and his betting book with entries from the race. After Cook's death, Palmer instructed Herring to collect Cook's winnings and use it to pay off some of his debts. See *The Times Report of the Trial of William Palmer* (Peschel Press, 2015).

CHAPTER XIX.

COOK AND PALMER AT RUGELEY — COOK'S ILLNESS — THE PILLS — A DEATH-BED SCENE.

IN SPITE OF WHAT WE have narrated above, Cook and Palmer were very soon friends again, and brother sportsmen. In the afternoon of Thursday, November 15, they started together for Rugeley, where Mr. Cook engaged a room at the Talbot Arms, exactly opposite to the snuggery inhabited by Mr. William Palmer. Thursday, in other respects, seems to have been a *dies non*,[1] but on Friday, Mr. Cook dined with Palmer and Jeremiah Smith at Palmer's house, returning to the Talbot in a state of perfect sobriety.

On the following morning, he felt qualmish and uncomfortable. He threw up a cup of coffee administered by the chamber-maid, and afterwards a basin of broth sent by Mr. Palmer.

It seems that Palmer desired a woman of the name of Rowley to go to an inn in Rugeley, the Albion, and get some broth. The woman got the broth, took it to Palmer's house, and put it in a saucepan on the kitchen fire to warm. She had something to do in the back kitchen, and went into the back kitchen — she saw no more of the broth, or Palmer, until Palmer, having poured it into a basin, brought it to her, told her to take it over to the Talbot Arms, and to tell any one to whom she might give it to take it up to Cook, and say Mr. Jerry Smith had sent it.

Throughout the whole of that day Palmer was constantly in and out, ministering to Cook a variety of things, and whenever he did administer anything to him, sickness invariably ensued. Dr. Bamford, aged 82, is called in, and sends a couple of opiate pills. The next morning he is again sent for.

---

[1] A legal term describing a day in which the courts do not sit or carry on business. In other words, a day in which nothing happened.

On this day (Sunday) some more broth is brought over from Palmer. This time it is tasted by the chamber-maid before it is taken into Mr. Cook's room. She merely drank a couple of tablespoonfuls. Within half an hour of that time the woman was taken violently ill; vomiting came on, which lasted five or six hours; she was obliged to go to bed at 12 o'clock in the day; she could not get up till 5 or 6 in the afternoon; and she vomited not less than twenty times.[2]

Palmer, during the Sunday, writes the following note to Mr. Jones, of Lutterworth, the friend whom Cook had seen off to the train on the day of Shrewsbury races:—

"NOVEMBER 18, 1855.

"MY DEAR SIR, — Mr. Cook was taken ill at Shrewsbury, and obliged to call in a medical man; since then he has been confined to his bed here with a very severe bilious attack, combined with diarrhea; and I think it advisable for you to come to see him as soon as possible.

"WILLIAM PALMER."

On Monday morning Cook was better and able to eat something, but he still lay stretched on his yellow-curtained bed at the Talbot Arms. In the afternoon he gets up for an hour or two and talks to his trainer and jockeys.

After seeing Cook for a few minutes in the morning, Palmer, it appears, hurried up to London to get his friend's accounts settled with respect to Shrewsbury races. Mr. Herring, to whom Cook had hinted his suspicions regarding the brandy-and-water, called on Palmer at his town lodging, 8, Beaufort-buildings, Strand, in compliance with a letter received from Palmer that morning.

"I inquired of him," states Mr. Herring, "how Mr. Cook was;" when he said, "Oh, he's all right; the physician had given him some calomel and recommended him not to come out, being a damp day," and added, "What I want to see you about is settling his account," holding out half a sheet of notepaper. I

---

[2] Elizabeth Mills testified at the trial about her reaction to the broth and Cook's decline and death in vivid detail. Her testimony can be found in *The Times Report of the Trial of William Palmer* (Peschel Press, 2015).

176 THE LIFE OF WILLIAM PALMER.

SHREWSBURY RACES.

rose slightly to take it, when he said, "You had better take it down," tearing some letter-paper and pushing it towards me at the time with pen and ink, saying, "What I have here will be a check against you."

Mr. Herring, it appears, held three £200 bills of exchange, one drawn by Mr. Cook and accepted by Palmer, the others drawn by Palmer and accepted by Cook. One of these had been settled at Shrewsbury; the remainder were now paid and cancelled. The various sums to be received amounted to £1,020, but of this £110 was refused, on the plea of a set-off.[3] He therefore wrote word to Mr. Cook, at Mr. Palmer's, Rugeley, to the effect that he had not been able to remit £350 he was to have sent to Mr. Padwick, but that he had duly sent a cheque for £450 to Mr. Pratt, the lawyer usually employed by Palmer in his monetary transactions. A telegraphic reply was directly returned by Palmer from the nearest station to Rugeley, requesting him to advance the amount necessary to make Mr. Padwick all right, and that he should be repaid on the Thursday. Mr. Herring prudently declined.

Subsequently, when the original memorandum sent by Palmer to Colwich was sought for, it appeared that his influence had availed to procure its restitution. Consequently, no legal proof exists that it was in his handwriting.

It was near upon 10 o'clock at night when Palmer arrived at Rugeley from London, yet at this late hour he hastened to call on a Mr. Newton, assistant to Mr. Salt,[4] a surgeon at Rugeley, whom he asked for three grains of strychnine. Newton

---

[3] A legal term meaning the party with the money could withhold payment to another party who owes money in return.
[4] Surgeons were addressed as Mr. because they did not undergo formal medical training at a university but learned their trade through apprenticeships. They were not even required to take an examination with the Surgeons' Company in London. Even if they passed, they received a diploma, not a degree, so they would still be addressed as Mr. Only physicians, who needed a degree in medicine, were entitled to be called Doctors. Palmer was a member of the MRCS (Royal College of Surgeons) and he put up a brass plate with "Mr. William Palmer" on his door. Only his notoriety has bestowed the title of Doctor on him.

weighed it accurately and gave it to him enclosed in a piece of paper. Palmer said nothing further but "Good night" and hurried off, taking it away with him.

On this same night Cook took two pills, which made him excessively ill. He screamed wildly, rolled his eyes about, and beat the bed-clothes with his hands while his head moved convulsively and his limbs soon after straightened.

Mr. Palmer, being sent for in haste, gave him some comforting words, two more pills, and a thick, dark-coloured draught, which smelt like opium. The sick man vomited almost immediately, but there was no appearance of the pills, and presently he fell into a refreshing slumber. The laudanum, if such it was, had been administered in too large a dose for the state of the stomach after so much irritation — otherwise it might have soothed him into a sleep from which there would have been no awaking.

During Tuesday, the 20th of November, Palmer, known not to have any large practice, goes to a chemist's shop in Rugeley, and buys 6 grs. of strychnine,[5] and 2 drs. of prussic acid.

---

[5] *Grs.* = grains, an obsolete unit of weight based on the size of a cereal seed. A standard aspirin tablet of 325 milligrams is the equivalent of five grains. A grain of pure strychnine is capable of killing a human. It seems like six grains would be overkill, but in the 1850s, drugs were nowhere near as pure as they are today. *2 drs. of prussic acid:*

In the afternoon of the same day, Mr. W.H. Jones, of Lutterworth, arrives to look after the sick man.

Old Dr. Bamford again called, and after seeing his patient, goes away with Palmer to prepare the necessary medicines. When he had made them up and put them into a box, Palmer asked him to write upon them the direction of how they were to be taken. This struck Bamford as being extraordinary, because, as Palmer himself was a medical man and was going to give the pills to the patient, there could be no necessity for writing the direction, which a medical man usually does when another medical man does not intervene to see the dose administered; but by Palmer's desire he did write the direction — "pills to be taken at bedtime." He put the box into a paper and sealed it up.

Three-quarters of an hour elapsed between the time the prisoner left Bamford and came to Cook. When he did come he gave Cook two pills; but before he gave them he opened the box, and called the attention of Mr. Jones to the direction, saying, in allusion to Mr. Bamford's handwriting, "how wonderful it was that a man of eighty should write so good and strong a hand." Vomiting ensued immediately after the pills had been administered, but the pills remained on the stomach.

This was at a little past eleven o'clock. Mr. Jones slept in the same room with his friend; the foot of the beds were opposite to each other, the room being sufficiently large, and Mr. Cook lying between the door and the window.

About midnight Mr. Jones undressed himself and turned in. He had not laid down above twenty minutes, when his friend called to him in alarm, and begged that Mr. Palmer might be sent for immediately. That gentleman was by his bedside within three minutes, foolishly volunteering the remark that he had never dressed so quickly in his life before. He then gave him two pills which he brought with him, saying, that they were ammonia pills — a preparation never kept ready made up, because of evaporation.[6]

Drs.=drachms, a unit of measurement roughly equal to 1/8 of a fluid ounce, or about a teaspoon. *Prussic acid* is a poisonous liquid containing hydrogen cyanidea. It is called today hydrocyanic acid.

[6] Ammonia is a chemical compound of nitrogen and hydrogen, noted for its pungent odor. It was used as an emetic and to relieve dyspeptic flatulence or heart palpitations. *Druitt's Surgeon's Vade-Mecum*

A terrible scene now ensued. Wildly shrieking, the patient tossed about in fearful convulsions; his limbs were so rigid that it was impossible to raise him, though he entreated that they would do so as he felt that he was suffocating. Every muscle was convulsed; his body bent upwards like a bow; they turned him over on his left side; the action of the heart gradually ceased and he was dead.

(1887) recommended keeping ammonia pills in a corked bottle lest they lost potency, but there's no indication that they couldn't be made up ahead of time.

CHAPTER XX.

COOK'S STEP-FATHER COMES TO RUGELEY — THE MISSING BETTING-BOOK — POST-MORTEM EXAMINATION — PALMER ATTEMPTS TO BRIBE THE POSTBOY — IS MORE FORTUNATE WITH THE POSTMASTER — TRIES IT ON WITH THE CORONER — IS ARRESTED FOR DEBT — IS FOUND GUILTY OF WILFUL MURDER.

COOK BEING NOW DEAD BEYOND all question, Palmer sets to work to possess himself of his remaining effects. He had already appropriated his winnings at Shrewsbury, with the exception of the Handicap Stakes; these he could not touch, as they were not payable till a week after the race and then only in London.

The evening that Cook expired, but before his actual decease, Palmer posted a cheque, which purported to be signed by Cook, to the secretary of the Jockey Club[1] for £350 on account of the said stakes. The day following, he writes off to Pratt, saying, "Mind, I must have Polestar;" and further, "should any one call upon you to know what monies Cook ever had from you, don't answer the question."

The breath was hardly out of Cook's body before Palmer orders someone to be sent for to lay the body out. The women on entering the room, find Palmer searching the pockets of a coat, which, there could be no doubt, was Mr. Cook's; they saw

---

[1] An aristocratic gentleman's club that started as an informal group of men interested in horseracing until it was formally founded in 1750. In reaction to the unregulated sport, the club began to assume an air of authority. In 1803, it published its rules for racing. By 1807, it was hearing evidence on disputed races and publishing the results. It also began sponsoring major races such as the 2,000 Guineas in competition with the Oakes and Derby. By the 1850s, the club was recognized by many local meetings as the ultimate authority on the conduct of races.

him hunt under the pillow and under the bolster; they saw some letters lying on the mantel-piece, which there was every reason to believe had been taken from the coat; on the following day, Palmer again rummages among Cook's things, under the pretence of seeking for a paper-knife which he had borrowed for him.

The death of Cook was communicated to his relatives in London. Palmer, when he heard what had been done, is reported to have exclaimed, "Good God! why, he has no relatives!"

On Friday, the 23rd, Mr. Stephens, who married Cook's mother, came down to Rugeley, and, after viewing the body of his relative, to whom he had been tenderly attached, asked Palmer about his affairs. Palmer assured him that he held a paper drawn up by a lawyer and signed by Cook stating that in respect of £4,000 worth of bills, he (Cook) was alone liable, and that Palmer had a claim to that amount against his estate. Mr. Stephens expressed his amazement and replied that there would not be 4,000 shillings for the holders of the bills. Subsequently Palmer displayed an eager officiousness in the matter of the funeral, taking upon himself to order a shell and an oak coffin. Mr. Stevens ordered dinner at the hotel for Bamford, Jones, and himself, and finding Palmer still hanging about, thought it but civil to extend the invitation to him. Accordingly they all sat down together.

After dinner, Mr. Stephens asked Jones to step upstairs and bring down all books and papers belonging to Cook. Jones left the room to do so, and Palmer followed him. They were absent about ten minutes, and on their return Jones observed that they were unable to find the betting-book[2] or any of the papers belonging to the deceased.

Palmer added, "The betting-book would be of no use to you if you found it, for the bets are void by his death." Mr. Stephens replied, "The book must be found;" and then Palmer, changing his tone, said, "Oh, I dare say it will turn up."

Mr. Stephens on this rang the bell, and when the housekeeper came, desired her immediately to go and take

---

[2] One witness at the trial described the book as "a dark book, with gold bands round the edges. It was not a very large book, rather more long than square, and had a clasp at one end."

possession of whatever there might be of Mr. Cook's; to lock the door, and allow no one to have access to the place until his return from London, where he had made up his mind to go to obtain the assistance of a solicitor.

On his arrival in London, he consulted his solicitor, who gave him a letter of introduction to Mr. Gardner,[3] a respectable gentleman practising in Rugeley. In returning from London the next day, on the train stopping for refreshment at Wolverton, he met Palmer, who was a passenger by the same train, having been up to London to pay some more money to Pratt, and Mr. Stephens communicated his determination to have a *post-mortem* examination. Palmer was particularly anxious to learn who were the persons who would be employed; Mr. Stephens did not inform him, but he did tell him he intended to employ a solicitor to inquire into his step-son's affairs; on which Palmer offered to recommend him one, an offer which Mr. Stephens thought proper to decline.

On Sunday, the 25th, Palmer goes to Dr. Bamford, and asks him for a certificate of the cause of Cook's death. Bamford replies, "Why should you ask me for it? He was your patient."

"No," said Palmer, "I would rather you gave the certificate." It was thereupon discussed what the certificate should be, and finally it was entered "apoplexy."[4]

On the same day, Palmer sent for Cheshire, and producing a paper purporting to bear the signature of Cook, asked him to attest it. Cheshire glanced over it. It was a document in which Cook acknowledged that bills to the amount of £4,000, or thereabouts, had been negotiated for his (Cook's) benefit, and in respect of which Palmer had received no consideration.

Cheshire refused; whereupon Palmer carelessly observed, "It is of no consequence; I dare say the signature will not be

---

[3] James Gardner testified during the trial's second day about the quality of the questions put to the witnesses during the inquest. In *The Poisoner*, Stephen Bates speculated that it was Gardner who passed along Rugeley gossip to the Attorney-General about Jere Smith's intimate relationship with Palmer's mother.

[4] The medical term for a stroke or a fit. Nowadays, it is used to describe a stroke, an inability to feel or move a part of the body due to a loss of blood flow to the brain, or a hemorrhage in a body cavity or organ.

disputed, but it occurred to me that it would look more regular if it were attested."

On the evening of the same day, Palmer writes another note to Pratt, urging him to be silent with reference to Cook's affairs. Here is the note in question:—

"(STRICTLY PRIVATE AND CONFIDENTIAL.)

"MY DEAR SIR, — Should any of Cook's friends call upon you to know what money Cook ever had from you, pray don't answer that question, or any other about money matters, until I have seen you. And oblige yours faithfully,

"WILLIAM PALMER."

About seven o'clock the same evening he sends for Mr. Newton, the person from whom he obtained the strychnia on the previous Monday. Newton thereupon goes to Palmer's house. Palmer was sitting by the kitchen fire reading. No one else was present.

He asked Newton to have some brandy and water, and then enquired of him the proper dose of strychnine to kill a dog, and also as to what would be the appearance of the stomach after death. Newton told him that there would be no inflammation, and that he did not think it could be found. Upon that Palmer snapped his finger and thumb in a quiet way, and exclaimed, as if communing with himself, "All right."

On the following day — Monday, the 26th of November, the *post-mortem* examination took place. Palmer, hearing that Newton was to assist, invited him beforehand to have some brandy, and persuaded him to drink a couple of glasses, neat. Palmer was present at the *post-mortem*, and seeing that the intestines and stomach presented a healthy appearance, could not refrain from observing to Dr. Bamford in a loud whisper, "Doctor, they won't hang us yet!"

The stomach and intestines were taken out and placed in a jar, and it was observed that Palmer pushed against the medical man who was engaged in the operation, and the jar was in danger of being upset. It escaped,[5] however, and was

---

[5] It did not. Palmer bumped Newton into Devonshire as he was transferring the stomach contents into a glass jar, pouring some of the fluid back into the body cavity.

covered with skins, tied down, and sealed.

Presently one of the medical men turned round, and finding that the jar had disappeared, asked what had become of it. It was found at a distance, near a different door from that through which people usually passed in and out, and Palmer exclaimed, "It's all right. It was I who removed it. I thought it would be more convenient for you to have it here, that you might lay your hands readily on it as you went out." When the jar was recovered it was found that two slits had been cut in the skins with a knife.

On the evening of the same day, Mr. Stephens having made up his mind that the stomach should be submitted to analysis by Professor Taylor,[6] engaged a fly[7] to convey him from the Talbot Arms, Rugeley, to the Stafford railway station, intending to carry the jars up to London himself. The fly was already horsed and waiting, and while the postboy who was to drive it was hurrying from his lodgings to the hotel, he encountered Palmer, who offered him a £10 note to upset the vehicle. The postboy firmly refused the tempting bribe.

According to rumours, which, however, we do not credit, Palmer was afterwards, in company with others, seen following the fly.

Mr. Stephens reached London safely, and gave the jars[8] into Professor Taylor's custody. The same evening that Mr. Stephens started off, Palmer was observed walking about the streets of Rugeley drunk! — drunk, too, as they say, for the first time in his life!

While Dr. Taylor was engaged with his analysis, the Coroner summoned a jury together, and opened an inquiry. At the first meeting the proceedings were merely formal, the body being only viewed and identified. Palmer appears by this time to have felt his position to be a doubtful one. He was a very reserved man to those who were not intimate with him;

---

[6] Alfred Swaine Taylor (1806-1880), toxicologist and the father of British forensic medicine. He became the first celebrity expert witness, conducting tests for poison and testifying at numerous murder trials.

[7] A light carriage drawn by a horse, used to ferry passengers or goods.

[8] There was only one jar, into which was thrown the stomach, slit open and inverted and the intestines which were not tied off.

nevertheless, while the inquests were going on, he treated everybody at the Talbot Arms to anything they would have.

His main trust was in his friend, the postmaster of the town, Mr. Cheshire, who, it will be remembered, was one of his referees in respect of "George Bates, Esq." It seems that Palmer used to place his carriage at the disposal of Mrs. Cheshire on Sundays, on which day that lady indulged in an afternoon drive, so that Cheshire owed him a good turn; this Cheshire proceeded to acquit himself of in the following fashion. Of course, from Cheshire's position, the correspondence passing to and fro between the solicitors and Dr. Taylor could be easily tampered with, and none but himself be the wiser. It was tampered with; and no doubt every letter that passed through the post-office referring to the case was shown to Palmer by Cheshire.

At any rate, we learn from Cheshire's own lips that Palmer called on him on Sunday, the 2d of December, and gave him a hint which he was not slow to take. He goes to Palmer next morning to tell him that nothing was up. Palmer was then in bed ill. Cheshire visits him again on the Wednesday, and this time with the joyful intelligence that no poison had been found; he having opened Dr. Taylor's letter to the solicitor to ascertain that fact.

"I knew they would not," said Palmer, "I'm as innocent as a baby."

No doubt this little bit of information helps to raise Palmer's spirits. He thinks that all he has to do now is to make it right with the Coroner, W. Webb Ward, Esq.; so, on the 8th December, he writes first of all a note to Mr. Frantz, poulterer of Stafford, ordering some "nice pheasants and a good hare," and then a note to the Coroner to accompany the said game. In this latter note he lets out, that he had seen "in black and white," Dr. Taylor's statement to the effect, that no poison had been found, and he coolly enough suggests to the Coroner, that he should like a verdict, "died of natural causes, and thus end it."

These notes Palmer commits into the hands of Mr. George Bates, who starts off to Stafford. He goes to Mr. Frantz, the dealer in game, who says he is a pheasant short of the order, but will send the other things to Bates, at the Junction Hotel.

Bates re-directs the parcel, and gives a lad 3d. to carry it to Mr. Ward's office. He next goes in search of Mr. Ward, whom he unearths in the smoking-room of the Dolphin Inn, which owns the only billiard-room in Stafford. George, having "tipped him a knowing wink," the Coroner came out to the foot of the billiard stairs, and there received the said letter.

On Thursday, the 13th, George Bates is again wanted on a similar errand. The adjourned inquest meets on the morrow, and Taylor's evidence will then come out. Palmer is still ill in bed, and when Bates arrives, he is sent to Thirlby (Ben that used to be at Salt's) to borrow a £5 note. This he came back with, but Palmer, in the meanwhile, seems to have thought the amount too little for his purpose. He therefore sets Bates to hunt for bank-notes in a looking-glass drawer.

George can only see one for £50, which Palmer, we suppose, thinks too much, and yet it is a question of life and death with him. At this juncture, a sheriff's officer is announced. So it has come to that at last; these bills, which he had set afloat, paying as much as 75 per cent per annum for discount, have at length entangled him in the meshes of the web.

Bates is now ordered to retire while Palmer holds some little conversation with the officer. When he comes back again, Palmer hands him a letter to take to W.W. Ward, Esq., which he is to be sure no one sees him deliver. George did not like so much secrecy, and he asked Mr. Palmer if he could not send someone else.

Palmer replied, "Why, George, as to this poor fellow Cook, they will find nothing in him; for he was the best pal I ever had in my life; and why should I have poisoned him?" and he added, "I am as innocent as you, George."

George thereupon goes off to Stafford. This time he catches William Webb Ward on the road between the Station and the Junction Hotel, and there slily slips the note into his hand. Not a word passed; both of them no doubt understood each other.

The next day, Friday, Dec. 14th, was a day of deep anxiety for William Palmer. Although matters looked black enough as they stood, still, until the Nemesian,[9] Dr. Alfred Taylor, came

---

[9] A variation of Nemesis, the Greek spirit of divine retribution

down to Rugeley, and threw the weight of his evidence into the scale, there was nothing more than vague, though serious, suspicion attaching to our sporting surgeon.

The witnesses had described Cook's death, with its minutest particulars; the medical evidence agreed that these particulars unmistakeably indicated tetanus. Dr. Taylor proved that that tetanus was produced by strychnine; and Charles Robert, in his turn, proved that he sold strychnine to Palmer only a day before Cook's death.

Palmer is summoned; the answer given is that he is too ill to attend — perhaps the sheriff's officers feared an escape.

Next day a verdict of "Wilful Murder" is returned, and Palmer's friend — the recipient of the "fine pheasant and a good hare" — the suspected recipient of the £5 note — W. Webb Ward, Esq., coroner for Staffordshire — makes out his warrant of commitment to the county prison.

Mr. Hatton, the local police superintendent, proceeds to Palmer's house, and arrests him. He is still in the custody of the sheriff's officers; and still too unwell to be removed. A guard of police officers is therefore left behind. So thoroughly did Palmer's friends believe in his innocence that when notice was given him of his arrest on the charge, a familiar companion of his, who was in the room at the time, was about to seize the officer by the throat, declaring that he would never allow Palmer to be taken away on such a diabolical charge. Such a proceeding would have availed Palmer nothing.

The police officers proceeded at once with their duty. Every article in the room was strictly examined; and a crowd of persons, whose murmuring voices could be distinctly heard in the miserable man's bedchamber, congregated around the house till midnight, in expectation of seeing him carried away to gaol.

Jerry Smith, the lawyer, saw him on the morning after the Coroner's jury had returned their verdict. He sent to see Jerry. It was some time before the latter could make up his mind to go; for, as he said, the news made him fall sick.

At last, when he recovered himself, he entered the room. Palmer was surrounded by policemen. Jerry, pointing to them,

---

against those who succumb to hubris.

said, "William! William! how is this?" Palmer could not answer him, but the tears trickled down his cheeks. This, the police say, is the only time they ever saw him affected, or betray any symptoms of emotion.

He, doubtless, did not pass one of the calmest nights in that well-known room in the old familiar house where he had lived so long — that room where he had, about a twelvemonth previously, gazed, though but for a moment, on the pale features of his dead wife for the last time. What would he give now to be able to re-call her — that she might whisper one word of comfort in his ear in his dire misery! — she who would have believed him innocent, though twenty juries pronounced him guilty; and, if guilty, would have brought him to repentance by the deep power of a woman's love. Alas! instead of her by his side, he sees the officers of justice crowded around his bed, watching for that slight change in his disorder which will warrant them in carrying him off a prisoner to Stafford gaol.

STAFFORD GAOL.

CHAPTER XXI.

PALMER'S FAREWELL — PALMER IN PRISON — HIS VOLUNTARY STARVATION — HIS FURNITURE SEIZED AND SOLD.

WE NEXT HEAR OF WILLIAM Palmer as a prisoner in Stafford gaol. Before, however, he was conveyed there, he took a farewell leave of Eliza Tharm, his maid-servant, throwing his arms round her neck, and requiting her illicit love with a £50 Bank of England note.

We have already spoken of the child to which she had given birth. There are dreadful reports current at Rugeley respecting it. The child, it seems, was sent out to nurse at Armitage, some two or three miles out of Rugeley, near the Canal Bridge. Some two or three days before Cook's death it is said that Palmer sent for the child, under the pretence that he wished to see that it was quite well. The reader will guess the result, the child was seized with convulsions while going home and died shortly after, or as some say, on its journey back.

When Palmer reached the prison he was still very ill; indeed he had risen from his bed to accompany the officers. Directly he arrived at the gaol he went to bed again. The Governor[1] took advantage of this to remove his clothes, for he had been directed to take them away, for fear that Palmer might have poison concealed on his person. Another suit of clothes was made expressly for him in the place of the old ones, but these Palmer declined to wear, and stated that he never would. From the great anxiety he evinced to have his own clothes, the officers felt persuaded that he had poison concealed in the seams or corners of either the coat, waistcoat, or trousers. Of course, a very small quantity of such a poison as

---

[1] Capt. William Fulford (1812-1886) had no experience in running a prison. He was commissioned into the Royal Artillery in 1831 and served in Corfu and Jamaica. He was sent home after contracting yellow fever in 1847.

he was wont to use would have sufficed.

When after a fortnight his own clothes were returned, the entire suit had previously been searched as carefully as possible. The seams were opened, and the garments were beaten and shaken sufficiently to remove any powder, were any concealed about them.

Palmer in his despondency appears on his first entry into the prison, to have determined on self-destruction. He remained in bed, refusing to take any food, simply swallowing a little water from time to time.

On the sixth day the Governor became alarmed by this obstinacy, and, at his morning's visit to the prison, he spoke to him, as he did, indeed, every day, arguing with him, and endeavouring to persuade him to take his food. Palmer constantly replied that he did not want anything, and that he was not hungry.

The Governor, finding him so determined, and seeing that the danger was imminent, resolved on forcing him to take nourishment. He procured a stomach-pump, and, ordering a basin of soup to be made, visited the prisoner. He once more asked him to take his food. Palmer again answered that he had no appetite.

The Governor replied that his looks were those of a healthy man, that his pulse was good, and that there was no apparent reason why he should not make the effort. Palmer still persisted in saying he should not eat.

The Governor reasoned with him, and told him, that if he did not take his food quietly, he should have to place the tube of the stomach-pump in his mouth, and inject the soup into his stomach. He pointed out to Palmer that his resistance was useless, for that in less than five minutes — if he was forced to have recourse to compulsory measures — he could oblige him to swallow the soup, as all he had to do was to summon his officers, (of whom there were fifty in the building), to place a small gag in his (Palmer's) mouth, and introduce the coil, and in less than five minutes the soup would be down his throat.

"In fact," added the Governor, "I shall just allow you the five minutes to consider whether you will take the food in the ordinary way or not."

After the five minutes had expired, Palmer seemed to

GATEWAY AT STAFFORD GAOL.

think better of the matter and took the soup, and ever since he has continued to eat his meals. At one time he requested that food might be sent to him from his own house, but of course this request was at once refused, in order to guard against any attempt being made to convey poison to him. He was told that he might order what he liked, but that it must be cooked in the prison.

The County Gaol and House of Correction[2] of Stafford has very much the appearance of a large, squat brick castle. At the corners of the building are round towers of red brick, and there are two outer walls of red brick adjoining two red inner walls. There is a red-hot glare about the pile, as if you saw it through red glass. The principal entrance is entirely built of stone, and it is quite refreshing to get near it, for it is like being in the cool shade.

---

[2] The HM Prison Stafford has been in nearly continuous operation since 1793. The complex is still surrounded by high red brick walls, but otherwise looks nothing like it did in Palmer's time.

The Governor's house is exactly opposite the porter's lodge, and has a little bit of a garden before it to enliven it; but the grass seems to know it is in prison, or else the ground is on criminal allowance, and allowed no luxuries such as manure; for the Governor's garden is not flourishing, and, beyond some remarkably fine flint stones, seems to grow nothing worthy of notice.

A pathway from hence leads to the debtors' airing court, a large piece of ground surrounded by wooden railings. The bake-house is next to the debtors' court; and through the windows, may usually be seen a vast amount of bread, not in square loaves such as freemen usually eat, but slabs of bread, like three-inch deal-planks,[3] sawn in small lengths of three feet, and piled together with the greatest order. A kind of grinding noise is heard, together with the hum of machinery. The power by which the mill-stones are put in motion is no other than a tread-wheel of 32-felon power, with poor wretches dressed in their prison gray, walking up "the endless stairs," which turns away beneath their feet.

Soon after Palmer's arrest, a solicitor of Birmingham arrived at Rugeley early one morning and demanded admittance into his house in virtue of a bill of sale for £10,400,[4] given by Palmer in the spring of 1855. The request was refused by the superintendent of police who was in charge of the papers and other things in the house and an entrance was subsequently effected by breaking a pane of glass and opening a window.

Arrangements were soon made for selling off the effects by public auction, and we gather from Mrs. Bennett, the next-door neighbour, that if it had been a nobleman's sale there couldn't have been more folks there. They came from Birmingham, and all round about. The sale, which, according to the catalogue, was to have occupied three days, was passed over between a morning and a night.

"The sale was too hurried," this lady said. "If they had

---

[3] A technical term for a board of a particular size usually sawn from a pine or fir log. The boards were thick, as big as 7 inches wide, 3 inches thick, and 6 feet long, but the actual size varied depending on the country it came from.

[4] Equivalent to £852,000 or $1.4 million today.

brought the things out into the open air, they would have fetched much more money; but they didn't give the bidding time. The books were almost given away, loads and loads of things went off from here to Birmingham. The furniture was very good indeed."

"His house was very handsomely furnished," observed an informant to us. "I know he gave forty guineas for a sideboard, and sixteen pounds for a cheffonier;[5] his chairs cost four guineas each. He had a very good taste in furniture. I am a cabinet-maker, and I have made many pieces of furniture under his directions. He had a very good taste indeed."

According to the catalogue of the sale, Palmer was possessed of 222 gallons of ale, and 67 dozen of port, and 43 gallons of spirits. He had more bottles in his cellar than in his surgery. He had 800 in the one, and only 137 in the other; but what matter where they were kept, since, doubtless, all were equally employed in his drugging business?

During the sale while the police were looking on, a deal box[6] was put up, with some fishing tackle and some pills. The auctioneer emphasized "pills," but the police did not think it worth their while to interfere. It is not at all improbable but that these might have been Bamford's pills thrown aside in a great hurry; for a medical man is not likely to keep his pills in a deal fishing-tackle box.

A prayer-book was purchased by a lady at the sale which had been presented to Palmer's wife by Colonel Brooks. Under the inscription, written in pencil, in Mrs. Palmer's handwriting, there was a long prayer for the safety of her child, beseeching most earnestly that he might not be cut off suddenly like the other four.

We wonder who bought "the handsome mahogany German bedstead, with panelled footboard, carved cornice, fringe, and figured damask hangings," on which poor Mrs. Palmer died!

---

[5] A piece of furniture similar to a sideboard but narrower and with doors enclosing the shelves. From the French word for rag-picker, suggesting that it was built to hold odds and ends.

[6] As mentioned above, deal is a technical term for a large board. So a deal box, and a deal fishing-tackle box, below, are boxes made from a deal-plank.

CHAPTER XXII.

THE SALE OF PALMER'S STUD AT TATTERSALL'S.

OPPOSITE THE GRAND ENTRANCE TO Hyde-park, where the carriages and horsemen enter, and where the mob stands to see the Queen go by, down by Decimus Burton's arch, with the horrible equestrian statue[1] of the late lamented F.M., on the top of it, is Tattersall's, the *sanctum sanctorum*[2] of sporting men; a haunt as familiar to the juvenescent Yorkshire tyke as to the best swell in London, a name as suggestive of good faith, honour, prompt payments, splendid horse-flesh, and noble company, as it is of swindling, robbery, "*non est's,*"[3] screws, and blackguards.

---

[1] Decimus Burton (1800-1881) was a prolific architect and garden designer. The arch in question is the Wellington Arch, designed to commemorate Britain's victories in the Napoleonic Wars. It was built to Burton's design between 1826 and 1830 and placed at the Hyde Park Corner entrance. In 1846, the arch was crowned with a statue of Field Marshal Arthur Wellesley, the Duke of Wellington (1769-1852), who commanded the British armies against Napoleon. At 30 feet tall, the statue showing Wellington on his horse and pointing was the largest equestrian statue in Britain. It was also completely out of proportion to the arch and many people suggested moving it. Queen Victoria privately agreed, but didn't want to risk offending Wellesley (who probably didn't give a damn one way or another) and ordered that it remain there throughout his lifetime. Wellington died in 1852, but they didn't get around to moving the statue until the arch was moved to its current location south of the park in 1882-83. The statue was replaced with a smaller, more elaborate statue depicting Nike, the winged goddess of victory, gently bestowing a laurel wreath on a military chariot being pulled by four horses and guided by a boy. The Wellington statue was moved to Aldershot, about 40 miles southeast of London, where the first permanent training camp for the British Army was founded.

[2] A Latin translation of the Biblical term "holy of holies," usually used to refer to the holiest spot in the Tabernacle of ancient Israel and later the temples in Jerusalem.

[3] A sheriff's writ that is returned when the person to be arrested or served with it cannot be found. From the shortened form of the Latin *non est inventus* for "[he] was not found defaulting."

There is a sporting air about the whole place, from the red-jacketed touts, who hang round the entrance, to the shrewd look of the auctioneer himself. Come down the yard, filling already, for the news that Palmer's nags are coming to the hammer has spread abroad; and hundreds whom business would never have tempted have strolled here through curiosity.

Here they are, gentle and simple, young and old, peers, gentry, tradesmen, and legs.[4] That tall old man, with the fine aristocratic face, and neck swathed in the thick white choker, is a clergyman, and as thorough a sportsman as ever stepped; the dirty little man in the brown coat, is a Viscount, and the tall, handsome roman-nosed man in the great coat with the fur collar, a butcher. Here comes the leviathan of the ring; this tall thin man, dressed entirely in black, with a blue-speckled handkerchief round his throat — he was a carpenter once, and his word is now good for £50,000.

In the stables you will find the acme of neatness and cleanliness; here to the right, is the subscription room, into which we must not go, and here, a public-house, for the bodily solace of these little grooms and jockies sprinkled here and there among the crowd.

It is Monday, January 14, 1856. The Rugeley poisoning cases are, of course, the ruling topic of conversation, and great was the interest excited by the presence of Mr. Hatton, chief of the Stafford constabulary, who, accompanied by Mr. W.V. Stephens, executor of the late John Parsons Cook, had come there to make inquiries relative to the money received of or paid to Mr. Cook. Notes, with certain indorsements on them, were known to have been in the possession of Mr. Cook, and information was requested respecting them. Ere Mr. Hatton takes his departure he causes the subjoined notices to be posted in the room, and a crowd, of course, soon collects to read them.

"Any gentleman who saw William Palmer in London on Saturday, the 24th of November, is earnestly requested to communicate with J.H. Hatton, Esq., chief of the county constabulary, Stafford; or with Mr. W.V. Stephens, No. 11, Campden-grove, Kensington, executor to the deceased."

---

[4] Short for blacklegs, the nickname for a dandy, professional gambler, or racecourse swindler, identified by his shiny black boots.

"Any gentleman who paid the late Mr. Cook money at Shrewsbury races, or who had, or witnessed any money transactions with him at that time, is earnestly requested to communicate with J.H. Hatton, Esq., chief of the county constabulary, Stafford, or with Mr. W.V. Stephens, &c."

It was on the Monday following that the brood mares, horses in training, and yearlings belonging to William Palmer of Rugeley were put up to auction at "the Corner." Many of the leading patrons of the turf, and most of the trainers from the north and south of England, were, of course, present; but a large majority of the miscellaneous assemblage consisted of persons whose motive was to satisfy a feeling of curiosity which the circumstances connected with the sale had excited.

In certain instances competition was sustained with much spirit and high prices were realised. In the aggregate, the sale amounted to £3,906.

Major Grove, Her Majesty's commissioner from the Royal paddocks, bought Trickstress for 230 guineas; but, strange to say, although he appeared to bid anxiously for Nettle — a decidedly superior animal — he at last let her go, Mr. F.L. Popham purchasing her for 430 guineas. Nettle, it will be remembered, was first favourite for the Oaks last year, but she fell over the chains soon after starting, and her jockey had his thigh fractured. The Chicken was "knocked down" for 800 guineas; the first bid was 300, and Mr. H. Hill spiritedly advanced the price, until he reached 780 guineas, when he stopped. The horse was ultimately sold to Mr. Harlock, who, it was understood, bought him for a "noble lord." For the 3 yr-old filly by Melbourne, out of Seaweed, Mr. Sargent gave 500 guineas. Staffordshire Nan was purchased for 300 guineas.

With regard to the 2-year-old brown colt by Sir Hercules, the auctioneer announced that a paper, signed by Palmer, had been handed to him, containing a promise on Palmer's behalf to pay the breeder of the colt 100 guineas on the first occasion of the animal's winning. This promise, however, the auctioneer stated, would, in no way, affect the sale, as the purchaser could pay the money or not, as he pleased.

Subjoined is a marked catalogue, with the names of the purchasers of the different lots affixed:

Doubt (foaled in 1846), by Gladiator, 81 guineas (Mr.

Blenkiron).

Trickstress, 8-yrs-old, 230 guineas (Prince Albert).

Duchess of Kent, 200 guineas (purchaser's name omitted).

Goldfinder's dam (foaled in 1843), 71 guineas (Mr. Parker).

Bay yearling colt by Touchstone — Duchess of Kent, 230 guineas (Mr. Padwick).

Bay yearling colt by Melbourne — Goldfinder's dam, 225 guineas (Mr. Blenkiron).

Brown yearling colt by Faugh-a-Ballagh — Doubt, 51 guineas (Mr. Nicholls).

Brown yearling filly by Touchstone — Maid of Lyme, 250 guineas (Mr. Padwick).

Brown colt 2-yrs-old by Sir Hercules — Lurley's dam, 105 guineas.

Bay filly 2-yrs-old (sister to Staffordshire Nan), 82 guineas (Mr. Hadland).

Brown filly 3-yrs-old by Melbourne — Seaweed, 590 guineas (Mr. Sargent).

Rip Van Winkle 3-yrs-old by the Flying-Dutchman, 70 guineas (Mr. Sargent).

Staffordshire Nan. 3-yrs-old, 300 guineas (Mr. Bryant).

Nettle, 4-yrs-old, 430 guineas (Mr. F. L. Popham).

THE CHICKEN.

CHAPTER XXIII.

PALMER'S HOUSE AT RUGELEY.

HE HOUSE IN WHICH PALMER lived stands exactly opposite to the Talbot Arms Hotel. It is a two-floored dwelling, with broad, modern windows, and faced with what builders call "rough cast," painted stone-colour. It is a comfortable place for an honest man to live in, and has, so says a neighbour, "some capital roomy rooms at the back."

It is not such a large house as that of Mr. Bennett, the shoemaker next door, nor has it so many outbuildings as those at "The Bell" [1] on the other side; but it has been painted and done up, and has a more "genteel" look, as if the surgeon wished to make some difference between his residence and the shops around. It has evidently been built as a superior kind of dwelling, for it stands back a few yards from the footway; a bit of turf, not bigger than a billiard-table, and a few evergreens, being enclosed by the iron railings in front.

Between the two front windows is the street-door, on which is still the brass plate of "Mr. William Palmer, Surgeon," but now grown rusty and dull, since Eliza Tharm has given over attending to it. Close against the party-wall of "The Bell" is the entrance to the surgery, with the knob of the night-bell sticking out from the door-post.

After the sale, all the shutters were closed, and as people passed by they used to look up at the windows, and point the rooms out to each other. "I've had many a glass of champagne in that room," says one. "That's where the devil used to sleep," says another; and all, cursing him, pass on.

The large window to the left of the door was that of the drawing-room. Here were "the handsome chimney glasses" and the fine-toned semi-grand pianoforte on which poor Mrs. William Palmer used to accompany herself when singing, —

---

[1] The pub, renamed the Pig and Bell, was closed in 2012 and replaced with a Chinese restaurant.

"for she was a sweet singer," as the people say. The room was well furnished. There was, to quote the words of the catalogue, the "rosewood couch, with spring seat, squab, and pillow, in blue damask, and the six elegant rosewood chairs *en suite*, and the very handsome mahogany bookcase, with plate-glass and sliding shelves," that Mrs. William Palmer used to sit and look at the long evening through, when her husband left her so much alone and was away at the race meetings.

The window to the right, on the first floor, belongs to the room in which the amiable and unfortunate lady expired. There she lay, extended on the "handsome German bedstead, with panelled foot-board, carved cornice and fringe, and figured damask hangings," with the half-conviction upon her that her husband had taken away her life, and fearing for the fate of the poor boy of seven she was parting from for ever.

Did Palmer ever sleep in that bed again? Did he see no other figures on the damask hangings besides those worked by the loom? It is known that he never would sleep alone from the time his wife died, and, perhaps, the prickings of his conscience forced him to make that partial confession of his guilt.

Palmer had a good cellar. He was a man who won hearts; and what begins a friendship so soon as a bottle of good old port? "He never drank himself, but he liked to see his friends enjoy themselves."

In the dining-room at the back, where, against the wainscotting, hung the portraits of "Marlow, the jockey," who broke his leg while riding "Nettle" for the Oaks, and "Goldfinder, the winner of the Derby." Palmer, seated on the plush velvet seat of one of the "Elizabethan carved oak chairs," would press the jovial group to try just one more bottle. Here it was that he thought "that just one glass of weak brandy-and-water wouldn't hurt Mrs. Thornton." Here, also, he sat and laughed with Bladon, passing round the bottle of "Fletcher's old port," and joking about heel taps![2]

At the back of the house stretches out the garden which covers some half-acre of land. It was well kept up — "in very good fettle," as a labourer called it. The low hedge that divided the courtyard from the garden was clipped with care, and the small garden in front of the stable, with a little bit of imitation rock-work, "to spruce it up," was thoroughly well attended to.

Palmer appears to have been a man who did not much care for flowers. He was more fond of leeks and spring onions, of which there are at least six beds. Cleanliness he liked, and so he kept his house well-painted, and his garden in order. A little patch, some twenty feet long and eight feet wide, was all the space he devoted to his flower-garden. The beds, cut out of the turf, are arranged in curious shapes, such as stars and lozenges, but beyond a few roots of pinks and drooping wallflowers, he did not attend to its floriculture.

There is a stable and coach-house, with a pear tree against the bricks, and a horse-shoe nailed to the door. In the courtyard before them Palmer's love of horses caused him to have every

---

[2] While drinking a toast with friends, it was common to cry "no heel taps!" to encourage everyone to finish their glass. A heel-tap is a layer of leather, a stack of which used to make the heel. During their drinking party at the Swan in Shrewsbury, Palmer might have used the same phrase to urge Cook to polish off his doctored glass of brandy.

improvement introduced that was useful and good. The large tank was of slate, and the rain water flowed into it, for he was too much in the society of grooms not to know that soft water was necessary to the animals' health.

In one corner next to a pigsty a manure tank was sunk, into which the slush of the stable and piggery drained, and there was a pump to raise up the liquid as it was required for the cultivation of the garden. The house is larger than would be imagined from its frontage. The dining-room runs far back, and has a little bit of grass and a few beds of flowers arranged before its window.

The whole of the building was locked up. Not a window, but the catch was turned over the sash to prevent the curious from raising it; not a door but the bolts were drawn and the lock fastened. The place seems to have been lately painted and done up. The whitewash was excessively clean, the little palings had been freshly pitched, and the woodwork repaired.

There were all the evidences of the house having been lately occupied. The brickwork partition outside the kitchen door, where the coals were kept, was still half full, and the old scuttle, in which they were carried into the house, was quietly rusting itself away into powder.

On the top of the coal-heap was the wooden top of an oyster-barrel with the card nailed to it, and the printed portion of "Lynn's oyster and fish warehouse," and the addition in ink of "7 paid," were still fresh and new. Old rope mats turned out of doors as worthless, and a broomtop with the hair worn off, were lying rotting in the yard.

Following the walk down the kitchen garden, where the clothes' poles and the cord along them form a kind of imitation telegraph, a bed of rhubarb was come to, just pushing with its new stalks and pale green leaves through the black mould. The bed was covered with manure, as if Palmer had prided himself on his rhubarb. Here was also to be found the first bed of leeks. A gooseberry and raspberry plantation of some forty trees appeared kept and pruned. The fruit-trees trained against the wall had not a bough loose.

On June 2nd, in the present year, a peripatetic photographer took up his quarters in the rear of Palmer's house, who forthwith issued the following announcement:—

> FOR A FORTNIGHT.
>
> PHOTOGRAPHIC PORTRAITS.
>
> **C. ALLEN,**
>
> Respectfully informs the Ladies, Gentry, and Inhabitants of Rugeley that he can produce
>
> **A VERY SUPERIOR PHOTOGRAPHIC PORTRAIT,**
>
> In Gilt and other Frames,
>
> *From One Shilling to One Guinea,*
>
> And solicits their patronage at the rear of the
>
> **Premises lately occupied by W. Palmer.**
>
> *Specimens may be seen at Mr. James's, Bookseller.*
>
> Commencing at 10 o'Clock Mornings, until 6 in the Evenings.
> RUGELEY, *June 2nd*, 1856.

The number of fashionably-dressed persons who journey over to Rugeley from the surrounding districts to obtain a sight of Palmer's house, is positively astounding. The photographer, no doubt, calculates upon a large proportion of these being seduced into returning home with such an interesting souvenir as their own portraits, actually taken off in Palmer's back garden.

It is not unlikely that Palmer's house will be pulled down. Old Masters, the landlord of the Talbot Arms, saw Lord Lichfield a day or two before Palmer's execution:

"Well, Masters," observed he, "What am I to do with that house?"

"I think, my Lord," replied Masters, "that you will have to pull it down."

"And I think so too," replied his lordship.[3]

---

[3] We don't know how long he held onto the building, but it stands today. Much modified, it houses two businesses.

CHAPTER XXIV.

VERDICTS OF WILFUL MURDER IN THE CASES OF ANN PALMER AND WALTER PALMER — PALMER AS A WITNESS AT WESTMINSTER — HE CHARGES HIS WIFE WITH FORGERY.

DURING THE TIME PALMER WAS attempting suicide by voluntarily starving himself in Stafford Gaol, the bodies of his wife, Ann Palmer, and of his brother, Walter Palmer, were being exhumed, and, after several adjourned inquests, verdicts of "Wilful Murder" were returned in both cases.

With respect to Mrs. Palmer, there is no manner of doubt but that she was poisoned by continual doses of antimony. No poison was found in the body of the brother; the lead coffin, and the length of time that had elapsed since his death, were sufficient to account for the evaporation of all traces of prussic acid — supposing that this deadly poison had been used to destroy Walter Palmer's life.[1]

The body of John Parsons Cook was also again exhumed in order that a more minute examination might be made of the condition of the spinal cord. The examination was proceeded with by Dr. Harland, Dr. Monckton, and Mr. Dawford, in the presence of two medical gentlemen, named by Mr. George Palmer, viz., Professor Bolton and Mr. Pemberton, of Birmingham. Both the body and coffin exhibited symptoms of decomposition. The spinal cord (which was alone the subject of

---

[1] During the inquest held at a Rugeley pub, the body had to be inspected by the jury. A hole was first bored into Walter Palmer's coffin. This turned out to be a dreadful mistake. The coffin had been hermetically sealed, so no air had been admitted. Instead of drying out and slowly decaying, Walter's body was swollen, black, partially liquefied, and reeking. Noxious fumes filled the pub, driving everyone out into the street and causing many on the jury to vomit. Once the vapors dissipated, they were able to return to the inquest. The smell lingered, however, and pub's owner had to re-sand the floors and replace the wallpaper to make it go away.

investigation) was in a state of preservation, which allowed a full and proper examination of its whole length. The spine was proved to be entirely free from disease.[2]

On January 21 of the present year, Palmer appeared at Westminster as a witness on a trial, in which Padwick was the plaintiff, and Palmer's mother the defendant. The action was to recover the amount of a bill of exchange for £12,000, which bill apparently bore the mother's acceptance. She was called to deny the handwriting, and other members of the family deposed to the same effect. Clerks in banks and solicitors were agreed that the bill was a forgery. Palmer, it seems, had put this bill into circulation, and he was at length called as a witness.

The scene was dramatic in the extreme — the court was crowded to suffocation, and most of those present were nervous with excitement in their eagerness to obtain a view of this individual.

The door of the judge's private room was thrown open, and Palmer appeared in court in the custody of an officer. He entered the witness box in a perfectly cool and collected manner, surveyed leisurely the crowded audience, to some of whom he nodded in a familiar way, and appeared to fix his attention on some person located near the learned counsel, who conducted the plaintiff's case. He was then sworn, and in a low, yet firm and distinct voice, answered the following questions put to him, betraying not the least hesitation or trepidation, and not at all moved by the gaze of the numerous audience, collected together to obtain a glimpse of so notorious an individual.

Mr. Edwin James, handing the bill of exchange to the witness, asked:— Is the signature "William Palmer," as the drawer of that bill, in your handwriting? — Palmer: Yes. And you applied to Padwick to advance you money on it? — I did. Who wrote Sarah Palmer's acceptance on it? — Anne Palmer. Who is she? — She is now dead. Do you mean your wife? — Yes. Did you see her write it? — Yes.

The witness was then removed in custody of the officer.

At this startling denouement, the counsel for the plaintiff saw no other course open to him than to retire from the case. A

---

[2] This examination was to forestall attempts by Palmer's defense to claim that Cook's health problems killed him.

verdict was, therefore, returned for the defendant,[3] and Palmer was hurried back to jail.

Shall we believe the statement which Palmer made with such cool deliberation — a statement, which every one present listened to with almost a shudder, while the man who made it was perfectly unmoved? No tender reminiscence connected with his dead wife could seal his lips if she were guilty; as no sense of justice — setting love altogether aside for her memory, could check him from calumniating[4] her, in the face of the world — if she were innocent. The secret lies between themselves, and the lips of both are now sealed.

Scoundrel as William Palmer was, he may, on some false pretence, have succeeded in persuading his wife to write the name of Sarah Palmer, in a feminine hand, across a blank piece of paper; or, he may have returned home some day, from one of his racing expeditions, and told her that he was a ruined

man — that he had staked his all on this last chance, and that fortune had not favoured him — that writs and lawyers' letters were pouring in upon him like hail; and, that to save their home, and what was dearer to her still, his good name, but one course was open; and, when he explained to her what that course was, we can imagine how she clasped her hands together in a fit of horror; but still, how in her love for him, trusting too as she did in him, as only woman trusts in man, and believing his protestations that the criminal act, he required her to perform, was the only way to save him, she was at length persuaded to write the requisite name with all the feminine skill she could command.

When, however, his increasing difficulties made it necessary for him to issue more of these so-called "securities," it was equally necessary that the signatures should all be the same handwriting. Did it so happen that the wife of William Palmer, in her deep affection for him she had sworn, at the altar, to love and obey, was once tempted to commit the crime of forgery, we can well conceive that in the hands of such a desperate and determined scoundrel as he has proved himself to be, it would have been impossible for her to recede. Henceforth she was in his power; and as the old proverb says, "Needs must when the Devil drives."

CHAPTER XXV.

WILLIAM PALMER IS TRIED FOR MURDER.

THE EXCITEMENT IN REFERENCE TO the Rugeley poisonings, for such was the designation given to the crimes with which Palmer was charged, rose to such a pitch in the immediate neighbourhood of Stafford, that it was considered the accused would not meet with a fair trial if tried at the assizes.[1] An application was therefore made to the Court of Queen's Bench, to allow the trial to take place in London, or at any rate in another county to that in which the crime was committed. This application was granted, but to admit of the trial taking place at the Central Criminal Court,[2] it was necessary to pass a special Act of Parliament. Sergeant Shee thus alluded to the circumstance at the opening of his speech in Palmer's defence:—

"The very circumstances under which we meet in this place are of a character to excite in me mingled feelings of encouragement and alarm. Those whose duty it is to watch over the safety of the Queen's subjects, felt so much apprehension lest the course of justice should be disturbed by the popular prejudice which had been excited against the prisoner — they were so much alarmed that an unjust verdict might, in the midst of that prejudice, be passed against him, that an extraordinary measure of precaution was taken, not only by her Majesty's Government, but also by the Legislature.

"An Act of Parliament, which originated in that branch of the Legislature to which the noble and learned Lord who presides here belongs, and was sanctioned by him, was passed to prevent the possibility of an injustice being done through an

---

[1] A criminal court session. Until 1972, assizes were held periodically, usually twice a year. The word assize is derived from the Old French word for session or legal action.

[2] A court building in central London that's also called the Old Bailey. The Old Bailey was located next to Newgate Prison, allowing a streamlined path for prisoners from conviction to execution.

adherence to the ordinary forms of law in the case of William Palmer.

"The Crown, also, under the advice of its responsible Ministers, resolved that this prosecution should not be left in private hands, but that its own law officer, my learned friend, the Attorney-General, should take upon himself the responsibility of conducting it. And my learned friend, when that duty was entrusted to him, did, what I must say, will for ever redound to his honour — he resolved that, in a case in which so much prejudice had been excited, all the evidence which it was intended to press against the prisoner should, as soon as he received it, be communicated to the prisoner's counsel.

"I must therefore tell my unhappy client, that everything which the constituted authorities of the land — everything which the Legislature and the law officers of the Crown could do to secure a fair and impartial trial has been done, and that if unhappily, an injustice should on either side be committed, the whole responsibility will rest upon my Lords and upon the jury."

On Wednesday, May 14, this long-deferred trial at length took place. We need not speak of it here,[3] further than to say, that after twelve days' protracted proceedings, the jury, on a brief consultation, came into court with a verdict of "Wilful Murder."

A letter has appeared in the *Times* newspaper, written by one of the jurymen, in correction of a report that was prevalent, to the effect that the jury remained out of court for a certain period of time with a view to give a greater appearance of decorum to their proceedings. The juryman in question writes:—

"On reaching the room there was a dead silence for about twenty minutes. A discussion of the facts that had been laid before us was then commenced, and it lasted for about ten minutes, after which each man took pen and paper, and wrote his decision and name, it having been agreed that no one should pronounce his opinion lest any other should receive a

---

[3] [Original footnote, modified for the updated edition—*Ed.*] See *The Times Report of the Trial of William Palmer* (426 p.p.) ~ PESCHEL PRESS — Price $19.99.

bias. The papers were then laid on the table; the foreman opened them and read them aloud, when "Guilty" was found to be the unanimous verdict. An earnest conversation then ensued, having no relation to William Palmer. This is a precise account of the proceedings of the jury.

"It is very material to the dignity of justice, and the jury's credit, that it should be known that no portion of our time was spent in sham; that no hollow pretence to appear decorous, on such a solemn occasion, was resorted to. Our situation was too dreadful, and too solemn to admit of humbug.

"It is quite untrue that we were absent a long time for the mere sake of appearances."

After sentence had been pronounced, and Palmer had been removed back to his cell, he complained to the Under-Sheriff that he had not received a fair trial. The Under-sheriff observed that he had no reason to complain, and reminded him that all the Judges agreed in the finding of the jury. Palmer's reply was, "Well, Sir, but that don't satisfy me."

During the charge of Lord Campbell, he repeatedly communicated verbally and by written messages, with Mr. John Smith, his solicitor, and the counsel conducting his case. After the learned Judge had concluded, he addressed a note to Mr. Smith, in which he stated that Lord Campbell's summing up was very unfair towards him, and that, consequently, the jury must be prejudiced against him. He added, however, the expression of his belief that they would find a verdict of not guilty.

When informed by the Under-Sheriff, after the sentence was passed, that he must prepare immediately to return to his former quarters in Stafford Gaol, he asked by what railway he was to be conveyed; and on being told that the London and North-Western was the usual and most direct route, he begged that he might be taken by the Great Western Railway, as he was so well known on the North-Western that he would be recognised all along the line. The Under-Sheriff informed him that his request could not be complied with, and he acquiesced without any further observation.

As it was suspected that the prisoner might attempt to commit suicide, and thus defeat the ends of justice, a new suit of clothes was prepared for him, which he was directed to put on immediately after his return to his apartment at Newgate. No person was allowed to see him or to communicate with him after the sentence was passed, except the Under-Sheriff and the authorities of the prison.

During the trial, the prisoner expressed a belief that one at least of the jurymen, whose "personnel" appeared to attract his attention, was not the man to return a verdict of guilty, and on more than one occasion, in his communications with his counsel and his solicitor, he alluded to this gentleman.

Before quitting the bench, the learned Judges signed the warrants for the removal of the prisoner to Stafford Gaol; and at twenty minutes to eight o'clock on the evening of his condemnation, two cabs drove up to Newgate, one of them entering the gaol gates, and the other remaining outside the governor's entrance. In a few minutes after, Palmer was brought out of the governor's door, placed in a cab, which, after the entrance of Mr. Weatherhead (the governor) and two officers, drove off as rapidly as possible. A great crowd had collected round the gaol gates, and when, a few seconds afterwards, the second cab was brought out empty, they saw that they had been deceived, and immediately ran after the first cab, and hooted the prisoner in the most excited manner.

The cab arrived at the Euston station in time for the eight o'clock train. At the station there was much excitement, Palmer having been recognised at the instant he arrived on the platform. He was thrust into the middle compartment of a first-class carriage, and the blinds were at once drawn across the windows. He was dressed in convict's costume,[4] his feet were ironed, the irons also being attached to one of the keepers, and his hands handcuffed. A cloak covered the whole.

Palmer arrived at Stafford late at night. Woollaston, the superintendent of the Stafford police, who was waiting to receive him, took one of his arms, and Weatherhead, the governor of Newgate, the other. Palmer looked rather fagged;

---

[4] The sole illustration of Palmer at his trial shows him in an ordinary civilian suit. Prisoners' outfits consisted of a blue-striped cotton shirt, trousers, waistcoat, and a plain coat with a stock (instead of a collar) that buttoned around the neck and over which the shirt collar folds. It looked different enough to be distinctive on the street without resorting to zebra-strip outfits worn by American convicts.

but it was difficult to distinguish faces, the night was so dark.

Palmer was almost the only one who spoke; he stepped in a puddle; "Dear me," said he, "it's very wet; have you had any rain down here?" Says Woollaston, "Yes, we have."

After a lapse of nearly five minutes he said, "I've had a wearying trial of it: twelve long days:" and when he stumbled he said, "Bother these chains; I wish they were off; I can't walk properly."

On Saturday, May 31, he was visited in his cell by his two brothers, George Palmer, the solicitor, and the Rev. Thomas Palmer. The latter begged earnestly that the prisoner would confess, if guilty.

"I fell on my knees before him," writes the brother in a letter to Lord Campbell;[5] "I implored him, by our past love and kindred, by our early recollections and hopes by our common faith, by all the duties which he owed to man and God, to disburthen his conscience if he were guilty, and not to enter before the presence of his Creator with a falsehood upon his lips. I adjured him to say, if he were guilty, or not guilty. Oh, my Lord! he did not wince; he did not change his noble composure: he spoke and looked all innocence. Calmly, earnestly, and solemnly he answered, and the seriousness of his words went into our hearts with the fullest persuasion of his perfect guiltlessness of blood."

On a subsequent occasion the Rev. T. Palmer again visited the convict, and more recently his sister, Sarah Palmer, came to see him. The interview between the prisoner and his sister was most affecting. She exhibited great distress, but he retained his usual composure of manner. He had some conversation with his sister respecting his little boy, expressing his anxiety respecting his welfare and prosperity in life. The poor little thing was ignorant of the doom awaiting his father, or, indeed, of his confinement in gaol, he being led to believe that he was ill at Birkenhead.[6] He says he is sure there must

---

[5] From *A Letter to the Lord Chief Justice Campbell*, a polemic attacking Campbell for the way he conducted the trial. Although it was credited to the Rev. Thomas Palmer, he denied any connection with the publication. It is suspected that one of Palmer's lawyers, Edward Kenealy, was behind it.

[6] A port near Liverpool, about 75 miles northwest of Rugeley. It was a

be something dreadful the matter with him, or that he would be certain to come home.

Poor little Willie Palmer is a nice boy, about seven years of age; he lifts his hat in an old-fashioned way when he is spoken to. He seems to be a general favorite with all who know him.

His father's miserable position was, of course, studiously concealed from him; and he did not become acquainted with it, until within a few days of Palmer's execution. It seems that a little boy (attending on his father, who was thatching a barn for old Mrs. Palmer) was playing with him. Willie made some reference to "Papa."

"Papa," said his little playmate; "your Papa is in Stafford jail."

Thomas Wright, the philanthropic foundryman, came over from Manchester, to see William Palmer in Stafford Jail, and, immediately after the old gentleman had gone, a rumour was spread about that Palmer had confessed; but one of the gaolers speaking about his confession said:—

"Well, sir, I haven't much to wager, but I'll bet every stick and stump I possess that Palmer does not confess after all. Why, he ate half-a-pound of steak last night for his tea, and complained of the milk not being good. I shall never forget the look he gave me when we took away his brush and tortoiseshell pocket-comb. We thought, you know, he might hurt himself with the comb. He went into such a passion. 'Send for the hairdresser,' he said, 'send for the hairdresser; I'll have every bit of my hair cut off."[7] And he did too. He looks so different, you can't imagine — so sharp. Yes, Mr. Wright may be a very good man, but I cannot imagine Palmer saying so much as he says he did. You mark my words, sir — and I've seen a good deal of him — he'll die hardened, and a coward."

---

center for shipbuilding and related industries.

[7] Two other stories have circulated to account for Palmer's shorn hair. In *The Times Report of the Trial of William Palmer* (Peschel Press, 2015): "At his request his light sandy hair had been closely cropped, which brought the whole configuration of his large round head and face into striking prominence." In *The Life and Career of Dr. William Palmer of Rugeley* (Peschel Press, 2014), his head was shaved after his execution so two death masks could be taken.

CHAPTER XXVI.

THE EXECUTION.

DURING THE LAST FEW DAYS of his existence, Palmer's general demeanour in no way changed. He took his meals regularly, and slept well. He maintained his self-possession; and the little conversation he had with those who visited him, or were in attendance upon him, evinced that his mind was somewhat subdued, but not depressed.

It seems that he attended chapel in the gaol twice on the Sunday preceding his execution, and these were the only occasions since his condemnation. The seat he occupied was screened from observation. The Rev. Mr. Goodacre, the chaplain of the prison, was with Palmer at frequent intervals, and did not cease to impress upon him the futility of expecting any remission of his sentence. The prisoner's brothers, George and Thomas, saw him several times during the week.

On Tuesday a beautiful Bible was received at the gaol, as a present to the prisoner by Mr. Serjeant Shee. The Bible was accompanied by a most affecting note from the learned Serjeant. The Bible and the note — melancholy *souvenirs* — will be kept by the family of the prisoner.

On Wednesday, June 11, Palmer expressed an anxious desire to see the Rev. Mr. Atkinson, the vicar of Rugeley, who has filled that office for many years, and who was, of course, well acquainted with the prisoner and his family. An intimation having been given to the rev. gentleman, of the prisoner's wish, he promptly acceded to it, and at once proceeded to Stafford, and was admitted to the prisoner's cell.

The interview lasted for a considerable time, and the conversation was believed to have reference to some of the prisoner's family affairs. Palmer was a good deal affected, and appeared to evince a state of mind much more in accordance with his fearful position than he had shown at any period since his trial and condemnation. Mr. Atkinson saw him again on the following day, and they had another long and earnest conversation. The prisoner was also visited on the same day by his brother-in-law, Mr. Heywood.

The prisoner's solicitor was extremely energetic in his endeavours to procure a reprieve, mainly on the plea of no strychnia having been found in Cook's body. Sir George Grey,[1] however, replied that he could "see nothing in the points pressed upon his attention to justify his interfering with the due course of the law."

Palmer when told by his solicitor that Sir George Grey had refused to grant a reprieve, his face grew suddenly pale, and it was some minutes before it recovered its usual florid expression.

Mr. Wright, the philanthropist, of Manchester, returned to Stafford again on Wednesday, on which day he had two interviews with Palmer, whom he saw again on the Thursday and Friday. The Rev. H[enry]. Sneyd also visited him. Each of these gentlemen endeavoured to bring the wretched man to a sense of the awful position in which he was placed. Palmer listened to everything the rev. gentleman and Mr. Wright said, with great attention marked by respect, but beyond this there was nothing to indicate that he was impressed by their exhortations. Palmer having spoken to the rev. Mr. Goodacre in high terms of Mr. Davis, the Ordinary of Newgate,[2] Mr. Goodacre communicated the fact to Mr. Davis, and that gentleman wrote to Palmer in a spirit of kindly advice. The letter wound up with a solemn but fruitless adjuration to Palmer to confess the justice of his sentence, and so make his peace with God and man.

Like all other appeals of a similar character, this appeal fell upon a deaf ear and a hardened heart. There was no perceptible emotion occasioned by its perusal, and probably no feeling at all was excited on his mind. But to talk of making

---

[1] Solicitor John Smith asked Home Secretary George Grey (1799-1882) to postpone the execution, challenging Charles Newton's testimony that he gave Palmer strychnine, Elizabeth Mills' character, the absence of two witnesses who could have testified about where the strychnine and Cook's winnings went, and the absence of strychnine found in Cook's body.

[2] The chaplain of the prison. An Ordinary is a clergyman given jurisdiction over an area that is not a parish.

peace with his Maker, under such circumstances as those in which Palmer found himself the day before the execution, appears to be an absurdity; for his cell was never empty for any length of time — visitor succeeded visitor in rapid succession; and the mind of the wretched criminal must have been too much occupied with them and their conversation, to fix his attention upon the things that appertain to another world. The day was fully taken up by the things of this life — the night only remained for religion and repentance. And night was devoted to sleep.

On Friday evening the final interview took place between Palmer and his brothers George and Thomas, who were accompanied by their sister. At this period all hope of a reprieve seemed to have passed away. Palmer appeared cheerful and serene; still there was now and then observable a slight twitching of the muscles at the corners of his mouth, and that restless play of the fingers which often seemed to occur involuntarily while he stood at the bar of the Old Bailey. The brothers took a sad farewell; the convict committing to their future care his only child; and it is rumoured that he extorted a promise from them that they would, for the sake of that child, quit their native country, and change their name. It is said that the Rev. Thomas Palmer earnestly entreated the prisoner to confess, if he were guilty, but he firmly and distinctly replied, "I have nothing to say, and nothing I shall say."

Contrary to expectation, no interview with his mother or his child took place, and it was believed that this was so by the prisoner's own desire.

In the morning Mr. Smith, his solicitor, was summoned by telegraph from London to Stafford, at Palmer's earnest request, and he arrived there at half-past 10 o'clock at night, when he had an interview with the convict, in the presence of Major Fulford, the governor of the gaol.

Palmer had declined to retire to rest until Smith came, and from that circumstance and the anxiety he had shown to have him sent for, it was supposed that he had some important communication to make to him; but it was not so.

On going into the cell, the Governor informed Palmer that if he had anything confidential to say on family affairs to Mr. Smith, he (the governor) would keep it a secret. The prisoner replied that he had not, and he hoped the governor would lose no time in publishing all he had said. He also added, all he had to say was to thank Mr. Smith for his great exertions — the officers of the prison for their kindness to him — and that Cook did not die from strychnine.

Major Fulford expressed a hope that in his then awful condition he was not quibbling with the question, and urged him to say "Aye" or "No," whether or not he murdered Cook. He answered directly, that Lord Campbell "summed up for poisoning by strychnine."

The governor retorted, it was of no importance how the deed was done, and asked him to say yes or no to the question.

Palmer said he had nothing more to add. He was quite easy in his conscience, and happy in his mind. This is the governor's version of the conversation; but upon the material point, Mr. Smith stated, just after leaving the convict, that what Palmer said to him was, "I am innocent of poisoning Cook by strychnine; and all I ask is, that you will have his body examined, and that you will see to my mother and boy."

Mr. Smith promised to fulfill his last behest, and parted with the prisoner, who presented him with a book, in which he wrote in a fair hand, "The gift of Wm. Palmer, June 13, 1856." The book is headed "The Sinner's Friend," [3] and a prelude, to which the prisoner referred, ran thus:—

> "Oh! where for refuge shall I flee,
> If Jesus had not died for me?"

---

[3] A conversion pamphlet written by John Vine Hall (1774-1860), a bookseller and religious writer. In 1812, a voice from the Lord told him "If thou wilt forsake thy sins they shall be forgiven." Hall devoted the rest of his life to sermonizing to anyone who would listen and translating into numerous languages (including Tahitian and Malagassy), publishing, and distributing "The Sinner's Friend" and other tracts. In addition to describing his conversion, Hall's autobiography frequently devolves into a list of encounters (for example: "Gave 'Sinner's Friend' to a Miss P. and seven others in various ways. All with prayer."). In the year Palmer was hung, Hall noted on his birthday "Jesus is the million, million times welcome occupant of my heart. This day commences my eighty-third year, full of health and life and fire."

Immediately after he had parted from the prisoner, Smith wrote to a friend as follows:—

"My interview ended in Palmer's making me pledge myself that Cook's body should be exhumed, and that he was never poisoned by strychnia. Palmer was as cool as though any ordinary question had been discussed.

"God help him!"

The convict retired to rest early in the morning, and slept two hours and a half, when he was visited again by Mr. Goodacre, the chaplain. Between five and six he took his breakfast, and made his gallows toilet with an unwavering serenity. There was no sign of repentance about him — no thought apparently of confession, possibly no feeling, not even the slightest, of compunction or remorse.

Breakfast over, the chaplain made his appearance in the cell to offer the final consolations of religion to the condemned, who was still quiet and resigned; and shortly afterwards came in the sheriff and other officials. As he was about to leave his cell for the last time, he said, in reply to the high sheriff, that he denied the justice of his sentence, and that he was a murdered man. These were about the last words he uttered.

Palmer walked (in the company of the sheriff) to the press-room, where he met Smith, the hangman[4] (from Dudley), and submitted as quietly to the final preparations for his execution as if he had been under the hands of a valet dressing for a dinner-party. In that sad place some of his relations met him. They had told him on the previous night that they would see him no more, alive or dead, and, save a few brief words of parting courtesy, he said nothing to sheriff, chaplain, or any one.

His bearing in the last supreme moments of his life elicited the amazement of all who witnessed it. When the fatal hour

---

[4] George "Topper" or "Throttler" Smith was himself a colorful character. Described by Stephen Bates in *The Poisoner* as "a stern, hatchet-faced Black Country nail-maker," he had been arrested for debt several times, and once for running naked through a village during a drunken spree. Wearing his trademark white smock and top hat, he had been Stafford's executioner for two decades. He was also something of a humanitarian; frequently he would run underneath the gallows and pull on the victim's legs to hasten his end.

arrived, the prison bell tolled forth the hour of his irrevocable doom, and the melancholy procession was formed which conducted him from his cell to his doom, he marched along with a jaunty air and a tripping gait, and, though the distance he had to traverse was considerable, he maintained this bold front to the last, stepped lightly up the stairs leading to the gallows, took his place on the drop, and confronted the vast multitude below, not without emotion, but without anything like bravado.

Palmer was received with a deafening round of curses, shouts, hootings, oaths and execrations from a crowd of from 20 to 30,000 people.[5] Cries, shrieks, groans, rose from the raging mob. The populace, infuriated, tore the air with clamours — "Murderer!" "Poisoner!" were loudly shouted and screamed in hideous mockery. The miners and colliers[6] seemed maddened with excitement.

Palmer cast just one look at the vast multitude around him. After a brief prayer with the chaplain, he turned to the hangman, had the rope put round his neck, and the long cap drawn over his face. He then shook hands with his executioner, said, in a low voice, "God bless you;" and as the last word issued from his lips the bolt was withdrawn, the drop fell, and, after a slight convulsion of the limbs, he hung lifelessly from the gallows. So well had everything been managed by the hangman, so nicely had the fatal cord been adjusted, and so clear was the fall of the drop, that death was all but instantaneous.

Palmer, contrary to all usage, was hung in the prison dress, but that was not intended as an indignity; it simply arose from the circumstance that the clothes in which he was tried were left in London, and no others had been since supplied.

His body hung the accustomed time, and then being cut down, was carried inside the prison, where Mr. Bridges, of

---

[5] Accounts of the crowd's reaction vary from catcalls to silence. Those nearest the gallows were probably the most vocal, while those farther away were more subdued. Most were probably miserable, considering that many of them had spent the night travelling to Stafford in a cold rain or drinking in a tavern, or both.

[6] Coal miners. Rugeley was the home of several open-pit mines, some of them owned by William Palmer's father.

Liverpool, immediately took a cast of the head, which he says is, phrenologically,[7] decidedly bad.

The body was afterwards, according to the letter of the sentence, buried within the precincts of the prison, and so passed from the sight of men for ever, the mortal remains[8] of William Palmer, the poisoner of Rugeley.

Early on the morning of Friday the intense anxiety with regard to it was manifested by the numbers pouring into Stafford from all directions. The trains were crowded and every successive arrival at the railway station augmented the number of visitors. During the day the town assumed more the appearance of some anticipated festivity than of the fearful judicial spectacle which was so shortly to take place. The streets, despite the torrents of rain which fell during nearly the whole of Friday, were unusually crowded. The public-houses were full, and in many of them the jocund song and merry dance were kept up with untiring energy, by numbers who had travelled far to glut their eyes with the death struggles of a fellow-creature.

One place of resort was the house where the hangman had located himself, every one being more or less anxious to obtain a sight of the man who was to be Palmer's executioner.

In the more immediate vicinity of the gaol raised platforms were erected on every available spot from which a sight of the gallows could be obtained. Twenty-three of these erections crowded the gaol and county-roads, the former of which runs parallel with the gaol; and the charge for admission to some of the front seats was as high as a guinea for each person; half a guinea was the ordinary rate, but back standing places were attainable for less money. In the county road the roof of one house was covered with boards, to afford a standing place from which the execution could be witnessed.

---

[7] The pseudoscience of judging a person's character by the shape of his skull. One practitioner, William Bally of Manchester (c.1799-c.1856), said the cast of Palmer's head, not surprisingly, showed a man "perfectly indifferent to honour or truth and . . . careless what became of the most intimate acquaintance or the nearest relative."

[8] Bodies of executed prisoners were dumped into unmarked graves. Palmer still rests somewhere within the grounds of HM Prison Stafford.

In other instances the luxurious produce of well-kept gardens was bartered away and trodden under foot, for the purpose of gratifying the morbid curiosity of the people.

As early as ten o'clock on Friday night, scores of persons had taken up their positions on some of these erections, expressing a determination to remain there until the drop fell; but the drenching rain soon compelled them to forego their determination, and seek shelter in some adjoining hostelry.

During the night, the streets were tolerably free from pedestrians, excepting those who arrived by the midnight mail trains, north and south; but as soon as the grey dawn dispersed the shadows of night, the whole town appeared to burst into renewed life and activity; the public-houses were gradually emptied of their occupants, and continuous stream of vehicles, from the four-in-hand[9] to the overladen pony-cart, poured into the town; these were also augmented by droves of pedestrians; and long before five o'clock every avenue leading to the gaol was choked up. The arrivals, however, did not cease until eight o'clock, when it was estimated that upwards of 20,000 strangers had assembled in the town.

The colliers from the neighbouring pits formed conspicuous objects in the midst of the crowd, where they were banded together in groups, and seemed determined to force their way near to the scaffold. The great preparations made by the magistrates and the police, to preserve order and prevent accident from pressure, were fully needed. As not one half of the congregated thousands could get a view of the scaffold, those who had not a sight of it struggled with all their might to improve their positions. The erection of the scaffold, hung with black cloth, was taken as a proof that the execution was not to be deferred; and this certainty gave increased eagerness to get near the spot, and, if possible, to hear the dying speech which it was supposed Palmer would deliver.

As the hour of eight drew near, the excitement of the mob increased, but still there was no disturbance, and the police were not called upon to interfere. Long before that time all persons who intended to see the execution had assembled, and

---

[9] A carriage pulled by four horses, requiring the driver to keep control of four sets of reins.

those of the crowd, who were in the most distant places, had made up their minds that it was impossible to better themselves, and were contented to know what was going on by the shouts of those in more favourable positions.

Amongst this immense crowd about 80,000 tracts, suitable to the occasion, and a number of bibles, were distributed by Mr. Radcliffe,[10] a gentleman from Liverpool, and others; and in several of the dissenting places of worship[11] continuous services were held during the night, on behalf of the unhappy culprit; whilst numberless preachers exercised their calling amongst the crowd during the early part of the morning.

The general impression amongst the authorities was that Palmer was advised not to confess in order that his memory might have the benefit of the doubt for the sake of his son.

The scaffold was a huge affair, somewhat resembling an agricultural machine, and hung with black cloth. Contrary to the usual custom in small country towns, it was not built upon the top of the prison, but was brought out in front, so as to encroach upon the road, and thus circumscribe the points occupied by the spectators. It was brought out from the jail about four o'clock in the morning.

Palmer's Executioner.

Smith, the man who was selected to execute the sentence of the law upon Palmer, is by trade a nailer;[12] he is a great, coarse, brutal fellow, standing about five feet ten inches; he has left his original trade since he became hangman. He executed Moore[13]

---

[10] Most likely Reginald Radcliffe (1825-1875), the son of an eminent lawyer who forsook the family business and turned to preaching in the streets. From there he turned to organizing people to attend race meetings, fairs, and executions to hand out tracts and preach.

[11] Any church that didn't belong to the Church of England, such as Catholic, Methodist, and Quaker.

[12] A man who makes nails, either by forging them in a blacksmith shop or cutting them with the aid of a specialized machine.

[13] On Oct. 25, 1852, the charred bodies of an elderly couple, John and Jane Blackburn, were found in the charred remains of Ash Flats, their home about three miles from Stafford. A bloody axe was found in the well by the back door, alongside the body of a dog belonging to their son, Henry Blackburn. Henry was taken into custody, but

for the murder of the Ash Flats, four years ago, and now pursues the precarious trade of a haggler.[14]

The earliest thing that is known of him is that he ran a race against time almost naked in a market town and was taken up immediately on accomplishing the disgusting feat and sent to jail.

He has been the Staffordshire hangman for sixteen years.

The rope with which Palmer was hung was made by a ropemaker of the name of Coates, who is also a porter at the Stafford station. All the men employed at the station had a hand in making it; and Coates, having an eye to the main chance, made thirty yards, cut the surplus length up into small pieces of about two or three inches, and hawked them about Stafford. In one instance, half-a-crown was obtained for about two inches.

A Prophecy Fulfilled

Mr. Maxwell, a big, loud-speaking man, a commercial traveller for J.&F. Pawson's, Saint Paul's-Churchyard, was in the habit of calling at Lloyd's Grand Junction Hotel, Stafford, and consequently knew Palmer whom, however, he had no great respect for.

One night, in the autumn of 1854, Palmer and a friend drop into the "Junction," and Palmer sees a letter in the cardrack by the side of the looking-glass addressed to Maxwell. He takes a pencil, and writes under it, "Hung at Stafford Jail." Presently Palmer and his friend go out to call upon Mr. Painter at the other side of the railway bridge; and, while they are gone, in comes Maxwell.

"Any letters?"

"Yes, sir; one in the commercial room." In goes Maxwell, takes the letter, discovers the insult, and swears and blusters like a trooper.

---

suspicion fell on an Irish laborer, Charles Moore, who wrote anonymous letters to the police describing the murders and blaming Blackburn. They were arrested, along with two of Moore's Irish friends, Edward Walsh and Peter Kirwan. Blackburn and Kirwan were found innocent, and Moore and Walsh guilty. Walsh was transported to Australia and Moore was hanged.

[14] A travelling peddler of small items.

"Why, Mr. Maxwell," says the landlord, "what on earth is the matter with you?"

"Matter enough," replies Maxwell, still in a great rage; "I'll never come into this house again. Who wrote that on my letter?" And he threw it on the table. Just then, back came Palmer and his friend.

"Well, it's only a joke, you know," said Palmer's friend. "To tell the truth, Palmer did it."

"Ah!" said Maxwell, with a sneer; "I thought so. Hung at Stafford Jail. Why, he knows I have told him that would be *his* fate, many a time."

BROADSIDE SOLD AFTER PALMER'S EXECUTION.

CHAPTER XXVII.

PALMER'S CHARACTER AND PECULIARITIES — PERSONAL APPEARANCE — RESEMBLANCE TO MANNING — THE POISONER'S HAND — EXTREME NEATNESS — HOSPITALITY AND GENEROSITY — GENERAL CHARACTER — FEAR OF SLEEPING ALONE.

HE APPEARANCE PALMER PRESENTED DURING his trial at the Central Criminal Court was that of a middle-aged country gentleman. He appeared to be of the middle height, and though not very stout, looked puffy. His neck was rather thick, but his appearance on the whole was pleasant and his expression rather good-natured than blood-thirsty. He seemed to be partly bald, and had flaxen hair through which the fair skin showed. He had smallish sandy whiskers, fat cheeks, and his countenance was entirely devoid of that forbidding expression which we are taught to look for in murderers.

Resemblance To Manning.

Inspector Field thought Palmer by no means unlike Manning.[1] His fair hair was rather more inclined to redness, and his chin was longer.

The Poisoner's Hand.

People in the neighbourhood of Rugeley talk a good deal of Palmer's hand. In the common room of the Talbot Arms we

---

[1] George Manning and his wife, Marie, were hanged in 1849 for killing their lodger and burying him under their kitchen floor. Dickens attended their hanging and was appalled: "I believe that a sight so inconceivably awful as the wickedness and levity of the immense crowd collected at that execution this morning could be imagined by no man, and could be presented in no heathen land under the sun."

heard three commercial gentlemen chatting together about this terrible hand that was so white and soft. Palmer, it seems, used to hold the wrist of the patient and feel the pulse in such a manner that his delicate hand might be seen to the best advantage.

There is something extremely horrible in the idea that the hand which drops the poison into the cup and then tenders it to the victim, should be round, white, and dimpled — such a one as you could not suspect of doing any injury.

Palmer, according to an intimate friend, had very "pretty" hands, and he was very fond of, and careful, of them. He would rub them to keep them white, and, when talking, would sit still picking or trimming his nails, and looking at his fingers. The hand was small, and almost womanly. It was round, plump, and dimpled, and he had a great objection to touching anything which could in any way soil or stain them. He did not wear rings, or show much of his shirt-cuff; but he was constantly washing his hands, and whenever he did, occupied much time in thoroughly drying them.

Extreme Neatness.

Palmer's love of order was something unusual — he was extremely neat in his dress — he had a great horror of anything approaching untidiness or slovenliness. "He was the cleanest man about a house I ever knew," remarked one of his friends.

Hospitality and Generosity.

Palmer was a hospitable man. He would give very good dinners, with champagne, and the best in the house. He only had three or four companions; but he was thought to be a humane man. The clergyman never called to see him upon a case of charity, but he'd give him a guinea.

"There was a man named William Hawton," observed an old sawyer at Rugeley, "who was clerk to Joseph Palmer, when he carried on the father's business. Hawton was taken very ill, and couldn't come to the yard for a long time."

"Well, sir, William Palmer was the man who sent him joints of meat, and things that he might want, lots of them, and money.

"Why, sir, Hawton told me himself that Palmer had lent him, or rather given him, now and again, a matter of more than ten pounds. He called it lending; but, bless you, it was only his kind way of doing it."

Another acquaintance gives him this sort of character:—

"Palmer was a very generous man; it is a mistake to say that he was at all abstemious — he was not; he would drink his share, but he never showed it in any way. If he was not a drunkard, he was the cause of drunkenness in others; I have seen the betting-men come reeling out of his house one after the other; he was very fond of company."

General Character.

The following particulars respecting Palmer's general character, were furnished to us by a gentleman in Rugeley, evidently a person of more than ordinary observation:—

"I don't think Palmer was the clever man the world takes him to be. He was rather a cunning and cold man. He was a man that never drank, but I don't think he was what I call a deep man. He could sit still and bite his nails, and listen to the conversation of others, and surmise plans of his own, but they were not of that deep character which you could suppose of a man in his position. Palmer was never drunk in his life. He was a perfectly sober man, kind and generous to all around; and his kindness disarmed his most near and dear friends as to suspicion. He was affectionate to his family, to his mother in particular; and a very many poor men (labourers) will long have reason to regret the present circumstances."

The landlord of the "Junction" at Stafford, says of Palmer:—

"I always took him for a very different sort of person to what he has turned out. He was most pleasant and affable. I never knew him to lose his temper. I never heard an oath or a bad word leave his lips.

"He never drank much. He used to dress very quietly; not at all like a sporting man. He always appeared very cool and collected, even during the race-time, whether he came home a loser or a winner. He was a man who appeared very quiet and thinking."

A betting man of some standing residing in the neighborhood told us that Palmer was a good-principled man as far as he knew him: "Of course, sir, he couldn't pay when he hadn't got the money; but he was a devil to speculate; and, bless you, knew as much about making a book as you yourself, sir. They talk about his being very clever; I don't believe he was clever. Why, I've heard people say that they wondered how he ever managed to win at all."

The "boots" at the "Junction," the man who fancied he had been poisoned by Palmer, says of him:—

"I've known Palmer ever since I remember. I come from about three miles off him. I'm from Colwich, and he Rugeley. I always took him for a very decent sort of fellow.

"Yes, there's no mistake about him. The least thing in the world as I ever did for him he's tip me a shilling. He never give less. If I was to just go, for instance, only as far as the station, he never gives less. Suppose he was to say, 'Here, Tom, order me a car, whilst I walk on to the house,' why, there was a shilling for only doing that.

"He didn't often stop long at our house when he came. Perhaps he'd come here of a night and take a car to go home to Rugeley in, and then he'd say to the postboy, 'Here, go and get a glass of gin,' or whatever it was.

"Sometimes he was merry, and sometimes he wasn't, just as he was took. Perhaps he'd come in and ask for a glass of liquor, whatever it might be. But I never see him a joking the maids, or anything of that sort."

The Rugeley sexton said:—

"I'm sure he is the last person in the town, as I should have suspected of such a thing as this. He was a religious man, and many's the time when I've had a sup of ale too much, he's chastised me for it. He'd say, 'Do keep yourself respectable, and don't go to them public houses. If you wants a drink of ale come here.'"

Palmer appears to have credit universally given him for his agreeable manners. He was always popular with the poor, and was liked by the public generally. Since he became a betting man he was never secretive of sporting news of value, and he seemed always glad to put money in the way of poor men eager for the excitement, sans the risk, of betting. These qualities obtained for him considerable influence in his own town, and in the sporting circles of the midland and northern counties.

He was, moreover, what has been called a liberal man. Ask the servants at the various hotels he frequented within thirty miles of his native town, and they will invariably speak of him as "a nice pleasant sort of gentleman." But he was never respected. Latterly, his companions were of rather a low class, and he only differed from them in his temperate habits and equable tact of manner.

If Palmer wanted a certificate from a surgeon, when in search of one of his many insurances, he would always go himself to get it; he would never sit down while it was being drawn out, but would stand over the surgeon and suggest minute alterations that individually were of no importance, but which at last materially altered the sense of the whole.

Fear at Sleeping Alone.

Palmer never could, or would, sleep by himself alone after his wife's death. Whenever he went to the races he used to get Jerry Smith, or somebody, to go along with him. At winter and summer he usually went to bed at eight o'clock; he used to make them go up with him to the bed-room, and allow them to have champagne, or anything they liked to drink, if they only stopped in the room with him.

William Palmer's Private Diary for the Year 1855.

PRINTED FROM AN OFFICIAL COPY
MADE FOR THE PURPOSES OF THE CROWN.

The book concludes with Palmer's diary, in reality his record of journeys, payments and appointments. It is notable to most people for its brief recording of Cook's death. For the rest of us, it is a day-by-day accounting of one man's life in mid-Victorian England, of little interest unless the reader knows that the man who bustles about paying his workers, buying hay for his horses, and dining at his mother's house regularly, was a multiple murderer hounded by debt. That so little of the private man appears in this record may be, itself, of interest.

Information about people show up repeatedly in the diary can be found below in alphabetical order. Those who appear once were given their own footnotes.

Crabb was a Rugeley solicitor who worked for Thomas Pratt, one of Palmer's London creditors.

Day was a Stafford doctor who examined Walter Palmer for the insurance company. He recommended the policy, but reversed himself later when he learned about the death of William Palmer's wife. He was present at Walter's death and testified at the inquest that he had died from apoplexy and digestive disease from too much drinking.

Tom Earwaker was one of Palmer's creditors. He would be paid £100 from Cook's winnings.

Lord Lichfield was Thomas Anson, the 2nd Earl (1825-1892), who served in the Commons for Lichfield from 1847 to 1854. Upon his father's death that year, he became an earl and moved to the House of Lords. He was also Lord-Lieutenant of Staffordshire (1863-1871). His family seat was Shugborough Hall, about 4 miles from Stafford. It still exists and can be toured.

William Saunders was Palmer's trainer and jockey.

Benjamin Thirlby was Palmer's former assistant who bought his practice. He was referee in evaluating Bates' fitness to be insured.

William Webb Ward was Staffordshire's coroner who would handle the Cook and Walter Palmer inquests, and who Palmer would attempt to bribe with £10 and a hamper of game.

T. Walkenden was hired along with his wife to mind Walter Palmer and, supposedly, keep him away from alcohol.

J. Weatherby could be James Weatherby (1810-1894), a member of the family that was intimately tied to Tattersall's and the Jockey Club. Another member of the family, Charles, a racing agent who handled Cook's betting account, would testify at the trial how Palmer attempted to get his hands on Cook's Shrewsbury winnings.

The book offers this commentary on Palmer's diary:

Note. — The expression the "Yard" is used to denote Mrs. Palmer's, sen., place of residence. "JERE" is an abbreviation for Jeremiah Smith; "BEN" refers to Mr. Thirlby; "ELIZA" is Eliza Tharm, Palmer's maid-servant; "WILLIE" is Palmer's little boy. The word "NERI," and the crosses prefixed to certain entries are private marks of Palmer's, no explanation of which has yet been suggested.

JANUARY, 1855.

1. MONDAY:— ....£ S. D.
    Went to Hednesford,[1] with Jere and Tom Earwaker. Mother, Sal. Walter, Jere, and Tom Earwaker dined.
    + Paid Crabb on account 5 0 0
    Cook and Brown, and Wm. Saunders called.
    + Paid Hyatt and Dalton.. 100 0 0

2. TUESDAY:—
    Smith and Tom Earwaker dined. Ann Heywood came.
    + Sent Josh. Saxon.. 32 0 0
    + Sent Mr. James Perkin... 12 10 0
    George, Ben, Walter, Jere, and Tom Earwaker to oysters. Will at Ben's, dinner and tea. Eliza and Jane went to a dance at the Talbot.

3. WEDNESDAY:—
    NERI Received a cheque from J. Weatherby for "Goldfinder,"
paid it into bank 300 0 0

---

[1] A small town near Cannock Chase, about 5 miles southwest of Rugeley. Palmer boarded his 17 horses there. That alone cost him £1,600 a year, plus the cost for food, training, transportation, jockey fees, and his own travels and bets.

NERI Paid Weatherby "Escape's" and "Morning Star's" entrances in the Liverpool Chase..10 0 0
Tom Earwaker, Willie, Annie Heywood, and I dined at the timber yard.
Eliza in bed.

4. THURSDAY:—
Wm. Saunders, James Eaton, Jere, and Tom Earwaker, here to dinner, and three bottles of wine. Eliza in bed.

5. FRIDAY:—
+ Paid Timmis balance of oats 5 0 0
Tom and I at yard to tea.

6. SATURDAY:—
Tom, Jere, and I went to Hednesford's to see some jumping.
Dined at the Keys.
Herbert Wright here.
+ Paid Walter for Mother (being all due up to day)..5 0 0
Paid Henry..0 14 0
——— Michael 0 12 0
——— Charles 0 2 6

7. SUNDAY:—
At home — sore throat. Tom and I at tea at the yard.

8. MONDAY:—
Tom Earwaker left here for London by the 8 o'clock train.
+ Paid Greensmith's bill..4 6 0
Sanders, Jere, and Charles Heywood here to dinner
++ Paid William Saunders for training..50 0 0
+ Paid Kaybe for tray and cord 0 17 0

9. TUESDAY:—
+ Paid Lord Lichfield's rent, he allowing £3 8s. 9d. for Income tax, and Hall's Acct 22 10 0
+ Paid Hall's Acct 1 11 0
+ Paid Markham's bill 1 14 0
+ Paid Mellard's bill 3 16 7
Eliza in bed yesterday and to-day — Exchanged dressing gown with Potts.

10. WEDNESDAY:—
+ Paid gas bill..0 14 2
Paid for coals 0 10 10
Eliza down stairs.
W. Ward called, gave him...1 0 0
Wm. Saunders and Charles Marlow called for two hours.

11. THURSDAY:—
+ Paid T. Southern's bill...2 19 0
+ Paid poor's rate...1 1 9
Ann Heywood gone to George's for a few days.
+ Paid Fortescue for turnips..1 3 4
+ Paid Fortescue for Saunders 3 10 0
Saunders and Jere Smith here to dinner — one bottle of wine.
+ Paid Jones for envelopes 0 6 6

12. FRIDAY:—
+ Paid Bennett's bill (after allowing 12s. for the Engine House) 4 4 0
+ Paid Simpson for Income Tax 2 18 4

13. SATURDAY:—
Saunders here to dinner.
Paid Henry 0 14 0
Paid Michael 0 10 0
——— Charles 0 3 0
Walter here in bed ill. 14th, signed a bill for £400 for Saunders, entirely as a matter of accommodation.

14. SUNDAY:—
At home with Walter. Willie at Yard to dinner and tea.

15. MONDAY:—
Went to London with Walter and Jere Smith by the 8 o'clock train. Expenses, &c. Slept at 7, Beaufort Buildings.[2]
Paid Pratt for Three bills 350 0 0
Went to the Lyceum.

16. TUESDAY:—
Went with Walter to see Dr. Hastings.
Returned home with Walter and Jerry Smith at half-past seven.

17. WEDNESDAY:—
Went to see Tom at the yard. Sent him some medicine. Jere and Walter here to dinner. Saunders here in the afternoon.
+ Paid Tunnicliffe's bill 0 8 10
++ Settled with Mrs. Robinson in full, and received a balance of 12s. 10d. from her through Jere.

18. THURSDAY:—
+ Paid Mr. Brown for hay 5 7 6
At home.
Walter went to Stafford, and stayed all day, till half-past four. Brother ill.

19. FRIDAY:—
+ Paid Whitworth for pork, steaks, and bran 0 10 9
+ Paid Hattersley for two gallons of gin 1 2 0
++ Received from Glover by Henry 15 0 0
Mother ill at home.

20. SATURDAY:—
Mother ill.
+ Paid Hatfield's bill 5 18 0
+ Paid Cox's bill 0 2 6
Paid Henry 0 14 0
——— Michael 0 12 0
Slept at the yard.

---

[2] Whenever he was in London, Palmer rented rooms at this place off The Strand. The building was torn down to build the Savoy Theatre, which opened in 1881.

21. SUNDAY:—
   At home — slept at yard.

22. MONDAY:—
   Mother ill in bed.
   Ben dined here.
   Willie all day at Eliza's.

23. TUESDAY:—
   Went to Stafford with Jere, and returned at 12 before 5.
   + Paid Ashmall's bill..8 13 0
   Willie all day at Ben's.
   + Paid J. Welis's bill 10 18 0
   +++ Myatt delivered gig harness — paid for 21st Feb. Walter gone to Stoke to buy dinner-service, &c., &c.
   Expenses...0 15 0

24. WEDNESDAY:—
   Went to Hednesford with Jere, and returned home for dinner.
   Jere and Walter dined.
   Mother still in bed.
   NERI. Mr. Milcrest died.[3]

25. THURSDAY:—
   Mother down stairs.
   Saunders, Smith, and Walter dined.

26. FRIDAY:—
   Fetched coals 0 9 9
   + Paid tithe 0 11 9
   Walter and Smith dined.
   Mother down stairs.
   + Paid Slater's bill 0 3 6

27. SATURDAY:—
   Walter gone with T. Walkenden to Stafford.
   + Paid Walter..1 0 0
   Willie at Ben's to dinner.
   Paid Henry...0 14 0
   ——— Michael 0 12 0
   ——— Charles..0 2 0
   Mother down stairs.

28. SUNDAY:—
   At church (sacrament).
   Willie poorly.

29. MONDAY:—
   At home.
   Lent Jere mare and gig to go to Hednesford.
   + Paid C. F. Wylde for Will's pinafore's[4] and coat................................0 8 0

---

[3] Possibly the father-in-law of his elder brother, Joseph Palmer.

[4] A sleeveless garment worn as an apron over the child's clothes and

30. TUESDAY:—
　　+++ Took Willie to Mrs. Salt's school.
　　+ Paid Walter 1 0 0
　　Dined at Ben's — he and Jere came and had 2 bott. after dinner.

31. WEDNESDAY:—
　　Very poorly in the house with cold.
　　+ Paid Crabb 5 0 0
　　Saunders, Jere, and Ben here to dinner and 4 bottles of wine.
　　Saunders got hurt going home.

FEBRUARY.

1. THURSDAY:—
　　In the house with a cold
　　+++ Charles Markham called.
　　Sam Cope called.
　　+ Paid Woolcott to Feb. 14 3 7
　　+ Paid Mrs. Barrett for Cope 1 0 0
　　+++ Received from Ben 30 0 0
　　+ Paid Mrs. Cook for making Will's shirts and material 0 10 8½

2. FRIDAY:—
　　In the house with a cold.
　　Charles Markham called.
　　++ Paid Tom Palmer 10 0 0
　　Eliza returned home, having gone home the day before.
　　Jere slept with me last night and to-night.

3. SATURDAY:—
　　Sent Henry to Stafford to see Willie.
　　Mr. Pratt came from London here to get receipts endorsed on Sun and Norwich Insurances.[5]
　　+ Walter here by 5 train and returned at half-past 7. Paid him 1 1 0
　　Sarah up twice about mother's illness.
　　Paid Henry 0 14 0
　　———— Michael 0 12 0

4. SUNDAY:—
　　At home with a bad cold.

5. MONDAY:—
　　++ Wm. Saunders sent Geo. Calloway's colt home.
　　At home with a cold.

---

could be removed easily and washed. Boys and girls were dressed in similar clothes until they were about 6 or 7 years old, Willie's age at this time.

[5] Three days before, Pratt had written to Palmer informing him that the Prince of Wales Office had agreed to insure Walter Palmer's life for £13,000 and warned him against trying for more so soon after his wife's death.

Jere here to dinner.
8th + Paid Crabb by Jere..5 0 0
Sarah called twice about her mother's medicine.

6. TUESDAY:—
In the house with a cold.
+ Fetched coals 0 10 3½
Jere and Ben gone to Hednesford to shoot for the gun.
15 dozn. wine come in from Pratt.

7. WEDNESDAY:—
+ Paid Wallbank for hams, &c 3 13 5½
In the house with a cold.
Jere and Ben packed the wine, gave them a bott sherry for trouble.

8. THURSDAY:—
In the house with a cold.
Jere Smith here to dinner.
+ Sent Fordham a cheque for 27 0 0
For riding Larley at Shrewsbury, and Whampton, and expenses..........19 18 6
My own, the remainder Saunders.
++ Paid Fordham for Saunders 7 11 6

9. FRIDAY:—
In the house with a cold.
+ Paid S. Timmis for wool 0 12 6
Jere, Walter, and Tom Walkenden here for dinner.
+ Paid Walter Palmer...1 0 0
+ Paid Jere for work done (all being due) 5 0 0

10. SATURDAY:—
In the house with a cold.
++ Lent Wm. Saunders..50 0 0
Advised Buxton's bill for 250 0 0
Received as balance of mother's 350*l.* bill..100 0 0
+ Paid Miss Manners for Willie's schooling 2 9 0
———— Emery..0 10 0
———— Henry 0 14 0
———— Michael 0 12 0

11. SUNDAY:—
In the house with a cold.
Jere here to dinner.

12. MONDAY:—
Out of doors again.
+ Paid Whitworth for cheese 6 10 0
George Bates and Jere Smith here to dinner off wild ducks.
Jere left at ¼ b. 6 p.m.

13. TUESDAY:—
+ Paid Salisbury for straw...17 14 0
+ Paid Wright's bill for shoeing..9 14 2
+ Paid Woodhouse for a pair of boots for myself and Jere Smith........1 12 0
Tom Palmer over
Called at the timber-yard for the first time after being ill.

+++ Sal gone visiting to Whampton.
++ Paid Walter (by Jere) 4 0 0
Gave Mr. Atkinson for alterations at school 2 0 0

15. THURSDAY:—
+ Paid Saml. Cope for oats 12 0 0
+ Paid George Palmer half a year's interest 15 0 0
+++ Lord Inges — he married to-day.
Jere Smith and Saml. Cope here to dinner.

16. FRIDAY:—
+ Paid Jno. Allen's bill 1 15 0
+ Fetched coals 0 7 7
Dined with Jere Smith at the Yard.

17. SATURDAY:—
Went to Stafford with Jere to see Willie — dined with Walter.
+++ Paid Mrs. Tunnicliffe on acc. for interest due April, 1855 .... 10 0 0
Paid Emery 0 10 0
+ Paid Jno. Wright's bill 13 0 0
Paid Henry 0 14 0
——— Michael 0 12 0
——— Chadbourne on acct. 1 0 0

18. SUNDAY:—
At church — Mr. Atkinson preached.
Dined at the Yard with Jere.

19. MONDAY:—
++ Paid Walter for mother 1 0 0
Lent Walter the mare to go to Armitage.
Walter and Jere Smith here to dinner.
+ Sent Dyke a bill at 2 months for 70 0 0

20. TUESDAY:—
Mr. Painter, Geo. Bates, and Jere Smith dined here; had 4 bottles of wine.
+ Paid Mr. Hullersley for wine bottles to bottle gin and brandy 1 8 0
Mrs. Bradshaw called, gave her 0 2 6
Jane called, and had tea and supper.

21. WEDNESDAY:—
+ Settled Myatt's accounts; paid him the balance 15 0 0

22. THURSDAY:—
Walter called, and had some soup.
Michael took 2 hams to his own house to cure for me.

23. FRIDAY:—
Mother not well; called 3 times.
++ Settled with Strawbridge; paid him 14 13 0

24. SATURDAY:—
Sent Henry to Stafford for Willie.
++ Walter here; paid him 3 0 0
Sal returned home from W'hampton.
Paid Emery.

—— Henry	0 14 0
—— Michael	0 12 0
—— Chadbourne	0 15 0

Commenced thawing.

25TH. SUNDAY:—
   At home with Willie.

26. MONDAY:—
   Sent Henry with Doubt to Rugby by the 8 o'clock train.
   Expenses ... 1 0 0
   Sent J. Warrington a bill at 2 Months for ... 210 0 0
   Willie and I dined at the Yard. Took Willie to School by the 3 o'clock train.
   ++ Paid Thomas Palmer ... 20 0 0

27. TUESDAY:—
   ++ Paid Walter Palmer ... 2 0 0
   + Paid Whitworth for Hams, &c. ... 2 6 0
   Jere Smith here to dinner. Hung the hams up.

28. WEDNESDAY:—
   Sent Charles to Brereton with some potatoes for Jane. Dined alone.
   + Paid Jere for M'Intosh.

MARCH.

1. THURSDAY:—
   Lent Henry the mare and cart to fetch coals.
   + Paid Charles for hay ... 9 5 6
   + Paid Sam Cope for Beans ... 2 6 0

2. FRIDAY:—
   Went with Ben to Hednesford, and returned at 5 o'clock.
   Emperor of Russia died.[6]
   H. Wright here to swear me to an affidavit before Mr. Atkinson.
   Planted my first peas.

3. SATURDAY:—
   Paid Carter for Insurance Ticket ... 1 0 0
   Went to Rugby to meet Pratt. Returned to Stafford to see Mr. Meeson and Walter.
   ++ Paid Walter (by Glover) ... 4 0 0
   Josh. Haywood retd. to Hayweed from Buxton.
   Paid Emery balance of account ... 0 18 0
   —— Chadbourne ... 2 0 0
   —— Henry ... 0 14 0
   —— Michael ... 0 12 0
   —— Charles ... 0 3 0

---

[6] Britain was in the middle of the Crimean War (1853-1856) against Russia, so an Englishman would be aware of Tsar Nicholas I (1796-1855). Under his rule, Russia expanded to its greatest extent, but the country would lose the war and undergo internal convulsions as reformers attempted to correct a corrupt system of governance.

4. SUNDAY:—
   At church — Mr. Atkinson preached.
   Dined at yard.

5. MONDAY:—
   3d. Henry fetched home "The Nuggett."
   4th. Jane called and had supper.
   Cook dined here.
   Drove to Colwich to meet the 13m. p. 2 train for Liverpool.
   Slept at the Stork.
   5th. Called to see Joseph at Liverpool.
   Dined at Joseph's.
   Slept at the Stork.

7. WEDNESDAY:—
   ++ Paid Escape's Stake in the Liverpool chase for Saunders 20 12 6
   ++ Saunders lost on Escape 10 0 0
   ++ Saunders lost on Keepsake 2 0 0
   Returned home with Ben by excursion train from Liverpool to Stafford, and then on by mare and gig at ¼ b. 1.

8. THURSDAY:—
   + Paid Walbank for hams, beef, &c 1 15 2½
   Cook and Saunders here to breakfast; lent them the mare and gig to go to Hednesford.
   Jane called and had luncheon.

9. FRIDAY:—
   8th. Sent Mr. Edwards 100 0 0
   Had breakfast at the yard.
   Sent Henry to Rugby to see "Doubt."
   Lent Sandon a desk 1 0 0

10. SATURDAY:—
    +++ Paid Walter Palmer (by Glover) 7 0 0
    Paid Chadbourne 2 0 0
    ——— Thomas Lyttler 1 10 0
    ——— Henry 0 14 0
    ——— Michael 0 12 0

11. SUNDAY:—
    At home.

12. MONDAY:—
    Dined at the yard. Saunders slept here, being on his way for Doncaster.

13. TUESDAY:—
    Went to Lichfield station for Doncaster, and back to Rugby at night, and slept there.
    +++ Paid Escape's Stake 15 10 0
    +++ Saunder's lost on Escape, forfeits at Doncaster 5 0 0
    Paid Morning Star's and Lusley's 8 10 0

14. WEDNESDAY:—
    Returned home by 10 train.
    Went to Hednesford with Saunders and stayed all day. Walter called, but I did not

see him.

15. THURSDAY:—
   Saunders called. Went to Colwich for Stafford and back at 5 o'clock to see Walter.
   Eliza cured two hams.

16. FRIDAY:—
   Mr. Halford came here at ten, and slept here.
   ++ Paid Walter (by Glover) 5 0 0

17. SATURDAY:—
   Went with Mr. Halford to Hednesford to try Smithmon.
   Paid Chadbourne 1 10 0
   ——— T. Lyttler...1 0 0
   ——— Henry 0 14 0
   ——— Michael 0 12 0
   ——— Charles..0 4 0

18. SUNDAY:—
   At home.
   Dined at the yard.

19. MONDAY:—
   Went to Hednesford to go with Saunders to Brown Hills, for Warwick.
   Returned to Birmingham in the evening, and on to York by mail train.

20. TUESDAY:—
   Went on to Bedals and Richmond, to Mr. Gill's to see "The Chicken." Returned to Derby by the mail train.

21. WEDNESDAY:—
   Returned home by 20m. to 10 train to Lichfield, then on here with Marlow's trap.
   Saunders and Marlow dined here.
   Fast day.

22. THURSDAY:—
   Went to Stafford by ½ p. 11 train, and dined with Mr. Painter.
   Wm. Saunders slept here on his way to Warwick.

23. FRIDAY:—
   Dined at the Yard.
   24th. Paid Brown for hay 6 19 0
   24th. Paid Masters for hay 3 7 6

24. SATURDAY:—
   Due to day to Tom Palmer...20 0 0
   ++ Paid Walter Palmer..5 0 0
   Paid Chadbourne 1 10 0
   ——— Henry 0 14 0
   ——— Michael 0 8 0

25. SUNDAY:—
   At home with a cold.
   Eliza gone home to tea.

26. MONDAY:—

Left for London by the 8 train to see Pratt, and returned to Northampton at ½ p. 6. Slept at the Angel.

27. TUESDAY:—
At Northampton. — Returned home by the ½ past 7 train.

28. WEDNESDAY:—
At home.
Walked to Brereton with George Bates.

29. THURSDAY:—
Paid Walter Palmer 1 0 0
Walter, Geo. Bates, and Jere dined here.
+ Paid school land rent 6 0 0
+ The Alderman called to see the colts.
Went to Colwich for Stafford, to see Mr. Painter.

30. FRIDAY:—
NERI. Fetched coals 0 10 2½
Went with Saunders to Lichfield; dined at the George hotel.

31. SATURDAY:—
Went with Saunders to Stoke, then to Stafford.
+ Paid Lloyd's bill 1 13 2
———— Chadbourne 2 6 0
———— T. Lyttler 1 0 0
———— Henry 0 14 0
———— Michael 0 12 0
———— Charles 0 3 0
Settled with Gardner up to this day.

APRIL.

1. SUNDAY:—
At church — son preached. Dined at the yard.

2. MONDAY:—
Went to Stafford to see Walter.
Paid Walter Palmer 5 0 0
———— J. Perkin 12 10 0
———— Keyte, for writing-desk 7 0 0
Saunders dined here.
Paid J. Cooper 37 13 4
+++ Sold Saunders a book-chest, or writing-desk 10 0 0
Paid Mrs. Welkden for washing 0 18 0

3. TUESDAY:—
Went to Hednesford to give C. Marlow the orders for Chicken and Nettle.
Jere dined here.
Sent H. Padwick[7] 100 0 0

---

[7] One of Palmer's major creditors. He would issue the writ that led to Palmer's arrest during the Cook inquest. Later, he would unsuccessfully sue Mrs. Palmer over a loan taken out over her forged signature.

Paid Shakeshaft for hay 9 9 6

4. WEDNESDAY:—
Went to Hednesford.
Paid Wm. Saunders (vide April 2nd 10*l*.) 50 0 0

5. THURSDAY:—
Willie came home.
Walter, Jere, and Saunders dined.
Willie at Geo's to tea.
Paid Walter Palmer 3 0 0
Went with Saunders to Lichfield to meet Kettle and the Chicken.

6. GOOD FRIDAY:—
At church with Willie.
Willie at Geo's to tea.
2nd sent brown colt and ch. filly from Mr. Painter's to Wm. Saunders to be trained.

7. SATURDAY:—
Went to Stafford to see Walter, Painter and Wright, of B'ham.
++ Paid Landor and Gardner —
++ Deposit on Inge's Land 50 0 0
Paid wages for the field 5 5 0
——— Henry 0 14 0
——— Michael 0 10 0

8. EASTER SUNDAY:—
At church.

9. MONDAY:—
Went with Jere to Hednesford, to see Nettle and Chicken; stayed all day.
Paid Walter Palmer 20 0 0

10. TUESDAY:—
Went by 8 train to Woodford.

11. WEDNESDAY:—
Returned from Woodford by Stafford at 6.10; then by fly.
Expenses with boys 10 0 0

12. THURSDAY:—
Walter dined here.
Paid Walter Palmer 2 0 0
Paid Fire Insurance 3 9 0

13. FRIDAY:—
Went with Saunders to Lichfield, to settle his account to April 1st, 1855, and find a balance due to me of 156 12 10

14. SATURDAY:—
Went to Birmingham by 8 train and back at 6.
Paid Field wages 4 4 0
——— Henry 0 14 0
——— Michael 0 12 0
——— Charles..0 6 0

HIS DIARY FOR 1855.   243

15. SUNDAY:—
    At Church — Mr. A's son preached.

16. MONDAY:—
    15th Paid Saunders.. 60 0 0
    Went with Saunders to Litchfield for York.
    Slept at the White Swan.
    Paid Walter Palmer (by Jere.) 20 0 0

17. TUESDAY:—
    At York.
    Slept at the White Swan.

18. WEDNESDAY:—
    Returned home at half-past 5.
    Paid Walter Palmer 1 1 6

19. THURSDAY:—
    Went to Stafford to see Day about Walter.
    Wm. Saunders here after dinner.
    19th bill, 3 months.

20. FRIDAY:—
    Went to London with Jere, and returned home at half-past 9.
    Paid for mother's bonnets, shawl's, and parasol.

21. SATURDAY:—
    Paid Dyke's bill (falls due) 70 0 0
    Went to Birmingham and back at half-past 5.
    Paid wages at Field.. 3 15 4
    ——— Henry.. 0 14 0
    ——— Michael.. 0 12 0
    ——— Charles 0 8 0
    ——— Walter Palmer 5 0 0

23. MONDAY:—
    Paid Wm. Saunders 100 0 0
    Went to Hednesford with Jere.
    Sent Henry with Goldfinder down to Teddington.

24. TUESDAY:—
    Went to Stafford with Keyte to order some things for Walter's house.
    Paid Walter Palmer 5 0 0
    Wm. Saunders and Ben here.
    Mr. Salt called to examine Jere for the Albion office.[8]

25. WEDNESDAY:—
    Paid Whitworth for hams and bacon.................................. 2 6 0
    ——— a County Court summons for Walter Palmer amounting to 3 11 9
    Jere Smith dined here.

26. THURSDAY:—

---

[8] We know nothing more about this, but if this is true, did Palmer intend to poison Jeremiah Smith as well?

Paid Sam Cope for oats 5 0 0
  Henry fetched the Duchess of Kent and foal from Mr. Painter's.
  Wm. Saunders, Ben, Jere, and Cook here to 3 bott. wine.
  Advised J. Warrington's bill for..210 0 0
  Went with Jere Smith to Hednesford.
  Paid Tom Palmer to March 25, 1855...20 0 0
  Sent Myatt...25 0 0
  Sold Mr. Saunders grey horse for..20 0 0

28. SATURDAY:—
  Paid J. Warrington's bill due.
  ——— Walter Palmer 5 0 0
  Went to Stafford.
  ++ Paid Mr. Saunders 10 0 0
  Sold Mr. Saunders bag of potatoes.
  Paid Field wages..1 12 0
  ——— Henry 0 14 0
  ——— Michael 0 12 0
  ——— Charles..0 6 0

29. SUNDAY:—
  Took H. Wright and Jere to Hednesford.

30. MONDAY:—
  Henry took the gig to Welhden's of Lichfield.
  Paid Wm. Saunders (by Jere)..5 0 0
  Started with Saunders and Cook by the ½ p. 11 train to Chester
  Slept at the White Lion.

MAY.

1. TUESDAY:—
  At Chester.
  Wm. Saunders lost at Chester...9 0 0

2. WEDNESDAY:—
  At Chester.

3. THURSDAY:—
  At Chester.

4. FRIDAY:—
  Returned home with Wm. Saunders at 9 o'clock, by fly from Stafford. Eliza here for the night.

5. SATURDAY:—
  Went to B'ham to see Wright.
  Went to Stafford to pay Mr. Painter for mare and foal......................400 0 0
  ++ Paid Walter Palmer..5 0 0
  ——— Field wages.
  ——— Henry 0 14 0
  ——— Michael 0 12 0
  ——— Charles..0 6 0

6. SUNDAY:—

At church — Mr. Atkinson preached — Dined at the yard.

7. MONDAY:—
   Went to Hednesford with Jere — dined at the yard.

8. TUESDAY:—
   Met Mr. Painter at the 8 train, and drove him to Hednesford — dined there.
   Goldfinder's dam foaled.

9. WEDNESDAY:—
   Went to Shrewsbury with Wm. Saunders by the ½ p. 11 train.
   Slept at the Raven.

10. THURSDAY:—
    Wm. Saunders lost at Shrewsbury, Lurley cup 15 0 0
    Slept at the Raven.

11. FRIDAY:—
    Returned home by 7 train to Stafford, then on by mare and carriage.
    12th Paid Walter 5 18 6

12. SATURDAY:—
    Paid Saml. Palmer's bill due.
    Went to Stafford with Wm. Saunders, and dined at Mr. Painter's.
    Went to Hednesford.
    Paid Henry 0 14 0
    ——— Michael 0 12 0
    ——— Charles 0 5 0
    Bought Staffordshire Nan and her sister from Meesom, and to give Wm. S. £25,
    £400 in all 375 0 0

13. SUNDAY:—
    At home. — Eliza here.

14. MONDAY:—
    Went to Hednesford with Jere.
    Dined at the Yard.
    Paid Wm. Saunders 90 0 0
    ——— Potts for Jere's clothes 2 12 6
    Henry fetched Meeson's yearling from Stafford.
    Paid Wm. Salt's deposit on land 160 0 0
    Eliza returned home.

15. TUESDAY:—
    Paid Hitchenson the balance of his account for painting 30 0 0
    ——— Pott's for a pair of trousers, and Henry's clothes 3 12 0
    ——— carriage of whiskey 0 6 6
    Dined at the yard.

16. WEDNESDAY:—
    Paid Wm. Turner for hay for Wm. Saunders 11 0 0
    Dined at Hednesford.

17. THURSDAY:—
    Mr. Painter, Wm. Bates, Wm. Saunders, and Jere, dined here.
    Sent Dorling a cheque for Chicken's stake at Epsom 5 0 0

18. FRIDAY:—
   Went with Jere Smith to Hednesford
   Henry took the Duchess to Stafford.
   Sent Weatherby a cheque for Nettle's stake for the Oaks 50 12 6
   Dined at the yard.
   Paid Brassington for 6 buckets 1 4 0

19. SATURDAY:—
   NERI. Paid Walter Palmer 5 0 0
   Went to Hednesford with Markham's gig — Saw Tom Walthew and Meeson.
   Paid Henry 0 14 0
   ——— Michael 0 12 0
   ——— Charles 0 6 0
   Eliza came.

20. SUNDAY:—
   At home. Eliza here.
   NERI. Paid Wm. Saunders 60 0 0
   Started by 8 o'clock train for Epsom.
   Paid Crabbe the balance of Pickard's ½ year's interest, due this month 4 8 9

22. TUESDAY:—
   At Epsom.

23. WEDNESDAY:—
   Wm. Saunders received from Dorling 15 0 0
   And lost on Dirk Haterick 10 0 0
   " " St. Hubert 5 0 0
   " " Nettle —

24. THURSDAY:—
   At Epsom.

25. FRIDAY:—
   At Epsom.
   Returned to London at 8 o'clock — Slept at Beaufort-buildings.

26. SATURDAY:—
   Returned home by the ½ past 7 train.
   Paid Chadbourne 0 19 0
   " " Henry 0 14 0
   " " Michael 0 12 0
   " " Charles 0 7 0

27. WHIT-SUNDAY:—
   At home.

28. MONDAY:—
   At home.
   Paid Walter Palmer 0 10 0
   Sold W. P. the carriage for 10 0 0
   Walter here to dinner.
   Sent Henry to Stafford to see dear Willie.

29. TUESDAY:—

Went to Hednesford and back per ½ past 11 train for Manchester, with Sarah and Saunders.
Slept at the Star.

30. WEDNESDAY:—
    At Manchester.
    Paid for Saunders at Manchester — St. Dunstan 3 0 0
    Sargent 2 0 0
    Bonnet 1 9 0

31. THURSDAY:—
    Returned home by the Express to Stafford, then on by gig with Saunders.
    ++ Paid Walter Palmer 2 0 0

JUNE.

1. FRIDAY:—
    Dined at the Yard.
    S. P.'s bill given.

2. SATURDAY:—
    Went to Stafford to see Buxton.
    Paid W. P. 1 0 0
    Paid Harland and Wogan's fees 2 2 0
    Dined at the Yard.
    Paid Henry 0 14 0
    ——— Michael 0 12 0
    ——— Charles 0 5 0

3. SUNDAY:—
    At home. Eliza came.

4. MONDAY:—
    Went by the 8 train to London with Saunders and George Whitehouse — then on to Ascot in the evening — slept at Mrs. Cook's.

5. TUESDAY:—
    At Ascot. Wm. Saunders lost on the Chicken 100 0 0

6. WEDNESDAY:—
    At Ascot.

7. THURSDAY:—
    At Ascot.
    9th Paid Walter at Ascot and London 7 0 0

8. FRIDAY:—
    At Ascot.
    Returned to London at 7 o'clock — slept at Beaufort-buildings.

9. SATURDAY:—
    Paid Buchannan's whiskey, to be advised to-day 29 10 1
    Returned home by the Express train to Stafford, then on by fly
    Paid Henry 0 14 0
    ——— Michael 0 12 0

10. SUNDAY:—
   At home.
   Dined at the yard.
   Went to Wednesford with Jere.

11. MONDAY:—
   At home with a bad head ache.
   Dined at the yard.
   Paid Phillips' ac. 5 10 0
   Paid Vernon for corks 0 8 6

12. TUESDAY:—
   Went to Birmingham by the 8 o'clock train, then on to Newton.
   Slept at the Leigh Arms.

13. WEDNESDAY:—
   At Newton.
   Won the gold cup with "Zarley."

14. THURSDAY:—
   At Newton.
   Won the Newton Cup with Zarley, and returned home by ½ p. 8 train to Stafford, then on by gig with Saunders.
   Willie retd. home from school.

15. FRIDAY:—
   Dined at the yard.
   Settled Hayward's Bond in full, by giving a cheque for the balance due, viz...22 17 0

16. SATURDAY:—
   Dined at the yard.
   Paid Henry...0 14 0
   ——— Michael 0 10 0
   ——— Charles
   Eliza came to see Willie.

17. SUNDAY:—
   At home.

18. MONDAY:—
   Received Edwards' rent to March, 1855...8 10 0
   Received from Glover..5 0 0
   Paid tithe 6 4 10
   Barbara called and stayed all night.

19. TUESDAY:—
   Paid Walter Palmer..2 0 0
   Eliza and Barbara went home in the carriage.
   Dined at the yard.
   Willie at Ben's all day.
   Sent Spittle a bill.

20. WEDNESDAY:—
   Neri.
   Sent Henry for Trickstress and foal, paid...31 10 6

Went to Hednesford to breakfast.
Paid Lord Lichfield's rent 22 10 0
Wm. Saunders, Ben, and Jere dined.
Wm. Saunders lost at Whist 1 8 0
+++
+++ Lent B. Thirlby 35 0 0

21. THURSDAY:—
Dined at yard.
Paid Crabbe 5 0 0

22. FRIDAY:—
Went to London by the 8 o'clock train.
Slept at Beaufort buildings.
Henry returned home with Trickstress and foal — expenses 1 12 6

23. SATURDAY:—
Returned from London by the 3 o'clock train.
Paid Henry 0 14 0
——— Michael 0 12 0
——— Charles 0 8 0

24. SUNDAY:—
At Church — Mr. Atkinson. Eliza came after dinner.

25. MONDAY:—
Wm. Saunders and Jere dined here, off goose.
Paid Walter Palmer 3 0 0

26. TUESDAY:—
Went by the 11 train from Lichfield for Newcastle. Slept at the Neville Hotel.
+++ Eliza confined of a little boy
++++ at 9 o'clock at night.

27. WEDNESDAY:—
At Newcastle.
Left Newcastle at 8 p. 7 and arrived at Derby at ½ p. 12. Slept at the Midland Hotel.

28. THURSDAY:—
Returned home from Derby by the 10 o'clock train.
Dined at the yard.

29. FRIDAY:—
Went to Hednesford with Willie and Ben; stayed dinner, and went round by Chorley.

30. SATURDAY:—
Willie and I dined at Jere's with Wm. Saunders.
Paid Henry 0 14 0
——— Michael 0 12 0
——— Charles 0 8 0

JULY.

1. SUNDAY:—

At Church; sacrament.
Dined at the yard.

2. MONDAY:—
    Paid Wm. Fortescue for cow, hay, straw, porter, and ale 26 7 0
    ——— T. Southern 1 15 0
Sent the 2 yearlings to Hednesford, by Henry and James Knott. Dined at the yard.

3. TUESDAY:—
    Paid Potts in full 4 6 6
    ——— Dewey for a bag of barley 1 0 0
Brewed 4 bushels of malt.
Paid Crabbe 5 0 0
Eliza came down stairs.

4. WEDNESDAY:—
2nd Mr. Atkinson left home for his holiday.
Dined at the yard.
Tom was there.
Paid Whateley's fee for Wm. Saunders 1 3 9

5. THURSDAY:—
Went with Jere to Worcester, and returned home at night by Stafford, then on by fly.

6. FRIDAY:—
Drove Jere and Willie to Lichfield.
The 7th. Paid Walter and Wright for Walter Palmer.

7. SATURDAY:—
Went to Birmingham with Jere — came back by Stafford — received Wright's rent (balanced after deducting Walter's account.)
    Paid Henry 0 14 0
    ——— Michael 0 12 0
    ——— Charles 0 6 6
Had supper with Cook, and Saunders, and Ben at Jere's.

8. SUNDAY:—
At Church — Mr. Atkinson, jun. did all.

9. MONDAY:—
Went to London and back the same day.

10. TUESDAY:—
Wm. Saunders dined here. Rode with Wm. Saunders to Lichfield to see Morning Star off for Mansfield.
    Paid W. S. to pay "The Star's" expenses 10 0 0

11. WEDNESDAY:—
Drove to Stafford for the 10 train for Liverpool.
Slept at the Stork.
+++ Henry fetched "Nettle."
+++ Home from Wm. Saunders'.

12. THURSDAY:—
At Liverpool.

Wm. Saunders received Morning's stake at Mansfield, amounting to 40 0 0

13. FRIDAY:—
Returned home by the 5 express from Liverpool, then on by gig home with G. to Whitehouse.

14. SATURDAY:—
Sent J. Edwards a cheque for £50 — for interest 50 0 0
Paid Henry 0 14 0
——— Michael 0 12 0

15. SUNDAY:—
At Church — Pittman read the prayers — Atkinson, jun., preached.

16. MONDAY:—
Went to Birmingham to see Wright, and returned back by Colwich at 3 o'clock.
Henry fetched home Doubt and her foal, expenses, &c., &c., &c. 74 0 0

17. TUESDAY:—
Dined at home.
Geo. Bates dined.
Eliza went to Stafford.

18. WEDNESDAY:—
Jere dined here — then went to Hednesford.
Paid Lander and Gardner —
For Mr. Inge's land... 450 0 0
— Possession 3 0 0
— Interest 1 8 0

19. THURSDAY:—
Saunders and Jere here to breakfast — then I went on with Saunders to Lichfield for Nottingham, but only got to Derby and back at night.

20. FRIDAY:—
Went to Shrewsbury to see Mr. Edwards; returned home at 8 o'clock.
Paid Jere Smith on account of Vetches.. 6 0 0

21. SATURDAY:—
Went to Birmingham, to see Mr. Wright.
Paid for Mowing — Hay-making.
——— Henry.. 0 14 0
——— Michael 0 12 0
——— Charles 0 3 0

22. SUNDAY:—
Willie went to Tom's at Coton with his Grandmama.
At home.

23. MONDAY:—
Went to London to see Pratt, and returned home with Jere by the 5 express.

24. TUESDAY:—
Went to Hednesford with Jere.
Went to Stafford, to see Dr. Harland, with Walter.
Paid Walter Palmer 17 0 0

25. WEDNESDAY:—
   At home.
   Sent Jere to Colwich station.

26. THURSDAY:—
   Henry fetched Willie home.
   George Whitehouse dined here.

27. FRIDAY:—
   At home.

28. SATURDAY:—
   Went to Stafford to see Walter.
   Paid Walter Palmer 3 2 0
   ——— Haymakers 1 3 9
   ——— Henry 0 14 0
   ——— Michael 0 12 0
   ——— Potts for Elis's clothes 3 3 6

29. SUNDAY:—
   ——— At home — Willie went to church, and to George's to tea.

30. MONDAY:—
   Paid Weatherby, for Wm. Saunders, for half Myrtle's stake in the Oaks, and at Liverpool 17 14 7½
   Wm. Saunders lost at Goodwood.[9]
   Went to London by 7 train from Lichfield for Goodwood.

31. TUESDAY:—
   At Goodwood.

AUGUST.

1. WEDNESDAY:—
   At Goodwood.

2. THURSDAY:—
   At Goodwood.
   Wm. Saunders lost at Goodwood 16 10 0

3. FRIDAY:—
   At Goodwood.
   Returned to Beaufort-buildings at ¼ b. 9.

4. SATURDAY:—
   Returned home at 10.
   Paid Southwell for venison 4 4 0
   Haymakers 2 0 0

---

[9] A horse-racing track in West Sussex. Unlike oval tracks, the Goodwood course travels straight for six furlongs. *The Spectator* magazine reported that the Thursday race was "Cup day." Palmer's horse was among only six that ran.

Henry 0 14 0
Michael 0 12 0

5. SUNDAY:—
    At Church — Mr. Freen read prayers — Sacrament.

6. MONDAY:—
    Went to Stafford to pay Willie's schooling 12 18 0
    Paid Walter Palmer (Glover) 2 0 0
    +++ Weaned the Duchess of Kent's foal.

7. TUESDAY:—
    Went to London by 5 o'clock train.

8. WEDNESDAY:—
    Went to Brighton races and returned to London in the evening.
    Returned to Stafford by the mail train. Slept at the junction.

9. THURSDAY:—
    Returned home by the 8 o'clock train.

10. FRIDAY:—
    Went to see Walter who was taken ill.
    Paid Walter Palmer 7 0 0

11. SATURDAY:—
    Went to see Walter twice, and returned home at night by fly.
    Paid Henry 1 4 0
    ——— Michael 0 12 0
    ++ I went to see Walter, and returned home by fly.

12. SUNDAY:—
    Mr. Dyke came.
    Jere dined. Mr. Dyke and I went to Wolverhampton with Southern's fly.

13. MONDAY:—
    Saunders lost on Lurley 20 0 0

14. TUESDAY:—
    Went by Stafford to see Walter. Came home by gig from Wolverhampton.

15. WEDNESDAY:—
    Went by Stafford to Wolverhampton, and returned by Stafford to see Walter, who was very ill.

16. THURSDAY:—
    Paid Fortescue for a barrel of beer 0 12 0
    Went to see Walter, who was very ill.
    Walter Palmer died at half-past two, p.m.

17. FRIDAY:—
    Went to Liverpool to tell Agnes, Eliza, and Joseph of Walter's death.
    Paid Meeson (in the train going to Liverpool) for oats 18 0 0

18. SATURDAY:—
    At home.

Paid Henry... 0 14 0
—— Chadbourne for thatching 0 8 6
—— Charles... 0 12 0

20. MONDAY:—
Went to Stafford to get Walter's certificate from Mr. Day.
Jere dined.
Settled with Glover, and received the balance.. 4 14 6

21. TUESDAY:—
Drove to Lichfield with Ben for Warwick. Slept at the Woolpack.

22. WEDNESDAY:—
At Warwick.
Returned home by luggage train at 20 p. 10.

23. THURSDAY:—
At home.
Jere dined here off pheasant.
Michael fetched coals from Brown Hills.

24. FRIDAY:—
Went to Hednesford with Cook and Jere.
7th. Paid Wm. Saunders... 100 0 0

25. SATURDAY:—
Saunders, Cook, Ben, Jere, and Geo. Bates here to dinner.[10]
Paid Henry... 0 14 0
—— Michael 0 12 0
—— Charles.

26. SUNDAY:
At home.
Jere dined.

27. MONDAY:—
++ Went to Stafford with
++ George and Tom, to
++ follow Walter to
++ his grave at Rugeley.
Dined at the yard.

28. TUESDAY:—
Went to Lichfield for York — stayed at the White Swan.

29. WEDNESDAY:—
At York.

---

[10] This was the dinner where Bates was pressured to sign the application for an insurance policy with the promise of being able to borrow £500 on it. If you're keeping score, Palmer by this time had tried to get policies taken out on Bates, Jere Smith, and his Stafford mistress, Jane Bergen.

30. THURSDAY:—
　　At York.

31. FRIDAY:—
　　At York.
　　Returned to Derby, and slept at the Midland.

SEPTEMBER.

1. SATURDAY:—
　　Sold the 2 yrs. old br. c. to Mr. Robinson, and delivered him to Armstrong, his trainer, this day.
　　Paid Henry 0 14 0
　　——— Michael 0 8 0

2. SUNDAY:—
　　At church — Mr. Coaney preached.

3. MONDAY:—
　　Mother, Sarah, George and Eliza started for Buxton at 7; lent them the mare and carriage.
　　Went to Hednesford with Jere.
　　Jere dined here.

4. TUESDAY:—
　　Went to Lichfield with Saunders for Derby; returned home in the evening.
　　Sold Wm. Saunders my half of Careless for 30 0 0
　　Paid Lurley's Stake 15 0 0

5. WEDNESDAY:—
　　At home.
　　Jere dined.
　　NERI. Paid for Jere for Crosbie's returned bill 12 0 0
　　27. Paid Southwell for Buck 4 0 0
　　Paid Jere Smith on Acc. of his law costs in Denman v. Saunders,
　　for Saunders 20 0 0
　　W. Bates, Geo. Bates, and Jere here to dinner.

7. FRIDAY:—
　　Went to Hednesford with Jere.
　　Paid Wm. Saunders 25 0 0
　　4th — Wm. Saunders lost on Little Nell, at Derby 5 0 0

8. SATURDAY:—
　　Went to London and back.
　　Paid Henry 0 14 0
　　——— Michael 0 12 0
　　——— Charles 0 5 0

9. SUNDAY:— AT HOME.
　　Jere and T. Walkenden dined.

10. MONDAY:—
　　Went to Lichfield with Wm. Saunders, for Doncaster.
　　Mother returned home from D. and Buxton.

11. TUESDAY:—
   At Doncaster.
   Wm. Saunders lost on Veteran and Midsummer 4 0 0

12 WEDNESDAY:—
   At Doncaster.
   William Saunders lost on the Chicken for Portland Plate 10 0 0

13. THURSDAY:—
   At Doncaster.

14. FRIDAY:—
   At Doncaster.
   Wm. Saunders lost on the Chicken for Don Stakes 10 0 0
   Returned home by way of Lichfield at 20 b. 11.

15. SATURDAY:—
   Went to Stafford.
   Dined with my Willie and Geo. Bates at Castle Terrace.[11]
   Paid Henry 1 4 0
   ——— Michael 0 8 0
   Eliza went home 16th to wake.
   Went to Hednesford — Mr. Cook dined.

17. MONDAY:—
   Drove Mr. Cook and Cheshire to Lichfield races — returned home at ½ p. 7, and supped with Jere.
   Eliza went with Barbara to the wake, and stayed all night.

18. TUESDAY:—
   Drove Mr. Cook to Hednesford, then on to Lichfield, and home in the evening.
   Eliza went to the races with Barbara.

19. WEDNESDAY:—
   Paid Crabb Mrs. Turnicliffe's interest, due in October next 14 8 9
   Paid Jno. Wright's bill 12 0 0
   Lent Jno. Wright on acc. of bill to Sep. 295 0 0
   Paid Perkins' interest, after deducting £2 18s. for income tax 9 12 0

20. THURSDAY:—
   Went to Stafford with Wm. Saunders, and returned home at 5 m. p. 8, P.M.
   Trickstress' foal died.

21. FRIDAY:—
   Geo. Bates and Jere Smith dined.
   NERI. Paid Wm. Saunders, for Nan's Stake, and expenses 10 0 0

22. SATURDAY:—
   Dined at the yard.
   Paid Henry 0 14 0
   ——— Michael 0 12 0
   ——— Charles 0 8 0

---

[11] Walter Palmer's home in Stafford.

23. SUNDAY:—
    Went to church with Cook — Mr. Atkinson.

24. MONDAY:—
    Went to London to see Pratt.
    Slept at Beaufort-buildings.
    Saunders sent the bay mare.

25. TUESDAY:—
    Returned home by the 10 train.

26. WEDNESDAY:—
    At home.
    27. Lent Myatt to go to London... 15 0 0
    Paid Crabb 5 0 0

27. THURSDAY:—
    Paid Jno. Timmiss for oats 10 18 0
    ——— Wenlock for straw 5 18 0
    Sam Cope dined.

28. FRIDAY:—
    Jere dined.
    Paid Bull for Paving.. 1 4 6

29. SATURDAY:—
    Received from James Webb for two years' rent, deducting 7*l*. 0s. 4d. for Property
    and Land-Tax 38 0 0
    Paid Henry 0 14 0
    ——— Michael 0 12 0
    ——— Charles 0 3 0

30. SUNDAY:—
    Went to Hednesford.

OCTOBER.

1. MONDAY:—
    Went to London, and from there to Chester.
    Slept at the White Lion.

2. TUESDAY:—
    At Chester.
    Wm. Saunders lost on Little Nell 5 0 0
    Beregina and Merrywing 7 0 0

3. WEDNESDAY:—
    At Chester.
    Wm. Saunders lost on Chicken and Crabstick 15 0 0
    And received from Topham for Chicken's stake
    Returned to Stafford, then on by fly with Cook.

4. THURSDAY:—
    At home.

5. FRIDAY:—
   At home.

6. SATURDAY:—
   Went to Lichfield for London with Mr. Cook.
   Paid Henry..0 14 0
   ——— Michael 0 12 0
   ——— Nailor 0 4 0

7. SUNDAY:—
   Went to Stafford.

8. MONDAY:—
   Went to Stafford to see Buxton and Day — Dined at the junction.

9. TUESDAY:—
   At home.
   Paid Robert Bentley 2 7 6

10. WEDNESDAY:—
    Went with Jere to Hednesford.

11. THURSDAY:—
    Willie's birth-day.
    Jere and George Bates here to dinner.
    Paid Pearson for oats28 12 0
    ——— Wm. for cheese0 13 0
    ——— for Nutt.

12. FRIDAY:—
    Went with Jere to Hednesford, then on with Wm. Saunders to Lichfield.

13. SATURDAY:—
    Went with Cook to Hednesford to try Polestar.
    Paid for getting up potatoes 0 15 9
    ——— Henry..0 14 0
    ——— Michael 0 12 0
    ——— Charles..0 3 0

14. SUNDAY:—
    Went with Willie to church — Sacrament.

15. MONDAY:—
    Sent Willie to school with T. Walkenden.
    Subpoenaed into County court.

16. TUESDAY:—
    Went by 8 train for Warwick.
    Slept at Woolpack.

17. WEDNESDAY:—
    At Warwick.
    Returned home by gig from Lichfield at ¼ p. 9.

18. THURSDAY:—

Paid Hopley for bricks.. 0 16 10
Mr. Clarke and Mason called to see the foals.

19. FRIDAY:—
Went with Mr. Cook to Hednesford to try "Nan," and in coming home the horse tumbled down — Eliza went to Stone.

20. SATURDAY:—
Mr. Cook, Mr. and Mrs. Walkenden breakfasted here.
Paid Henry 0 14 0
——— Michael.. 0 12 0
——— Tom Palmer... 5 0 0

21. SUNDAY:—
Left for London by 30 p. 12 train.

22. MONDAY:—
Left Eastern Counties Station for Newmarket at 8 o'clock.
Slept at Pettit's.

23. TUESDAY:—
At Newmarket.

24. WEDNESDAY:—
At Newmarket.
Chicken won, beating Ld. Alfred and 15 others.

25. THURSDAY:—
At Newmarket.

26. FRIDAY:—
At Newmarket.
Returned to London with Geo. Whitehouse, to B. Buildings at ½ p. 10.

27. SATURDAY:—
Went to see Pratt, and paid him £250 on acc. of £2,000 bill.
Returned home at ½ p. 7.
Paid Henry 0 14 0
——— Michael.. 0 12 0
——— Charles 0 4 0

28. SUNDAY:—
At home.

29. MONDAY:—
Jere dined, then rode with me to Lichfield for Worcester.
Slept at the Bell Inn.

30. TUESDAY:—
At Worcester.
Returned home by fly from Lichfield at ½ p. 9.

31. WEDNESDAY:—
At home with a bad cold.
Jere dined.
Charles and Henry brewed 14 bushels of malt.

NOVEMBER.

1. THURSDAY:—
   At home with a bad cold.

2. FRIDAY:—
   At home with a bad cold.
   Charles and Henry brewed.
   Eliza and Barbara went to see the horsemanship, &c.

3. SATURDAY:—
   Went with Ben to Hednesford to see Chas. Marlow.
   Paid Henry 0 14 0
   ——— Michael 0 12 0
   ——— Charles 0 3 6

4. SUNDAY:—
   At home.

5. MONDAY:—
   At home.

6. TUESDAY:—
   Went to Liverpool with Cook, Jere, and Saunders.
   Paid Saunders 10 0 0
   Slept at the Stork.

7. WEDNESDAY:—
   At Liverpool.
   Saunders lost on Chicken 50 0 0
   Saunders lost on Staffordshire Nan 50 0 0

8. THURSDAY:—
   At Liverpool.
   Paid Wm. Saunders 20 0 0
   Returned home by fly from Stafford.

9. FRIDAY:—
   Went to London by 12 m. b. 5 train.
   Slept at B. Buildings.

10. SATURDAY:—
    Returned home by B'ham.
    Paid Henry 0 14 0
    ——— Michael 0 12 0
    ——— Charles 0 4 0

11. SUNDAY:—
    At home.
    Mr. H — A. preached farewell.

12. MONDAY:—
    At home.
    Jere dined.

13. TUESDAY:—
  Drove with Cheshire to Stafford, with George's poney for Shrewsbury.
  Returned home at night with Wm. Saunders.

14. WEDNESDAY:—
  Went to Colwich with George's poney for Shrewsbury.
  Slept in the Raven.

15. THURSDAY:—
  Retd. home with Cook and Myatt, by fly from Stafford.

16. FRIDAY:—
  Cook and Jere dined here.

17. SATURDAY:—
  Cook ill in bed.
  Dined with Jere.
  Paid Henry 0 14 0
  —— Michael 0 12 0
  —— Harriman 0 18 0

18. SUNDAY:—
  At home.
  Cook ill in bed.

19. MONDAY:—
  Went to London to pay Pratt 700 0 0
  Returned home by fly from Stafford.
  Sat up with Cook all night.

20. TUESDAY:—
  Attending on Cook all day.
  Dined at the yard.
  Sat up with Cook all night.

21. WEDNESDAY:—
  ++++ Cook died at 1 o'clock this morning.
  Jere and Wm. Saunders dined.
  Sent Bright a 3 months' bill.

22. THURSDAY:—
  Paid Spilsbury for hay for Wm. Saunders 32 19 9
  —— Spilsbury for my hay 13 2 6
  —— Burnett for spirits 13 13 0

23. FRIDAY:—
  Cook's friends and Jones came, and I dined with them at Masters'.[12]

---

[12] "Jones" was William Jones of Lutterworth, who knew Palmer and Cook from the racing field. A surgeon, he had been summoned by Palmer to attend to Cook and was present at his death. He testified that Cook had his betting-book, which went missing after his death, and that Palmer said he and Cook owed £3,000 to £4,000 and he hoped Mr. Cook's friends would help pay it off.

24. SATURDAY:—
Went to Lichfield for London, and returned home at ½ p. 7.
Mr. Stevens came at ½ p. 7.
Paid Harriman..0 18 0
——— Henry 0 14 0
——— Michael 0 12 0
——— Charles...0 8 0

25. SUNDAY:—
At church — Hamilton preached.
Dined, yard.

26. MONDAY:—
Attended a P.M. examination on poor Cook, with Drs. Harland, Mr. Bamford, Newton, and a Mr. Devonshire.

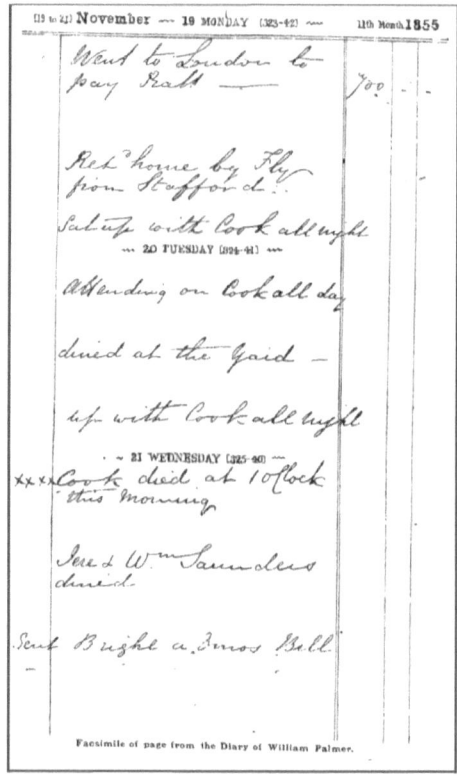

DIARY PAGE COVERING NOV. 19-21.

The Jane Letters

William Palmer

With his wife safely interred in the family vault, Palmer began an affair in early 1855 with Jane Bergen, the daughter of the chief superintendent of the Stafford Rural Constabulary. Over the course of the year they passed a number of messages between them. Bergen's side of the correspondence was lost, but Palmer's notes surfaced after his execution. They were first mentioned in George Fletcher's The Life & Career of Dr. William Palmer of Rugeley *(Peschel Press, 2014), but he refused to quote from them, saying they were written in "a most lascivious, degrading style." Fortunately, the 34 letters were stored in the William Salt Library in Stafford, and we can follow the course of the affair from infatuation to disillusionment that ended in Jane's blackmailing of Palmer.*

Remember that during the Jane affair, Palmer was also carrying on with his housemaid Eliza Tharm. On June 26, 1855, Eliza gave birth to Palmer's son, who most likely died at Palmer's hands on Dec. 13. It is believed that Jane had her abortion around the beginning of August of that year.

An unknown hand numbered the letters, but the Salt library placed Letters 16 and 17 after Letter 28 believing that's where they belong. This practice was followed here.

-1-

MY DEAR MISS JANE,

I shall not be able to meet you at the Station but if you come straight to the back of the Grand Stand I will meet you <u>accidentally</u> and will take care that you have a pleasant day.

YOURS FAITHFULLY,
WM. PALMER

RUGELEY, TUESDAY MORNING

-2-

MY DEAR JANE,

How are you this morning? I shall see you this afternoon and then — 'As soon as night shall fix her seal upon the eyes and lips of men, oh dearest! I shall panting steal to nestle in thine arms again.'[1]

---

[1] From "An Ode Upon Morning" by Thomas Moore (1779-1852), an

YOURS,
WM. PALMER

-3-

MY DEAR JANE,
I cannot possibly be with you on Tuesday but you may expect me on Wednesday evening. Will that do for you?

YOURS,
WM. PALMER

-4-

MY DEAR JANE,
Break your journey on Saturday — book — to Rugeley — come to my surgery with your handkerchief to your face — no one will be in but <u>myself</u>. I will perform an <u>operation</u> on you and you can have a snack and go on by the next train.

YOURS,
WM. PALMER

-5-

MY DEAR JANE,
Send the enclosed note to Frantz by an errand lad, he will bring back a lobster, etc. I am coming tonight to help you eat it.

YOURS,
WM. PALMER

-6-

MY DEAR JANE,
If Mrs K. calls on you or sends anybody poking into your affairs you will know what to do.
Mum's the word.

YOURS,
W.P.

-7-

MY DEAR JANE,
I can't today, will try tomorrow.

Irish poet, songwriter, and entertainer.

Is your cold better?

YOURS,
WM. PALMER

-8-

MY DEAR JANE,

I missed you — were you there? I shall be at Shrewsbury on Friday. Drop me a line.

YOURS,
W.P.

-9-

MY DEAR JANE,

No note for me at Shrewsbury. I hope you are well. I shall call on Monday,

YOURS,
WM. PALMER

-10-

MY DEAR JANE,

Will you send the enclosed note to Frantz and give me my supper tonight.

YOURS,
W.P.

-11-

MY DEAR JANE,

I meant to have called before leaving the town to ask you to meet me at Lichfield next week. Will you?

Write by return.

YOURS,
W.P.

-12-

MY DEAR JANE,

You are the right sort. Be near the west door of the Cathedral[2] at 11 o'clock on Wednesday — and leave the rest to

---

[2] The medieval cathedral at Lichfield in Staffordshire.

me.

YOURS,
W. P.

-13-

MY DEAR JANE,
   How do you feel today?
   <u>Hope you slept well last night.</u>

YOURS,
W.P.

THURSDAY MORNING

-14-

MY DEAR JANE,
   Don't see Waddell[3] until I have seen *you* which will be in the course of a few days.

YOURS,
W.P.

-15-

Jane has told Palmer that she fears she is pregnant. Note that Letters 16 and 17 have been placed after Letter 28.

MY DEAR JANE,   <u>BURN THIS</u>
   Don't trouble yourself — we can wait for a couple of months <u>and see</u>. All can be made right easily. And I can drop in at <u>any</u> time? I shall be over on Saturday.

YOURS,
W.P.

-18-

MY DEAR JANE,
   I ran against Mrs. W. and Mrs. T. just now — they said they were going to call on you and had I seen you lately? Yes —

---

[3] Possibly Dr. Cornelius Waddell, who lived on Tipping Street in Stafford. It's possible that Palmer tried to insure Jane's life, which would require an examination by a doctor. This might be the same Waddell who had examined Walter Palmer for a policy and warned the insurance company against insuring his life.

<u>I had been to ask you for slips of your pansies for my mother.</u>

You will get this before they arrive — <u>hadn't you better tell them where I passed the night?</u>

YOURS,
WM. PALMER

-19-

MY DEAR JANE,   <u>BURN THIS</u>

I knew Waddell would find you all right. Of course *he* did not discover anything. Did he ask for a kiss? Or did he take one without asking?

YOURS,
W.P.

SUNDAY MORNING

-20-

Dr. Waddell intends to tell the insurance company that Jane should not be insured.

MY DEAR JANE,   <u>BURN THIS</u>

I think the Devil is in it. Waddell says you had better not propose — that means that he will report unfavourably — so there will be a difficulty raising the needful[4] for you as intended — though I am pressed you shall not suffer.

YOURS,
W.P.

-21-

MY DEAR JANE,

A lady asked me just now how I liked last night's concert. I said very well but I preferred a duet which followed.

So I did — rather — did you?

YOURS,
W.P.

-22-

---

[4] We know that two of Palmer's victims were told he could raise money for them if they let themselves be insured. It appears that Jane Bergen narrowly escaped being another one of his victims.

My dear Jane,

I do not know what to make of your last letter — 'What do I intend'? Well I think it would be better to see and tell you. Shall I come on Sat. evy [evening]?

Yours,
W.P.

-23-

My dear Jane,

I think you are rather out of temper. You would not let me come on Saturday — and you do not say when I may. I wish you would fix a time.

Any day but Thursday next week will do for me.

Yours,
Wm. Palmer

-24-

My dear Jane,

I can't make you out — of course I am sorry that you are unwell. Perhaps the face ache is caused by <u>that</u>. I shall be over tomorrow.

Yours,
Wm. Palmer

-25-

In this letter, Palmer uses "dentist" as a euphemism for an abortionist. Ascot is a reference to a horse racing event in Berkshire. Cooke could be Stafford chemist James Cook, who did business from Foregate Street in Stafford.

My dear Jane,   BURN THIS

Ascot tomorrow so I must repeat by letter what I said to you on Sunday because I wish you very much to do it — it wont hurt you worth mentioning and as I said you have had toothache and Cooke is known as the best dentist in Stafford. Your handkerchief to your mouth — and you can't talk will do it.

He won't keep you ten minutes. Say the word and I will write to him and you will only have to ask him to draw the tooth that hurts you. He will know where to look for it!!!

So don't be surprised at what he may do.

<u>The man is as silent as death</u> and you may depend on him. Send word that I may write to him there's a dear girl.

YOURS,
WM. PALMER

P.S. You see I am <u>not</u> afraid 'to write as I speak' because I am sure that you will burn this as you have burnt the others.

W.P.

-26-

MY DEAR JANE,   <u>BURN THIS</u>

You are a good plucked one. I have written to Cooke — do just as he tells you — send me word how you get on.

YOURS,
W.P.

-27-

Palmer presents a gift to Jane for her troubles.

MY DEAR JANE,   <u>BURN THIS</u>

All's well that ends well. I am glad that you were so little hurt — in a week or two you will be all right again. I enclose halves of two £5 notes. Say you have got them and I will send the others.

YOURS,
W.P.

-28-

MY DEAR JANE,   <u>BURN THIS</u>

I am deucedly sorry to hear that you are so unwell — but you have got rid of the <u>cause</u> and now as old Tylecote[5] would say the effects will cease.

Remaining halves enclosed — send me word you have them and that you are better.

YOURS,
W.P.

-16-

MY DEAR JANE,   <u>Burn this</u>

---

[5] The doctor Palmer was apprenticed to early in his medical career.

I enclose the halves of four £5 notes. Acknowledge receipt and I will forward the others — <u>they can't be traced.</u>

YOURS,
W.P.

-17-

MY DEAR JANE,   <u>Burn this</u>
Enclosed are the remaining halves — drop me a line by return to York to say they are all right.

YOURS,
WM. PALMER

-29-

Walter Palmer died on Aug. 16 and his funeral was on Aug. 20.

MY DEAR JANE,
Walter's funeral went off very well.
I caught sight of you at the window — when shall I call? Hope you are all right now?

YOURS,
WM. PALMER

-30-

MY DEAR JANE,
Your letter is hard to understand. What queer things are people saying? Some damned chatterboxes can't mind their own business and are looking after mine, are they? You can't say I have used you ill. Let us speak of a man as we find him is my motto.
Please write and say why you think I "had better not call for a few weeks."

YOURS,
WM. PALMER

-31-

One of the few dated letters, which tells us that on this day Cook's horse Polestar won at Shrewsbury and Palmer's horse lost. He returned to Rugeley to find Jane's response to Letter 30. He writes her a letter and returns to Shrewsbury. At a drinking party that evening at The Raven, Cook falls ill.

RUGELEY, NOV. 13TH 1855

MY DEAR JANE,

It's <u>damned hard</u> for a fellow to find his friends turning against him and I was surprised to learn that you have never burned one of my letters — I cannot do what you ask.

<u>I should not mind giving £30 for the whole</u> of them though I am hard up at present. If you agree you shall have the money in the course of a week or ten days.

I enclose the only letter of yours I can find.

I shall always think with pleasure of our intimacy and can say with Moore:

"We've had some happy hours together
But joy must change its wing
And Spring would be but gloomy weather
If we had nothing else but Spring."[6]

Oblige me with an early reply and believe me, Dear Jane,
YOURS TRULY,
WM. PALMER

-32-

Palmer settles for £40, which in purchasing power is worth about £3,300 or $4,710 today.

NOV. 19TH

MY DEAR JANE,

I am agreeable to split the difference and will send you £40 in notes tomorrow or the day after and shall expect you — <u>honour bright</u> — to let me have the letters on return of Bearer.
YOURS,
WM. PALMER

-33-

NOV. 21ST

MY DEAR JANE,

Enclosed you have halves of eight fivers. Please acknowledge receipt and I will send remainders.

---

[6] From "A Parting" by Thomas Moore.

In great haste.

> YOURS,
> WM. PALMER

-34-

On this day Palmer took the train to London. On the way back, he met Stevens and is told of the inquest on Cook.

> NOV. 24TH 1855

MY DEAR JANE,
   Remaining halves of notes enclosed.
   Please keep letters for me until I send for them.

> YOURS,
> WM. PALMER

P.S. You have no reason to be unfriendly to me, remember.
W.P.

ONE OF PALMER'S NOTES PASSED TO HIS ATTORNEYS DURING HIS TRIAL.

On Duty with Inspector Field

Charles Dickens

Charles Frederick Field (1805-1874), who investigated Palmer's application to insure George Bates, had a long familiarity with criminals and their ways. He joined London's Metropolitan Police force when it was formed in 1829, rose to inspector and moved to the Detective Branch in 1846, retiring as its chief in 1852. The year before he became chief of the Detective Branch, Charles Dickens shadowed him on the job and wrote this essay, which appeared in the June 14, 1851, edition of Household Words. During the writing of Bleak House, *Dickens would use Field as his model for Inspector Bucket.*

HOW GOES THE NIGHT? SAINT Giles's clock is striking nine. The weather is dull and wet, and the long lines of street lamps are blurred, as if we saw them through tears. A damp wind blows and rakes the pieman's fire out, when he opens the door of his little furnace, carrying away an eddy of sparks.

Saint Giles's clock strikes nine. We are punctual. Where is Inspector Field? Assistant Commissioner of Police is already here, enwrapped in oil-skin cloak, and standing in the shadow of Saint Giles's steeple. Detective Sergeant, weary of speaking French all day to foreigners unpacking at the Great Exhibition,[1] is already here. Where is Inspector Field?

Inspector Field is, to-night, the guardian genius of the British Museum. He is bringing his shrewd eye to bear on every corner of its solitary galleries, before he reports "all right." Suspicious of the Elgin marbles, and not to be done by cat-faced Egyptian giants with their hands upon their knees, Inspector Field, sagacious, vigilant, lamp in hand, throwing monstrous shadows on the walls and ceilings, passes through the spacious rooms. If a mummy trembled in an atom of its dusty covering,

---

[1] A massive trade goods fair held at the Crystal Palace from May 1 to October 11, 1851. Considered the first World's Fair, it displayed inventions, wares, and people in their native costumes from 28 nations to more than 6 million people. The centerpiece building, the cast-iron and plate-glass Crystal Palace was built in only nine months and was considered a triumph of design and construction.

Inspector Field would say, "Come out of that, Tom Green. I know you!" If the smallest "Gonoph"[2] about town were crouching at the bottom of a classic bath, Inspector Field would nose him with a finer scent than the ogre's, when adventurous Jack lay trembling in his kitchen copper. But all is quiet, and Inspector Field goes warily on, making little outward show of attending to anything in particular, just recognising the Ichthyosaurus[3] as a familiar acquaintance, and wondering, perhaps, how the detectives did it in the days before the Flood.

Will Inspector Field be long about this work? He may be half-an-hour longer. He sends his compliments by Police Constable, and proposes that we meet at St. Giles's Station House, across the road. Good. It were as well to stand by the fire, there, as in the shadow of Saint Giles's steeple.

Anything doing here to-night? Not much. We are very quiet. A lost boy, extremely calm and small, sitting by the fire, whom we now confide to a constable to take home, for the child says that if you show him Newgate Street, he can show you where he lives — a raving drunken woman in the cells, who has screeched her voice away, and has hardly power enough left to declare, even with the passionate help of her feet and arms, that she is the daughter of a British officer, and, strike her blind and dead, but she'll write a letter to the Queen! but who is soothed with a drink of water — in another cell, a quiet woman with a child at her breast, for begging — in another, her husband in a smock-frock, with a basket of watercresses — in another, a pickpocket — in another, a meek tremulous old pauper man who has been out for a holiday "and has took but a little drop, but it has overcome him after so many months in the house" — and that's all as yet. Presently, a sensation at the Station House door. Mr. Field, gentlemen!

---

[2] A thief. It could have come from the Hebrew *gannabh,* the French *gniaffe,* and even low Glaswegian *gnaff.*

[3] A fish-lizard hybrid from the late Triassic and early Jurassic periods. Mary Anning (1799-1847), a fossil collector and paleontologist, discovered a complete fossil in 1811 in the cliffs at Lyme Regis in southwest England. It was one of the first finds to raise questions about the earth being older than the 6,000 years calculated from Genesis. The British Museum purchased the skeleton in 1819.

Inspector Field comes in, wiping his forehead, for he is of a burly figure, and has come fast from the ores and metals of the deep mines of the earth, and from the Parrot Gods of the South Sea Islands, and from the birds and beetles of the tropics, and from the Arts of Greece and Rome, and from the Sculptures of Nineveh, and from the traces of an elder world, when these were not. Is Rogers ready? Rogers is ready, strapped and great-coated, with a flaming eye in the middle of his waist, like a deformed Cyclops.[4] Lead on, Rogers, to Rats' Castle![5]

How many people may there be in London, who, if we had brought them deviously and blindfold, to this street, fifty paces from the Station House, and within call of Saint Giles's church, would know it for a not remote part of the city in which their lives are passed? How many, who amidst this compound of sickening smells, these heaps of filth, these tumbling houses, with all their vile contents, animate, and inanimate, slimily overflowing into the black road, would believe that they breathe THIS air? How much Red Tape[6] may there be, that could look round on the faces which now hem us in — for our appearance here has caused a rush from all points to a common centre — the lowering foreheads, the sallow cheeks, the brutal eyes, the matted hair, the infected, vermin-haunted heaps of rags — and say, "I have thought of this. I have not dismissed the thing. I have neither blustered it away, nor frozen it away, nor tied it up

---

[4] A metaphor for the bull's-eye lantern that policemen carried or attached to their belts.

[5] A notorious lodging-house frequented by thieves, prostitutes, and orphans, in the squalid St. Giles area. Newgate criminals on their way to "dance the jig" at Tyburn were allowed to stop there for a final bowl of ale. The Castle was torn down in 1845 to make way for New Oxford Street, but it wasn't until the 1950s that the area was redeveloped and the last of the urban poor were moved on.

[6] At first look, it appears that he's talking about the rope of bureaucracy that prevents things from getting done. The phrase was already in use, popularized in *Alice* (1838), a novel by that icon of novelists, Edward Bulwer-Lytton. But the sentence doesn't seem to make sense. But "red tape" (or red ribbon) was also used to describe brandy (with gin called "blue tape"). Used that way, it appears that Dickens was more likely asking, "How drunk do you have to be before you'll admit that such people living in these horrible conditions exist within walking distance of where you live?"

and put it away, nor smoothly said pooh, pooh! to it when it has been shown to me?"

This is not what Rogers wants to know, however. What Rogers wants to know, is, whether you WILL clear the way here, some of you, or whether you won't; because if you don't do it right on end, he'll lock you up! "What! YOU are there, are you, Bob Miles? You haven't had enough of it yet, haven't you? You want three months more, do you? Come away from that gentleman! What are you creeping round there for?"

"What am I a doing, thinn, Mr. Rogers?" says Bob Miles, appearing, villainous, at the end of a lane of light made by the lantern.

"I'll let you know pretty quick, if you don't hook it. WILL you hook it?"

A sycophantic murmur rises from the crowd. "Hook it, Bob, when Mr. Rogers and Mr. Field tells you! Why don't you hook it, when you are told to?"

The most importunate of the voices strikes familiarly on Mr. Rogers's ear. He suddenly turns his lantern on the owner.

"What! YOU are there, are you, Mister Click? You hook it too — come!"

"What for?" says Mr. Click, discomfited.

"You hook it, will you!" says Mr. Rogers with stern emphasis.

Both Click and Miles DO "hook it," without another word, or, in plainer English, sneak away.

"Close up there, my men!" says Inspector Field to two constables on duty who have followed. "Keep together, gentlemen; we are going down here. Heads!"

Saint Giles's church strikes half-past ten. We stoop low, and creep down a precipitous flight of steps into a dark close cellar. There is a fire. There is a long deal table. There are benches. The cellar is full of company, chiefly very young men in various conditions of dirt and raggedness. Some are eating supper. There are no girls or women present. Welcome to Rats' Castle, gentlemen, and to this company of noted thieves!

"Well, my lads! How are you, my lads? What have you been doing to-day? Here's some company come to see you, my lads! — THERE'S a plate of beefsteak, sir, for the supper of a fine young man! And there's a mouth for a steak, sir! Why, I should be too proud of such a mouth as that, if I had it myself! Stand up and show it, sir! Take off your cap. There's a fine young man for a nice little party, sir! An't he?"

Inspector Field is the bustling speaker. Inspector Field's eye is the roving eye that searches every corner of the cellar as he talks. Inspector Field's hand is the well-known hand that has collared half the people here, and motioned their brothers, sisters, fathers, mothers, male and female friends, inexorably to New South Wales.[7] Yet Inspector Field stands in this den, the Sultan of the place. Every thief here cowers before him, like a schoolboy before his schoolmaster. All watch him, all answer when addressed, all laugh at his jokes, all seek to propitiate him. This cellar company alone — to say nothing of the crowd surrounding the entrance from the street above, and making the steps shine with eyes — is strong enough to murder us all, and willing enough to do it; but, let Inspector Field have a mind to pick out one thief here, and take him; let him produce that ghostly truncheon from his pocket, and say, with his business-air, "My lad, I want you!" and all Rats' Castle shall be stricken with paralysis, and not a finger move against him, as he fits the handcuffs on!

Where's the Earl of Warwick? — Here he is, Mr. Field! Here's the Earl of Warwick, Mr. Field! — O there you are, my Lord. Come for'ard. There's a chest, sir, not to have a clean shirt on. An't it? Take your hat off, my Lord. Why, I should be ashamed if I was you — and an Earl, too — to show myself to a gentleman with my hat on! — The Earl of Warwick laughs and uncovers. All the company laugh. One pickpocket, especially, laughs with great enthusiasm. O what a jolly game it is, when Mr. Field comes down — and don't want nobody!

So, YOU are here, too, are you, you tall, grey, soldierly-looking, grave man, standing by the fire? — Yes, sir. Good evening, Mr. Field! — Let us see. You lived servant to a nobleman once? — Yes, Mr. Field. — And what is it you do now; I forget? — Well, Mr. Field, I job about as well as I can. I left my employment on account of delicate health. The family is still kind to me. Mr. Wix of Piccadilly is also very kind to me when I am hard up. Likewise Mr. Nix of Oxford Street. I get a trifle

---

[7] A province in Australia where convicts were transported.

from them occasionally, and rub on as well as I can, Mr. Field. Mr. Field's eye rolls enjoyingly, for this man is a notorious begging-letter writer. — Good night, my lads! — Good night, Mr. Field, and thank'ee, sir!

Clear the street here, half a thousand of you! Cut it, Mrs. Stalker — none of that — we don't want you! Rogers of the flaming eye, lead on to the tramps' lodging-house!

A dream of baleful faces attends to the door. Now, stand back all of you! In the rear Detective Sergeant plants himself, composedly whistling, with his strong right arm across the narrow passage. Mrs. Stalker, I am something'd that need not be written here, if you won't get yourself into trouble, in about half a minute, if I see that face of yours again!

Saint Giles's church clock, striking eleven, hums through our hand from the dilapidated door of a dark outhouse as we open it, and are stricken back by the pestilent breath that issues from within. Rogers to the front with the light, and let us look!

Ten, twenty, thirty — who can count them! Men, women, children, for the most part naked, heaped upon the floor like maggots in a cheese![8] Ho! In that dark corner yonder! Does anybody lie there? Me sir, Irish me, a widder, with six children. And yonder? Me sir, Irish me, with me wife and eight poor babes. And to the left there? Me sir, Irish me, along with two more Irish boys as is me friends. And to the right there? Me sir and the Murphy fam'ly, numbering five blessed souls. And what's this, coiling, now, about my foot? Another Irish me, pitifully in want of shaving, whom I have awakened from sleep — and across my other foot lies his wife — and by the shoes of Inspector Field lie their three eldest — and their three youngest are at present squeezed between the open door and the wall. And why is there no one on that little mat before the sullen fire? Because O'Donovan, with his wife and daughter, is not come in

---

[8] Many types of cheeses, such as Gorgonzola, are made with the help of small white worms commonly called maggots. For example, a Sardinian sheep milk cheese called "casu marzu" is fermented by introducing the eggs of the cheese fly. The eggs hatch and the larvae eat the cheese and break down its fats in its digestive system. Of course, you have to eat the cheese while the maggots are still alive. Eating it with dead maggots would be gross.

from selling Lucifers!⁹ Nor on the bit of sacking in the nearest corner? Bad luck! Because that Irish family is late to-night, a-cadging in the streets!

They are all awake now, the children excepted, and most of them sit up, to stare. Wheresoever Mr. Rogers turns the flaming eye, there is a spectral figure rising, unshrouded, from a grave of rags. Who is the landlord here? — I am, Mr. Field! says a bundle of ribs and parchment against the wall, scratching itself. — Will you spend this money fairly, in the morning, to buy coffee for 'em all? — Yes, sir, I will! — O he'll do it, sir, he'll do it fair. He's honest! cry the spectres. And with thanks and Good Night sink into their graves again.

Thus, we make our New Oxford Streets, and our other new streets, never heeding, never asking, where the wretches whom we clear out, crowd. With such scenes at our doors, with all the plagues of Egypt tied up with bits of cobweb in kennels so near our homes, we timorously make our Nuisance Bills and Boards of Health, nonentities, and think to keep away the Wolves of Crime and Filth, by our electioneering ducking to little vestrymen and our gentlemanly handling of Red Tape!

Intelligence of the coffee-money has got abroad. The yard is full, and Rogers of the flaming eye is beleaguered with entreaties to show other Lodging Houses. Mine next! Mine! Mine! Rogers, military, obdurate, stiff-necked, immovable, replies not, but leads away; all falling back before him. Inspector Field follows. Detective Sergeant, with his barrier of arm across the little passage, deliberately waits to close the procession. He sees behind him, without any effort, and exceedingly disturbs one individual far in the rear by coolly calling out, "It won't do, Mr. Michael! Don't try it!"

After council holden in the street, we enter other lodging-houses, public-houses, many lairs and holes; all noisome and offensive; none so filthy and so crowded as where Irish are. In one, the Ethiopian party are expected home presently — were in Oxford Street when last heard of — shall be fetched, for our delight, within ten minutes. In another, one of the two or three Professors who drew Napoleon Buonaparte and a couple of mackerel, on the pavement and then let the work of art out to a

---

⁹ Matches.

speculator,[10] is refreshing after his labours. In another, the vested interest of the profitable nuisance has been in one family for a hundred years, and the landlord drives in comfortably from the country to his snug little stew in town. In all, Inspector Field is received with warmth. Coiners and smashers[11] droop before him; pickpockets defer to him; the gentle sex (not very gentle here) smile upon him. Half-drunken hags check themselves in the midst of pots of beer, or pints of gin, to drink to Mr. Field, and pressingly to ask the honour of his finishing the draught. One beldame in rusty black has such admiration for him, that she runs a whole street's length to shake him by the hand; tumbling into a heap of mud by the way, and still pressing her attentions when her very form has ceased to be distinguishable through it. Before the power of the law, the power of superior sense — for common thieves are fools beside these men — and the power of a perfect mastery of their character, the garrison of Rats' Castle and the adjacent Fortresses make but a skulking show indeed when reviewed by Inspector Field.

Saint Giles's clock says it will be midnight in half-an-hour, and Inspector Field says we must hurry to the Old Mint in the Borough. The cab-driver is low-spirited, and has a solemn sense of his responsibility. Now, what's your fare, my lad? — O YOU know, Inspector Field, what's the good of asking ME!

Say, Parker, strapped and great-coated, and waiting in dim Borough doorway by appointment, to replace the trusty Rogers

---

[10] Pavement artists like those seen in *Mary Poppins* seem to be a recent innovation in Palmer's time. They were not mentioned in Mayhew's exhaustive (and exhausting to read) *London Labor and London Poor* (1851). One magazine writer speculated that it was a byproduct of the Great Exhibition at the Crystal Palace, where huge numbers of visitors created an appreciative and paying audience. In *Epoch* magazine of 1891, householders who objected to having their pavement turned into an open-air art gallery were advised to "express [his objections] at once, for when the pictures are completed the artist is not at all disposed to move away. Nor is he apt to be pacified when the irate landlord tells him that he can take his pictures along with him."

[11] *Coiners* are counterfeiters, while *smashers* pass the funny money. You might say they're two sides of the same coin. (In case you were wondering, a smasher also breaks the windows at jewelers and banks and grabs what he can, but that was used only in the U.S.)

whom we left deep in Saint Giles's, are you ready? Ready, Inspector Field, and at a motion of my wrist behold my flaming eye.

This narrow street, sir, is the chief part of the Old Mint, full of low lodging-houses, as you see by the transparent canvas-lamps and blinds, announcing beds for travellers! But it is greatly changed, friend Field, from my former knowledge of it; it is infinitely quieter and more subdued than when I was here last, some seven years ago? O yes! Inspector Haynes, a first-rate man, is on this station now and plays the Devil with them!

Well, my lads! How are you to-night, my lads? Playing cards here, eh? Who wins? — Why, Mr. Field, I, the sulky gentleman with the damp flat side-curls, rubbing my bleared eye with the end of my neckerchief which is like a dirty eel-skin, am losing just at present, but I suppose I must take my pipe out of my mouth, and be submissive to YOU — I hope I see you well, Mr. Field? — Aye, all right, my lad. Deputy, who have you got upstairs? Be pleased to show the rooms!

Why Deputy, Inspector Field can't say. He only knows that the man who takes care of the beds and lodgers is always called so. Steady, O Deputy, with the flaring candle in the blacking-bottle, for this is a slushy back-yard, and the wooden staircase outside the house creaks and has holes in it.

Again, in these confined intolerable rooms, burrowed out like the holes of rats or the nests of insect-vermin, but fuller of intolerable smells, are crowds of sleepers, each on his foul truckle-bed coiled up beneath a rug. Holloa here! Come! Let us see you! Show your face! Pilot Parker goes from bed to bed and turns their slumbering heads towards us, as a salesman might turn sheep. Some wake up with an execration and a threat. — What! who spoke? O! If it's the accursed glaring eye that fixes me, go where I will, I am helpless. Here! I sit up to be looked at. Is it me you want? Not you, lie down again! and I lie down, with a woful growl.

Whenever the turning lane of light becomes stationary for a moment, some sleeper appears at the end of it, submits himself to be scrutinised, and fades away into the darkness.

There should be strange dreams here, Deputy. They sleep sound enough, says Deputy, taking the candle out of the blacking-bottle, snuffing it with his fingers, throwing the snuff into the bottle, and corking it up with the candle; that's all I know. What is the inscription, Deputy, on all the discoloured sheets? A precaution against loss of linen. Deputy turns down the rug of an unoccupied bed and discloses it. STOP THIEF!

To lie at night, wrapped in the legend of my slinking life; to take the cry that pursues me, waking, to my breast in sleep; to have it staring at me, and clamouring for me, as soon as consciousness returns; to have it for my first-foot on New-Year's day, my Valentine, my Birthday salute, my Christmas greeting, my parting with the old year. STOP THIEF!

And to know that I MUST be stopped, come what will. To know that I am no match for this individual energy and keenness, or this organised and steady system! Come across the street, here, and, entering by a little shop and yard, examine these intricate passages and doors, contrived for escape, flapping and counter-flapping, like the lids of the conjurer's boxes. But what avail they? Who gets in by a nod, and shows their secret working to us? Inspector Field.

Don't forget the old Farm House, Parker! Parker is not the man to forget it. We are going there, now. It is the old Manor-House of these parts, and stood in the country once. Then, perhaps, there was something, which was not the beastly street, to see from the shattered low fronts of the overhanging wooden houses we are passing under — shut up now, pasted over with bills about the literature and drama of the Mint, and mouldering away. This long paved yard was a paddock or a garden once, or a court in front of the Farm House. Perchance, with a dovecot in the centre, and fowls pecking about — with fair elm trees, then, where discoloured chimney-stacks and gables are now — noisy, then, with rooks which have yielded to a different sort of rookery. It's likelier than not, Inspector Field thinks, as we turn into the common kitchen, which is in the yard, and many paces from the house.

Well, my lads and lasses, how are you all? Where's Blackey, who has stood near London Bridge these five-and-twenty years, with a painted skin to represent disease? — Here he is, Mr. Field! — How are you, Blackey? — Jolly, sa! Not playing the fiddle to-night, Blackey? — Not a night, sa! A sharp, smiling youth, the wit of the kitchen, interposes. He an't musical to-night, sir. I've been giving him a moral lecture; I've been a talking to him about his latter end, you see. A good many of these are my pupils, sir. This here young man (smoothing down the hair of one near him, reading a Sunday paper) is a pupil of mine. I'm a teaching of him to read, sir. He's a promising cove, sir. He's a smith, he is, and gets his living by the sweat of the brow, sir. So do I, myself, sir. This young woman is my sister, Mr. Field. SHE'S getting on very well too. I've a deal of trouble with 'em, sir, but I'm richly rewarded, now I see 'em all a doing so well, and growing up so creditable. That's a great comfort, that is, an't it, sir? — In the midst of the kitchen (the whole kitchen is in ecstasies with this impromptu "chaff") sits a young, modest, gentle-looking creature, with a beautiful child in her lap. She seems to belong to the company, but is so strangely unlike it. She has such a pretty, quiet face and voice, and is so proud to hear the child admired — thinks you would hardly believe that he is only nine months old! Is she as bad as the rest, I wonder? Inspectorial experience does not engender a belief contrariwise, but prompts the answer, Not a ha'porth[12] of difference!

There is a piano going in the old Farm House as we approach. It stops. Landlady appears. Has no objections, Mr. Field, to gentlemen being brought, but wishes it were at earlier hours, the lodgers complaining of ill-convenience. Inspector Field is polite and soothing — knows his woman and the sex. Deputy (a girl in this case) shows the way up a heavy, broad old staircase, kept very clean, into clean rooms where many sleepers are, and where painted panels of an older time look strangely on the truckle beds. The sight of whitewash and the smell of soap — two things we seem by this time to have parted from in infancy — make the old Farm House a phenomenon, and connect themselves with the so curiously misplaced picture of the pretty mother and child long after we have left it, — long after we have left, besides, the neighbouring nook with something of a rustic flavour in it yet, where once, beneath a low wooden colonnade still standing as of yore, the eminent Jack Sheppard[13] condescended to regale himself, and where, now, two

---

[12] Half-penny's worth, a small amount indeed. The word is also slang in the north of England for a silly or stupid person, such as a "daft ha'porth."

[13] A notorious thief and multiple prison escapee (1702-1724) whose

old bachelor brothers in broad hats (who are whispered in the Mint to have made a compact long ago that if either should ever marry, he must forfeit his share of the joint property) still keep a sequestered tavern, and sit o' nights smoking pipes in the bar, among ancient bottles and glasses, as our eyes behold them.

How goes the night now? Saint George of Southwark answers with twelve blows upon his bell. Parker, good night, for Williams is already waiting over in the region of Ratcliffe Highway, to show the houses where the sailors dance.

I should like to know where Inspector Field was born. In Ratcliffe Highway, I would have answered with confidence, but for his being equally at home wherever we go. HE does not trouble his head as I do, about the river at night. HE does not care for its creeping, black and silent, on our right there, rushing through sluice-gates, lapping at piles and posts and iron rings, hiding strange things in its mud, running away with suicides and accidentally drowned bodies faster than midnight funeral should, and acquiring such various experience between its cradle and its grave. It has no mystery for HIM. Is there not the Thames Police!

Accordingly, Williams leads the way. We are a little late, for some of the houses are already closing. No matter. You show us plenty. All the landlords know Inspector Field. All pass him, freely and good-humouredly, wheresoever he wants to go. So thoroughly are all these houses open to him and our local guide, that, granting that sailors must be entertained in their own way — as I suppose they must, and have a right to be — I hardly know how such places could be better regulated. Not that I call the company very select, or the dancing very graceful — even so graceful as that of the German Sugar Bakers, whose assembly, by the Minories, we stopped to visit — but there is watchful maintenance of order in every house, and swift expulsion where need is. Even in the midst of drunkenness, both of the lethargic kind and the lively, there is sharp landlord supervision, and

---

exploits made him popular with the poor. He wrote an autobiography, thought to have been ghosted by Daniel Defoe, and inspired John Gay to create Macheath for *The Beggar's Opera* (1728). His popularity was revived with the novel *Jack Sheppard* (1840) by William Harrison Ainsworth (1805-1882), which itself formed the basis of a popular musical.

pockets are in less peril than out of doors. These houses show, singularly, how much of the picturesque and romantic there truly is in the sailor, requiring to be especially addressed. All the songs (sung in a hailstorm of halfpence, which are pitched at the singer without the least tenderness for the time or tune — mostly from great rolls of copper carried for the purpose — and which he occasionally dodges like shot as they fly near his head) are of the sentimental sea sort. All the rooms are decorated with nautical subjects. Wrecks, engagements, ships on fire, ships passing lighthouses on iron-bound coasts, ships blowing up, ships going down, ships running ashore, men lying out upon the main-yard in a gale of wind, sailors and ships in every variety of peril, constitute the illustrations of fact. Nothing can be done in the fanciful way, without a thumping boy upon a scaly dolphin.

How goes the night now? Past one. Black and Green are waiting in Whitechapel to unveil the mysteries of Wentworth Street. Williams, the best of friends must part. Adieu!

Are not Black and Green ready at the appointed place? O yes! They glide out of shadow as we stop. Imperturbable Black opens the cab-door; Imperturbable Green takes a mental note of the driver. Both Green and Black then open each his flaming eye, and marshal us the way that we are going.

The lodging-house we want is hidden in a maze of streets and courts. It is fast shut. We knock at the door, and stand hushed looking up for a light at one or other of the begrimed old lattice windows in its ugly front, when another constable comes up — supposes that we want "to see the school." Detective Sergeant meanwhile has got over a rail, opened a gate, dropped down an area, overcome some other little obstacles, and tapped at a window. Now returns. The landlord will send a deputy immediately.

Deputy is heard to stumble out of bed. Deputy lights a candle, draws back a bolt or two, and appears at the door. Deputy is a shivering shirt and trousers by no means clean, a yawning face, a shock head much confused externally and internally. We want to look for some one. You may go up with the light, and take 'em all, if you like, says Deputy, resigning it, and sitting down upon a bench in the kitchen with his ten fingers sleepily twisting in his hair.

Halloa here! Now then! Show yourselves. That'll do. It's not you. Don't disturb yourself any more! So on, through a labyrinth of airless rooms, each man responding, like a wild beast, to the keeper who has tamed him, and who goes into his cage. What, you haven't found him, then? says Deputy, when we came down. A woman mysteriously sitting up all night in the dark by the smouldering ashes of the kitchen fire, says it's only tramps and cadgers here; it's gonophs over the way. A man mysteriously walking about the kitchen all night in the dark, bids her hold her tongue. We come out. Deputy fastens the door and goes to bed again.

Black and Green, you know Bark, lodging-house keeper and receiver of stolen goods? — O yes, Inspector Field. — Go to Bark's next.

Bark sleeps in an inner wooden hutch, near his street door. As we parley on the step with Bark's Deputy, Bark growls in his bed. We enter, and Bark flies out of bed. Bark is a red villain and a wrathful, with a sanguine throat that looks very much as if it were expressly made for hanging, as he stretches it out, in pale defiance, over the half-door of his hutch. Bark's parts of speech are of an awful sort — principally adjectives. I won't, says Bark, have no adjective police and adjective strangers in my adjective premises! I won't, by adjective and substantive! Give me my trousers, and I'll send the whole adjective police to adjective and substantive! Give me, says Bark, my adjective trousers! I'll put an adjective knife in the whole bileing of 'em. I'll punch their adjective heads. I'll rip up their adjective substantives. Give me my adjective trousers! says Bark, and I'll spile the bileing of 'em!

Now, Bark, what's the use of this? Here's Black and Green, Detective Sergeant, and Inspector Field. You know we will come in. — I know you won't! says Bark. Somebody give me my adjective trousers! Bark's trousers seem difficult to find. He calls for them as Hercules might for his club. Give me my adjective trousers! says Bark, and I'll spile the bileing of 'em!

Inspector Field holds that it's all one whether Bark likes the visit or don't like it. He, Inspector Field, is an Inspector of the Detective Police, Detective Sergeant IS Detective Sergeant, Black and Green are constables in uniform. Don't you be a fool, Bark, or you know it will be the worse for you. — I don't care, says Bark. Give me my adjective trousers!

At two o'clock in the morning, we descend into Bark's low kitchen, leaving Bark to foam at the mouth above, and Imperturbable Black and Green to look at him. Bark's kitchen is crammed full of thieves, holding a CONVERSAZIONE there by lamp-light. It is by far the most dangerous assembly we have seen yet. Stimulated by the ravings of Bark, above, their looks are sullen, but not a man speaks. We ascend again. Bark has got his trousers, and is in a state of madness in the passage with his back against a door that shuts off the upper staircase. We observe, in other respects, a ferocious individuality in Bark. Instead of "STOP THIEF!" on his linen, he prints "STOLEN FROM Bark's!"

Now, Bark, we are going up-stairs! — No, you ain't! — YOU refuse admission to the Police, do you, Bark? — Yes, I do! I refuse it to all the adjective police, and to all the adjective substantives. If the adjective coves in the kitchen was men, they'd come up now, and do for you! Shut me that there door! says Bark, and suddenly we are enclosed in the passage. They'd come up and do for you! cries Bark, and waits. Not a sound in the kitchen! They'd come up and do for you! cries Bark again, and waits. Not a sound in the kitchen! We are shut up, half-a-dozen of us, in Bark's house in the innermost recesses of the worst part of London, in the dead of the night — the house is crammed with notorious robbers and ruffians — and not a man stirs. No, Bark. They know the weight of the law, and they know Inspector Field and Co. too well.

We leave bully Bark to subside at leisure out of his passion and his trousers, and, I dare say, to be inconveniently reminded of this little brush before long. Black and Green do ordinary duty here, and look serious.

As to White, who waits on Holborn Hill to show the courts that are eaten out of Rotten Gray's Inn, Lane, where other lodging-houses are, and where (in one blind alley) the Thieves' Kitchen and Seminary for the teaching of the art to children is, the night has so worn away, being now almost at odds with morning, which is which, that they are quiet, and no light shines through the chinks in the shutters. As undistinctive Death will come here, one day, sleep comes now. The wicked cease from troubling sometimes, even in this life.

Judge Hawkins' Memoirs

Sir Henry Hawkins

Although Sir Henry Hawkins (1817-1907) never met Palmer, he did relate this second-hand story in The Reminiscences of Sir Henry Hawkins, Baron Brampton *(1904). Hawkins had a long legal career as a barrister and judge, eventually reaching the High Court of Justice (1876-1898). He presided over several notorious murder trials, including Thomas Neill Cream (1850-1892), who poisoned several prostitutes, and Albert Milsom and Henry Fowler for the Muswell Hill murder of 1896. But he earned his reputation as a "hanging judge" at the notorious 1877 trial of four members of the Staunton family in the death of Harriet Staunton. Hawkins' bias against the defendants was so pronounced that a public outcry organized by author Charles Reade (1814-1884) successfully saved them from the gallows.*

I WAS TRAVELLING ONE DAY ON circuit from London to Norwich. It was shortly after the Rugeley poisoning case; and a word or two on that matter may be necessary in order to explain the conversation which I could not help overhearing between two fellow-travellers, who were evidently bookmakers returning from the races.

William Palmer was a surgeon practising at Rugeley in Staffordshire. He was a great racing man, and owned one or two racers. A young gentleman of considerable fortune had taken to the turf, and owned horses. Palmer and he became intimate as companions — in short, they were at Shrewsbury races, where Palmer lost and Cook won. The latter had considerable sums of money to receive on bets, and Palmer, desirous of getting hold of it, poisoned the poor man with strychnine, took possession of his betting-book and papers, received all moneys due, and then had him hastily buried. Ultimately suspicion fell on Palmer; he was tried for the murder, and hanged. There was little doubt he had murdered several others for the sake of the money for which he had insured their lives, notably his wife and mother,[1] whose name

---

[1] It was actually his mother-in-law, not his mother. He did forge his mother's name to several bills.

he had forged to several bills.

One of the men in the railway-carriage I knew by sight. His name was Kirby — a rough, good-natured, honest sort of man, I believe, as anyone in a small way of book-making of that day. His companion was a stranger. Everybody at that time talked of Palmer the Rugeley poisoner, for he had just been hanged.

"Bill," said Kirby, "I knowed that there Palmer; did you?"

"No," said Bill, "don't know as ever I did."

"Well, I had dealings with him, and a nice sort of fellow he was, only nobody never could get any money from him."

After a pause he continued: "Well, he owed me a matter o' five-and-twenty pound, and I wrote, I suppose, a dozen letters to him, perhaps more; but it was no good, and so at last I sent him a stinger. I knowed what to say to him, for I had 'eeard a bit from the ostler at the public where I stopped. He told me as Palmer persuaded him to let him insure his life, which the fool did, and next time he see Palmer the doctor gave him a drink that nearly made old Sam kick the bucket there and then.

"After I sent the letter, Palmer asked me to come over one day and he'd settle with me. So over I goes, and when I gets to his house was asked into a little room, and left there by myself for a goodish while. On the table was a decanter of sherry wine and a glass. I was putty thirsty, of course, but I didn't touch the wine. Howsomever, there it was to help myself if I'd a mind to. Presently in comes the doctor with a pleasant smile, a friendly shake of the hand, and a 'Very glad to see you, Kirby! How are you getting on, Kirby? A glass o' sherry, Kirby? it will do you good after your walk.'

"I shall be glad to have one, Mr. Palmer, if you'll join me," I ses, for a thought come to me about Sam the ostler.

"No," he says, "thankee, Kirby, I never drink sherry."

"No more don't I, Mr. Palmer," I ses; and then I asked him if it was agreeable to him to pay what he owed.

"No," says he, "Kirby, it is not quite agreeable at present — but — are you sure you won't take a glass of sherry, Kirby?"

"Quite, sir," I ses, "thankee all the same; I ain't no sherry drinker, Mr. Palmer."

"What will you take?" ses he; "you must have something."

"No sir, thankee, my little account's all I wants."

"Well, if you won't take anything," ses he, "you may as well have a look round my little farm. I've got some nice little pigs to show you."

Well, when we got to the sty, there was as nice a farrer as you could see.

"I'll tell you what it is, Kirby," ses he: "you've been very good lettin' that little account of ours stand over, and I'll make you a present of one of these sucking-pigs, and my cook shall send him over all ready for roasting."

"No, thankee, sir," I ses again; "I ain't come for no pigs." I weren't going to have his damned sherry and poisoned pig.

Such was Kirby's story, and I have no doubt he was doomed to death by Palmer. Some time after, when I was a Judge and at the Stafford Assizes, I was talking with Major Talford, the governor of the gaol where Palmer was hanged, and he told me that Palmer talked freely about his case while waiting execution; that he said all through the trial he expected an acquittal, and even after the Judge's terrible summing up, hope did not desert him.

"But," he added, "when the jury returned into court, and I saw the cocked-up nose of the perky little foreman, I knew it was a gooser with me."

On the morning of the execution the path from the condemned cell to the gallows was wet and muddy, it having rained during the night, and Palmer minced along like a delicate schoolgirl, picking his way and avoiding the puddles. He was particularly anxious not to get his feet wet.

The prejudice against Palmer in Staffordshire was such that an Act of Parliament was passed to remove the trial from that county to the Central Criminal Court, an invasion of local venue never before known. I may also add that at that time there was no known test for the discovery of strychnine in the body, and Palmer was convicted entirely upon the symptoms preceding death, and especially the peculiar arching of the body after. It is now discoverable in every organ of the system.

During the trial, while the Lord Chief Justice Campbell was examining an expert doctor so as to test his evidence, which was in favour of Palmer, the prisoner wrote on a slip of paper which he handed down to his junior counsel, Johnny Gray, these words: "I should like to give just such a dose to that old devil!" meaning Campbell.

Judge Kenealy's Memoirs

Edward Kenealy

Edward Kenealy (1819-1880) was junior counsel for Palmer during his trial and wrote about it in his posthumous Memoirs of Edward Vaughan Kenealy (1908). The Irish-born Trinity College graduate rose through the ranks of English law until his defense of Tichborne claimant Arthur Orton during his perjury trial in 1873. His behavior — abusing witnesses and judges and in the process making the trial the longest in English legal history — was so extreme that the jury censured his behavior and he was disbarred. The Tichborne case became an obsession with him. He was elected to the Commons the next year, where he sought a Royal investigation of the case (he lost by a vote of 433 to 3) and wrote a nine-volume account of the affair. He lost his seat in the 1880 general election and died shortly thereafter.

IN THE SPRING OF 1856 I was engaged as one of the junior counsel for the defence of William Palmer. This remarkable criminal, who was indicted for one and suspected of having committed fourteen or fifteen cold-blooded, hideous murders, was a man whose image is still fresh in my mind, so striking and characteristic was his personality.

His face bore the impress of honesty, calm, passionless and truthful. At first I was somewhat deceived by the clear look of sincerity which characterised him, but on closer acquaintance I observed that whensoever my eyes met his he quickly dropped his lids as though he feared lest I might read there something he wished to conceal. From a habit of closely scanning the features of witnesses during cross-examination my eyes have acquired a steady, searching look, which I am told by those who have been under fire is not easy to withstand if there be need for concealment. Palmer was one of those who could not return my gaze; he invariably drooped and seemed uncomfortable.

Otherwise he displayed the greatest composure on every occasion. His manners were courteous, bland and sympathetic. Yet there was something in their very smoothness which reminded me of some creeping reptile; not repulsive, on the contrary attractive, but suggestive of the gliding, stealthy movements of a snake.

He entered the room with a gentle tread, making no sound, like a man walking over a thick carpet. Gliding forward he laid in one's grasp a soft small hand which seemed to slip from the touch so soon as taken.

His voice was low and unctuous, almost tender. One acquainted with him can picture this gentle, quiet man inviting his victim, in the most soothing, seductive tones, to drink the fatal draught. One can picture the poor wife, whom he so fondly and assiduously tended, taking her food from him, almost conscious of its nature, yet submitting to the deadly meal which was offered in so seductive, so caressing a fashion.

He would allow no other but his own hand to administer her food, his solicitude appeared to be so great. She grew weaker and more feeble. As her strength declined his attentions were redoubled, and she passed from the world, her dying moments soothed by the hand from which she had been daily drinking the draught of death.

Four out of the five children who were born to him died very shortly after their birth from unaccountable fits of sickness which speedily exhausted them.

Palmer turned to profitable account the lessons he had received on toxicology at his medical college (he was a doctor), and seems to have been wonderfully successful in his fatal dosing. Although so many members of his family died under suspicious circumstances, no suspicion seems to have been aroused until the number of his victims was considerable, or perhaps until "grown bold by custom" he took less pains to conceal his guilt.

His wife seems to have had an intuition that some ill fate attended her offspring, and when the like sickness carried off one after another, she resigned herself to the fact that their death would be speedy, even before their birth had taken place.

William Palmer cultivated his deadly instincts and the science of accomplishing them, until he acquired a perfect insensibility to human suffering, and was able, under pretence of relieving, to further administer the drug which gave rise to his victim's insufferable tortures.

There is something peculiarly horrible in the evidence given concerning the death-bed scene of Cook.

This miserable wretch was dosed with strychnia until his

whole frame was cramped and writhing under its terrible influence. Every muscle of his body was convulsed, the contraction of his limbs being such that he assumed the shape of a bow, resting on head and heels. His intellect retained its full vigour so that he was acutely sensitive to the agony which racked him.

Cook had been his most intimate friend and companion, yet Palmer could witness and aggravate these tortures. His wife was a woman of kind and affectionate nature, who had always been gentle and submissive. There had been no disagreement between them. He treated her all through with apparently the tenderest consideration, apart from the fact that he poisoned her mother, her four little babies, and last of all her unsuspecting self.

He was present at her death and gave her poison within an hour of its occurrence. He killed her in a manner more merciful than that which he chose for his friend. He did not subject her to the horrible convulsant action of strychnia. But it was probably chance, or a fear that suspicion might be aroused if all his victims died with similar symptoms, which made Palmer select the various drugs employed. Had he been content with the poison by which his brother was removed it is probable no jury could have found him guilty, as after the time which elapsed before the bodies were subjected to examination no trace of it could have been found.

As it was, there was difficulty in proving that Cook had met his death other than by disease, to which the tetanic symptoms were attributed. The body of Mrs. Palmer was completely saturated with antimony; there could have been no doubt after the analytical investigation as to the manner of her death.

I was present at post-mortem examinations of the three of his victims whose remains were tested for poison. There was great public interest excited in the case and I was anxious to gain as much information as possible by personal investigation.

Mrs. Palmer when exhumed was in a fair state of preservation, although the corpse had been buried for more than a year. This was owing to the antiseptic properties of the drug which was found in all the tissues of her body. She was very pale and attenuated, but decay had made but little progress.

Palmer was indicted for the murder of his friend Cook as this was more difficult to prove. Had they failed to convict him of this there would not have been the least trouble in hanging him for the murder of his wife.

Cockburn,[1] who was then Attorney-General and prosecuted for the Crown, got the credit for this arrangement which gave the prisoner no loop-hole of escape. I have no doubt that it was his suggestion.

Another proceeding damning to Palmer's chances was that of bringing the case to London for trial. Had it been tried by a local jury they would never have convicted. But by removing it to London so much and such universal interest was excited that every investigation had to be made, and the detailed circumstances published in full, laying bare the prisoner's life and character to the scant mercy of public opinion.

In his own neighbourhood Palmer was such a general favourite and had so many personal friends and acquaintance that no verdict of "Guilty" could have been obtained. The Trial would have attracted little notice and all would have passed off quietly.

I have now not the least doubt but that Palmer committed not only the murder for which he was tried, but probably the dozen others of which he was suspected, yet he was hanged on evidence very conflicting, especially in regard to medical witnesses on whose reports the chief strength of the prosecution rested.

That he had a "fair, impartial Trial" cannot be maintained.

Lord Campbell had prejudged him and was determined to convict. On the first day of the proceedings he showed an unfairness which gradually increased, until his conduct can be

---

[1] Sir Alexander Cockburn (1802-1880) directed the prosecution of Palmer and eventually rose to become Lord Chief Justice, a post he held for 21 years. He had a reputation as a womanizer — the lifelong bachelor left behind a daughter and a son — and publicity-seeker. As a judge, he made sure he was chosen for many high-profile trials, such as the Tichborne Case, the Henry Wainwright murder case (he killed his mistress and was caught after attempting to move her dismembered body through London), and the Fenians' 1867 Clerkenwell Prison bombing that killed 12.

justly described by no other word than infamous. Not so much in language as by look, tone and gesture, highly significant and dramatic, did his Lordship convey to the Jury his assurance of the prisoner's guilt.

During Shee's speech for the defence everything in Palmer's favour was met by frowns and by dagger looks from Campbell, while he made a point of writing down fully everything against, noting scarcely anything to the prisoner's advantage.

His proposition of a pleasant country excursion for the Jury can hardly be looked upon other than unduly to influence these gentlemen, who are easily flattered into coinciding with a Judge when he shows so plainly what verdict he desires.

Cockburn remarked shortly after the commencement of the Trial that he could "see Palmer's death in Jack Campbell's face." This was the impression conveyed by the Chief's features to everybody present during his summing-up, and indeed from the very first day he assumed an expression of intense hatred toward the guilty wretch.

On the last day of the Trial Palmer passed the following notes to me: "Did not Campbell sum up sufficiently plain for the jury to say that I am guilty? All I can say if they do, they are great liars. Wm. P." and "If I had a book I would send it at Campbell's head, for I think he behaves ill."

Of Mr. Justice Cresswell I cannot speak too highly, both with respect to the consideration and fairness he showed to all and of the quiet dignity of his demeanour. On several important occasions illegal evidence would have been admitted, had it not been for his firm and just interference. His conduct throughout was most impartial, fair and honourable.

Amidst the injustice and bad feeling shown by his confreres on the Bench he may truly be said to have set an estimable example of that judicial purity and justice which we are taught to believe exists in the heart of all ministers of the law.

Jorrick Goes to the Races

Robert Smith Surtees

Early in the editing of this book, I had decided to write an essay about horse racing in Palmer's time. Then I came across Jorrick's Jaunts and Jollities *by Robert Smith Surtees and realized I didn't have to. It conveyed better than anything I could write the feel of attending a popular source of amusement in the Victorian era.*

Surtees (1805-1864) was an editor, novelist and sporting writer. There were plenty of better writers at that time, but he captured his era in a rough and memorable fashion, and his books are still being rediscovered and enjoyed today. Jorrick *became a touchstone in British literature, popping up in the most unusual places: Rudyard Kipling's* Stalky & Co. *(1899); Siegfried Sassoon's autobiographical novel* Memoirs of a Fox-Hunting Man *(1928); Virginia Woolf's* Mrs. Dalloway *(1925); and Evelyn Waugh's* Brideshead Revisited *(1945). The R.S. Surtees Society, founded in 1979, continues to celebrate the man and his works today.*

In this excerpt, Jorrick is in Newmarket. He had befriended a Frenchman called "the Baron," and met a Yorkshireman who convinced him to attend a local race meet. The text has not been edited, except for breaking up long paragraphs into a more readable format.

BUT RACE HOUR APPROACHES, AND people begin to assemble in groups before the "rooms," while tax-carts, pony-gigs, post-chaises, the usual aristocratical accompaniments of Newmarket, come dribbling at intervals into the town. Here is old Sam Spring in a spring-cart, driven by a ploughboy in fustian, there the Earl of—— on a ten-pound pony, with the girths elegantly parted to prevent the saddle slipping over its head, while Miss——, his jockey's daughter, dashes by him in a phaeton with a powdered footman, and the postilion in scarlet and leathers, with a badge on his arm. Old Crockey puts on his greatcoat, Jem Bland draws the yellow phaeton and greys to the gateway of the "White Hart," to take up his friend Crutch Robinson; Zac, Jack and another, have just driven on in a fly. In short, it's a brilliant meeting!

Besides four coronetted carriages with post-horses, there are three phaetons-and-pair; a thing that would have been a phaeton if they'd have let it; General Grosvenor's dog-carriage, that is to say, his carriage with a dog upon it; Lady Chesterfield and the

Hon. Mrs. Anson in a pony phaeton with an out-rider (Miss——
will have one next meeting instead of the powdered footman);
Tattersall in his double carriage driving without bearing-reins;
Old Theobald in leather breeches and a buggy; five Bury butchers
in a tax-cart; Young Dutch Sam on a pony; "Short-odds Richards"
on a long-backed crocodile-looking rosinante; and no end of
pedestrians.

But where is Mr. Jorrocks all this time? Why eating brawn in
the "Rutland Arms" with his friend the Baron, perfectly
unconscious that all these passers-by were not the daily visables
of the place.

"Dash my vig," said he, as he bolted another half of the
round, "I see no symptoms of a stir. Come, my lord, do me the
honour to take another glass of sherry." His lordship was nothing
loath, so by mutual entreaties they finished the bottle, besides a
considerable quantity of porter.

A fine, fat, chestnut, long-tailed Suffolk punch cart mare—
fresh from the plough—having been considerately provided by the
Yorkshireman for Mr. Jorrocks, with a cob for himself, they
proceeded to mount in the yard, when Mr. Jorrocks was
concerned to find that the Baron had nothing to carry him. His
lordship, too, seemed disconcerted, but it was only momentary; for
walking up to the punch mare, and resting his elbow on her hind
quarter to try if she kicked, he very coolly vaulted up behind Mr.
Jorrocks.

Now Jorrocks, though proud of the patronage of a lord, did
not exactly comprehend whether he was in earnest or not, but the
Baron soon let him know; for thrusting his conical hat on his
brow, he put his arm round Jorrocks's waist, and gave the old
mare a touch in the flank with the Chinese boot, crying out —
"Along me, brave garcon, along ma cher," and the owner of the
mare living at Kentford, she went off at a brisk trot in that
direction, while the Yorkshireman slipped down the town
unperceived.

The sherry had done its business on them both; the Baron,
and who, perhaps was the most "cut" of the two, chanted the
Marsellaise hymn of liberty with as much freedom as though he
were sitting in the saddle. Thus they proceeded laughing and
singing until the Bury pay-gate arrested their progress, when it
occurred to the steersman to ask if they were going right.

"Be this the vay to Newmarket races?" inquired Jorrocks of the pike-keeper.

The man dived into the small pocket of his white apron for a ticket and very coolly replied, "Shell out, old 'un."

"How much?" said Jorrocks.

"Tuppence," which having got, he said, "Now, then, you may turn, for the heath be over yonder," pointing back, "at least it was there this morning, I know."

After a volley of abuse for his impudence, Mr. Jorrocks, with some difficulty got the old mare pulled round, for she had a deuced hard mouth of her own, and only a plain snaffle in it; at last, however, with the aid of a boy to beat her with a furze-bush, they got her set a-going again, and, retracing their steps, they trotted "down street," rose the hill, and entered the spacious wide-extending flat of Newmarket Heath.

The races were going forward on one of the distant courses, and a slight, insignificant, black streak, swelling into a sort of oblong (for all the world like an overgrown tadpole), was all that denoted the spot, or interrupted the verdant aspect of the quiet extensive plain. Jorrocks was horrified, having through life pictured Epsom as a mere drop in the ocean compared with the countless multitude of Newmarket, while the Baron, who was wholly indifferent to the matter, nearly had old Jorrocks pitched over the mare's head by applying the furze-bush (which he had got from the boy) to her tail while Mr. Jorrocks was sitting loosely, contemplating the barrenness of the prospect.

The sherry was still alive, and being all for fun, he shuffled back into the saddle as soon as the old mare gave over kicking; and giving a loud tally-ho, with some minor "hunting noises," which were responded to by the Baron in notes not capable of being set to music, and aided by an equally indescribable accompaniment from the old mare at every application of the bush, she went off at score over the springy turf, and bore them triumphantly to the betting-post just as the ring was in course of formation, a fact which she announced by a loud neigh on viewing her companion of the plough, as well as by upsetting some half-dozen black-legs[1] as she rushed through the crowd to greet her.

---

[1] Nickname for a dandy, professional gambler, or racecourse swindler, identified by his shiny black boots.

Great was the hubbub, shouting, swearing, and laughing,— for though the Newmarketites are familiar with most conveyances, from a pair of horses down to a pair of shoes, it had not then fallen to their lot to see two men ride into the ring on the same horse,— certainly not with such a hat between them as the Baron's.

The gravest and weightiest matters will not long distract the attention of a black-leg, and the laughter having subsided without Jorrocks or the Baron being in the slightest degree disconcerted, the ring was again formed; horses' heads again turn towards the post, while carriages, gigs, and carts form an outer circle.

A solemn silence ensues. The legs are scanning the list. At length one gives tongue.

"What starts? Does Lord Eldon start?"

"No, he don't," replies the owner.

"Does Trick, by Catton?"

"Yes, and Conolly rides — but mind, three pounds over."

"Does John Bull?"

"No John's struck out."

"Polly Hopkins does, so does Talleyrand, also O, Fy! out of Penitence; Beagle and Paradox also—and perhaps Pickpocket."

Another pause, and the pencils are pulled from the betting-books. The legs and lords look at each other, but no one likes to lead off.

At length a voice is heard offering to take nine to one he names the winner.

"It's short odds, doing it cautiously. I'll take eight then," he adds — "sivin!" but no one bites.

"What will anyone lay about Trick, by Catton?" inquires Jem Bland.

"I'll lay three to two again him. I'll take two to one — two ponies to one, and give you a suv. for laying it."

"Carn't" is the answer.

"I'll do it, Jem," cries a voice.

"No, you won't," from Bland, not liking his customer.

Now they are all at it, and what a hubbub there is!

"I'll back the field — I'll lay — I'll take — I'll bet — ponies — fifties — hundreds — five hundred to two."

"What do you want, my lord?"

"Three to one against Trick, by Catton."

"Carn't afford it — the odds really arn't that in the ring."

"Take two — two hundred to one."

"No."

"Crockford, you'll do it for me?"

"Yes, my lord. Twice over if you like. Done, done."

"Do it again?"

"No, thank you."

"Trick, by Catton, don't start!" cries a voice.

"Impossible!" exclaim his backers.

"Quite true, I'm just from the weighing-house, and —— told me so himself."

"Shame! shame!" roar those who have backed him, and "honour — rascals — rogues — thieves — robbery — swindle — turf-ruined" — fly from tongue to tongue, but they are all speakers with never a speaker to cry order.

Meanwhile the lads have galloped by on their hacks with the horses' cloths to the rubbing-house, and the horses have actually started, and are now visible in the distance sweeping over the open heath, apparently without guide or beacon.

The majority of the ring rush to the white judge's box, and have just time to range themselves along the rude stakes and ropes that guard the run in, and the course-keeper in a shooting-jacket on a rough pony to crack his whip, and cry to half a dozen stable-lads to "clear the course," before the horses come flying towards home.

Now all is tremor; hope and fear vacillating in each breast. Silence stands breathless with expectation — all eyes are riveted — the horses come within descrying distance — "beautiful!" three close together, two behind.

"Clear the course! clear the course! pray clear the course!"

"Polly Hopkins! Polly Hopkins!" roar a hundred voices as they near. "O, Fy! O, Fy!" respond an equal number. "The horse! the horse!" bellow a hundred more, as though their yells would aid his speed, as Polly Hopkins, O, Fy! and Talleyrand rush neck-and-neck along the cords and pass the judge's box.

A cry of "dead heat!" is heard. The bystanders see as suits their books, and immediately rush to the judge's box, betting, bellowing, roaring, and yelling the whole way. "What's won? what's won? what's won?" is vociferated from a hundred voices. "Polly Hopkins! Polly Hopkins! Polly Hopkins!" replies Mr. Clark with judicial dignity. "By how much? by how much?" "Half a head — half a head," [2] replies the same functionary.

"What's second?" "O, Fy!" and so, amid the song of "Pretty, pretty Polly Hopkins," from the winners, and curses and execrations long, loud, and deep, from the losers, the scene closes.

The admiring winners follow Polly to the rubbing-house, while the losing horses are left in the care of their trainers and stable-boys, who console themselves with hopes of "better luck next time."

After a storm comes a calm, and the next proceeding is the wheeling of the judge's box, and removal of the old stakes and ropes to another course on a different part of the heath, which is accomplished by a few ragged rascals, as rude and uncouth as the furniture they bear. In less than half an hour the same group of anxious careworn countenances are again turned upon each other at the betting-post, as though they had never separated.

But see! the noble owner of Trick, by Catton, is in the crowd, and Jem Bland eyeing him like a hawk.

"I say, Waggey," cries he (singling out a friend stationed by his lordship), "had you ought on Trick, by Catton?"

"No, Jem," roars Wagstaff, shaking his head, "I knew my man too well."

"Why now, Waggey, do you know I wouldn't have done such a thing for the world! no, not even to have been made a Markiss!" a horse-laugh follows this denunciation, at which the newly created marquis bites his livid lips.

The Baron, who appears to have no taste for walking, still sticks to the punch mare, which Mr. Jorrocks steers to the newly formed ring aided by the Baron and the furze-bush. Here they come upon Sam Spring, whose boy has just brought his spring-cart to bear upon the ring formed by the horsemen, and thinking it a pity a nobleman of any county should be reduced to the necessity of riding double, very politely offers to take one into his carriage.

Jorrocks accepts the offer, and forthwith proceeds to make himself quite at home in it. The chorus again commences, and Jorrocks interrogates Sam as to the names of the brawlers.

---

[2] [Original footnote] No judge ever gave a race as won by half a head; but we let the whole passage stand as originally written.—*Ed.*

"Who be that?" said he, "offering to bet a thousand to a hundred."

Spring, after eyeing him through his spectacles, with a grin and a look of suspicion replies, "Come now — come — let's have no nonsense — you know as well as I."

"Really," replies Mr. Jorrocks most earnestly, "I don't."

"Why, where have you lived all your life?"

"First part of it with my grandmother at Lisson Grove, afterwards at Camberwell, but now I resides in Great Coram Street, Russell Square — a werry fashionable neighbourhood."

"Oh, I see," replies Sam, "you are one of the reg'lar city coves, then — now, what brings you here?"

"Just to say that I have been at Newmarket, for I'm blowed if ever you catch me here again."

"That's a pity," replied Sam, "for you look like a promising man—a handsome-bodied chap in the face—don't you sport any?"

"O a vast! — 'unt regularly — I'm a member of the Surrey 'unt — capital one it is too — best in England by far."

"What do you hunt?" inquired Sam.

"Foxes, to be sure."

"And are they good eating?"

"Come," replied Jorrocks, "you know, as well as I do, we don't eat 'em."

The dialogue was interrupted by someone calling to Sam to know what he was backing.

"The Bedlamite colt, my lord," with a forefinger to his hat.

"Who's that?" inquired Jorrocks.

"That's my Lord L——, a baron-lord — and a very nice one — best baron-lord I know — always bets with me — that's another baron-lord next him, and the man next him is a baron-knight, a stage below a baron-lord — something between a nobleman and a gentleman."

"And who be that stout, good-looking man in a blue coat and velvet collar next him, just rubbing his chin with the race card — he'll be a lord too, I suppose?"

"No, — that's Mr. Gully, as honest a man as ever came here, — that's Crockford before him. The man on the right is Mr. C——, who they call the 'cracksman,' because formerly he was a professional housebreaker, but he has given up that trade, and turned gentleman, bets, and keeps a gaming-table.

This little ugly black-faced chap, that looks for all the world like a bilious Scotch terrier, has lately come among us. He was a tramping pedlar — sold worsted stockings — attended country courses, and occasionally bet a pair. Now he bets thousands of pounds, and keeps racehorses. The chaps about him all covered with chains and rings and brooches, were in the duffing line — sold brimstoned sparrows for canary-birds, Norwich shawls for real Cashmere, and dried cabbage-leaves for cigars. Now each has a first-rate house, horses and carriages, and a play-actress among them.

"Yon chap, with the extravagantly big mouth, is a cabinet-maker at Cambridge. He'll bet you a thousand pounds as soon as look at you. The chap on the right of the post with the red tie, is the son of an ostler. He commenced betting thousands with a farthing capital. The man next him, all teeth and hair, like a rat-catcher's dog, is an Honourable by birth, but not very honourable in his nature."

"But see," cried Mr. Jorrocks, "Lord—— is talking to the Cracksman."

"To be sure," replies Sam, "that's the beauty of the turf. The lord and the leg are reduced to an equality. Take my word for it, if you have a turn for good society, you should come upon the turf. — I say, my Lord Duke!" with all five fingers up to his hat, "I'll lay you three to two on the Bedlamite colt."

"Done, Mr. Spring," replies his Grace, "three ponies to two."

"There!" cried Mr. Spring, turning to Jorrocks, "didn't I tell you so?"

The riot around the post increases. It is near the moment of starting, and the legs again become clamorous for what they want. Their vehemence increases. Each man is in extremis.

"They are off!" cries one. "No, they are not," replies another. "False start," roars a third. "Now they come!" "No, they don't!" "Back again."

They are off at last, however, and away they speed over the flat. The horses come within descrying distance. It's a beautiful race — run at score the whole way, and only two tailed off within the cords. Now they set to — whips and spurs go, legs leap, lords shout, and amid the same scene of confusion, betting, galloping, cursing, swearing, and bellowing, the horses rush past the judge's box.

The Physiology
of the London Medical Student

Albert Richard Smith

In 1841, during Punch *magazine's first year, it ran a lively 12-part series detailing the education of a medical student in London, from his first day in class to the celebration after passing his examinations. Although exaggerated for comic effect, the excerpts below would have seemed familiar to Palmer. Its author, Albert Richard Smith (1816-1860) was a former medical student who abandoned his calling for writing. He was an early contributor to* Punch *and to* Bentley's Miscellany *and was one of the most popular humorists of his time. His writings and lectures after ascending Switzerland's Mont Blanc helped popularize mountaineering in Britain (he also co-founded the Alpine Club, mentioned in Chapter V). He visited Constantinople, the Near East, and Hong Kong, and published books about his travels. He died at age 43 of bronchitis.*

The New Man.

NO SOONER DO THE GEESE become asphyxiated by torsion of their cervical vertebrae, in anticipation of Michaelmas-day; no sooner do the pheasants feel premonitory warnings, that some chemical combinations between charcoal, nitre, and sulphur, are about to take place, ending in a precipitation of lead; no sooner do the columns of the newspapers teem with advertisements of the ensuing courses at the various schools, each one cheaper, and offering more advantages than any of the others; the large hospitals vaunting their extended field of practice, and the small ones ensuring a more minute and careful investigation of disease, than the new man purchases a large trunk and a hat-box, buys a second-hand copy of Quain's Anatomy, abjures the dispensing of his master's surgery in the country, and placing himself in one of those rattling boxes denominated by courtesy second-class carriages, enters on the career of a hospital pupil in his first season.

The opening lecture introduces the new man to his companions, and he is easily distinguished at that annual gathering of pupils, practitioners, professors, and especially old hospital governors, who do a good deal in the gaiter-line, and applaud the lecturer with their umbrellas, as they sit in the front row.

The new man is known by his clothes, which incline to the prevalent fashion of the rural districts he has quitted; and he evinces an affection for cloth-boots, or short Wellingtons with double soles, and toes shaped like a toad's mouth, a propensity which sometimes continues throughout the career of his pupilage. He likewise takes off his hat when he enters the dissecting-room, and thinks that beautiful design is shown in the mechanism and structure of the human body — an idea which gets knocked out of him at the end of the season, when he looks upon the distribution of the nerves as "a blessed bore to get up, and no use to him after he has passed."

But at first he perpetually carries a *Dublin Dissector*[1] under his arm; and whether he is engaged upon a subject or no, delights to keep on his black apron, pockets, and sleeves (like a barber dipped in a blacking-bottle), the making of which his sisters have probably superintended in the country, and which he thinks endows him with an air of industry and importance.

The new man, at first, is not a great advocate for beer; but this dislike may possibly arise from his having been compelled to stand two pots upon the occasion of his first dissection. After a time, however, he gives way to the indulgence, having received the solemn assurances of his companions that it is absolutely necessary to preserve his health, and keep him from

---

[1] An anatomy textbook first published in 1831. It concisely explained what the medical student will find as he dissects a body, much in the same way a tourist guidebook describes a city. It also provided instructions for opening the thorax, abdomen, and the head, using the cold, precise language found in a Chilton auto-repair manual:

"Let the student (having provided himself with a heavy hammer, strong in the claws) take hold of the head in his left hand, and with the right commence striking steadily, beginning about half an inch above the superciliary ridge, and continuing it round on a line with the incisions in the temporal muscle, terminating a little above the occipital ridge."

After that, the anonymous physician who wrote the book reassures us that "no danger is to be apprehended of wounding the brain in this proceeding." For the sake of your digestion, I won't mention why you needed a hammer "strong in the claws."

getting the collywobbles in his pandenoodles — a description of which obstinate disease he is told may be found in *Dr. Copland's Medical Dictionary*,[2] and *Gregory's Practice of Physic*,[3] but as to under what head the informant is uncertain.

The first purchase that a new man makes in London is a gigantic note-book, a dozen steel pens on a card, and a screw inkstand. Furnished with these valuable adjuncts to study, he puts down every thing he hears during the day, both in the theatre of the school and the wards of the hospital, besides many diverting diagrams and anecdotes which his fellow-students insert for him, until at night he has a confused dream that the air-pump in the laboratory is giving a party, at which various scalpels, bits of gums, wax models, tourniquets, and foetal skulls, are assisting as guests — an eccentric and philosophical vision, worthy of the brain from which it emanates.

But the new man is, from his very nature, a visionary. His breast swells with pride at the introductory lecture, when he hears the professor descant upon the noble science he and his companions have embarked upon; the rich reward of watching the gradual progress of a suffering fellow-creature to convalescence, and the insignificance of worldly gain compared with the pure treasures of pathological knowledge; whilst to the riper student all this resolves itself into the truth, that three draughts, or one mixture, are respectively worth four-and-sixpence or three shillings: that the patient should be encouraged to take them as long as possible, and that the thrilling delight of ushering another mortal into existence, after being up all night, is considerably increased by the receipt

---

[2] James Copland (1791-1870) was a Scottish physician and Fellow of the Royal Society. He wrote a number of medical books, including the three-volume *Dictionary of Practical Medicine*, which promoted circumcision and suggested that socialism caused insanity.

[3] *Elements of the Theory and Practice of Physic* (1826) by George Gregory (1790-1853) a physician who served in the Royal Navy during the Napoleonic Wars and afterwards practiced medicine and wrote books as well as articles for medical journals. The book, written for medical students, broke down diseases into categories such as acute, inflammatory, and chronic, and described their symptoms and treatment.

of the tin for superintending the performance; i.e. if you are lucky enough to get it.

It is not improbable that, after a short period, the new man will write a letter home.

"MY DEAR PARENTS,—

I am happy to inform you that my health is at present uninjured by the atmosphere of the hospital, and that I find I am making daily progress in my studies. I have taken a lodging in —— (Gower-place, University-street, Little Britain, or Lant-street, as the case may be,) for which I pay twelve shillings a week, including shoes. The mistress of the house is a pious old lady, and I am very comfortable, with the exception that two pupils live on the floor above me, who are continually giving harmonic parties to their friends, and I am sometimes compelled to request they will allow me to conclude transcribing my lecture notes in tranquillity—a request, I am sorry to say, not often complied with. The smoke from their pipes fills the whole house, and the other night they knocked me up two hours after I had retired to rest, for the loan of the jug of cold water from my washhand-stand, to make grog with.

"Independently of these annoyances, I get on pretty well, and have already attracted the notice of my professors, who return my salutation very condescendingly, and tell me to look upon them rather as friends than teachers. The students here, generally speaking, are a dissipated and irreligious set of young men; and I can assure you I am often compelled to listen to language that quite makes my ears tingle.

"I have not been to the theatres yet, nor do I feel the least wish to enter into any of the frivolities of the great metropolis. With kind regards to all at home, believe me,

"YOURS AFFECTIONATELY,
"JOSEPH MUFF."

Of His Gradual Development.

FOR THE FIRST TWO MONTHS of the first winter session the fingers of the new man are nothing but ink-stains and industry. He has duly chronicled every word that has fallen from the lips of every professor in his leviathan note book; and his desk teems with reports of all the hospital cases, from the burnt housemaid, all cotton-wool and white lead, who set herself on fire reading penny romances in bed, on one side of the hospital, to the tipsy glazier who bundled off his perch and spiked himself upon the area rails on the other. He becomes a walking chronicle of pathological statistics, and after he has passed six weeks in the wards, imagines himself an embryo hunter.

The new man does not enter much into society. He sometimes asks a few other juniors to his lodgings, and provides tea and shrimps, with occasional cold saveloys for their refection, and it is possible he may add some home-made wine to the banquet. Their conversation is exceedingly professional; and should they get slightly jocose, they retail anatomical paradoxes, technical puns, and legendary "catch questions," which from time immemorial have been the delight of all new men in general, and country ones in particular.

But diligent and industrious as the new man may be, he is mortal after all, and being mortal, is not proof against temptation. The new man firmly withstands all inducements to irregularity until his first temptation appears in the form of the Cyder-cellars — the convivial Rubicon which it is absolutely necessary for him to pass before he can enrol himself as a member of the quiet, hard-working, modest fraternity of the Medical Student of our London Hospitals.

We have arrived at an important point in our physiology — the first launch of the new man into the ocean of his London life, and we pause upon its shore. He has but definite ideas of three public establishments at all intimately connected with his professional career — the Hall, the College, and the Cyder-cellars.

The new man and his friends arrive beneath the beacon which illumines the entrance of the tavern. He descends the stairs in an agony of anticipation, and feverishly trips up the six or eight succeeding ones to arrive at the large room. A song has just concluded, and he enters triumphantly amidst the thunder of applause, the jingling of glasses, the imperious vociferations of fresh orders, and an atmosphere of smoke that pervades the whole apartment, like dense clouds of incense burning at the altar of the genius of conviviality.

The new man is at first so bewildered, but as he collects his ideas, he contrives to muster sufficient presence of mind to order a Welsh rabbit,[4] and earnestly contemplates the scene around him. There is the room which so vividly recurs to him, when he is sitting up all night at a bad case in the mud cottage of a pauper union. There are its blue walls, its wainscot and its pillars, its lamps and ground-glass shades, within which the gas jumps and flares so fitfully; its two looking-glasses, that reflect the room and its occupants from one to the other in an interminable vista. The professional gentlemen all laying their heads together at the top of the table to pitch the key of the next glee; and the waiters bustling up and down with all sorts of tempting comestibles; and the gentleman in the Chesterfield wrapper smoking a cigar at the side of the room, while he leans back and contemplates the ceiling, as if his whole soul was concentrated in its smoke-discoloured mouldings.

The new man is in ecstasies; he beholds the realization of the Arabian Nights, and when the harmony commences again, he is fairly entranced.

At first, he is fearful of adding the efforts of his laryngeal "little muscles with the long names" to swell the chorus; but, after the second glass of stout and a "go of whiskey," he becomes emboldened, and when the gentleman with the bass voice sings about the Monks of Old,[5] what a jovial race they were, our friend trolls out how "they laughed, ha, ha!" so lustily, that he gets quite red in the face from obstructed

---

[4] A snack consisting of melted cheddar cheese in a savory sauce served over toasted bread. The ingredients varied according to taste and included beer, ale, Worcestershire sauce, and cayenne pepper. Also called Welsh rarebit. Thought to be called this because at the time the word was coined in the early 18th century, most Welsh were poor, and this was as close to a rabbit as they could find.

[5] A song in six stanzas by William Jones and Stephen Glover (1813-1870). It begins:

Many have told of the monks of old,
What a saintly race they were;
But 'tis more true that a merrier crew
Could scarce be found elsewhere;
For they sung and laugh'd,
And the rich wine quaff'd,
And lived on the daintiest cheer.

jugulars.

The precise hour at which the new man arrives at home, after this eventful evening, has never been correctly ascertained; having a latch-key,[6] he is the only person that could give any authentic information upon this point; but, unfortunately, he never knows himself.

The first lecture the next morning fails to attract him; he eats no breakfast, and when he enters the dissecting-room about one o'clock, his fellow-students administer to him a pint of ale, with some Cayenne pepper thrown into it, which he is assured will set to rights the irritable mucous lining of his stomach.

The effect of this remedy is to send him into a sound sleep during the whole of the two o'clock anatomical lecture; and awakened at its close by the applause of the students, he thinks he is still at the Cyder-cellars, and cries out "Encore!"

Of the Manner in Which the First Season Passes.

FROM THE PERIOD OF OUR last Chapter our friend commences to adopt the attributes of the mature student. His notes are taken as before at each lecture he attends, but the lectures are fewer, and the notes are never fairly transcribed; at the same time they are interspersed with a larger proportion of portraits of the lecturer, and other humorous conceits. He proposes at lunch-time every day that he and his companions should "go the odd man for a pot;" and the determination he had formed at his entry to the school appears somewhat difficult of being carried into execution.

It is at this point of his studies that the student commences a steady course of imaginary dissection: that is to say, he keeps a chimerical account of extremities whose minute structure he has deeply investigated (in his head), and received in return various sums of money from home for the avowed purpose of paying for them. If he really has put his name down for any heads and necks or pelvic viscera at the commencement

---

[6] A door key consisting of a rod with a notched paddle at the end. This is a forerunner of the tumbler lock used today. Boarding houses typically locked up when the owner went to bed, so our student was fortunate to be given a latch-key.

of the season, when he had imbibed and cherished some lunatic idea "that dissection was the sheet-anchor[7] of safety at the College," he becomes a trafficker in human flesh, and disposes of them as quickly as he can to any hard-working man who has his examination in perspective.

He now assumes a more independent air, and even ventures to chalk odd figures on the black board in the theatre. He has been known, previously to the lecture, to let down the skeleton that hangs by a balance weight from the ceiling, and, inserting its thumb in the cavity of its nose, has there secured it with a piece of thread, and then, placing a short pipe in its jaws, has pulled it up again.

His inventive faculties are likewise shown by various diverting objects and allusions cut with his knife upon the ledge before him in the lecture-room, whereon the new men rest their note-books and the old ones go to sleep. His favourite position at lecture is now the extremity of the bench, where its horse-shoe form places him rather out of the range of the lecturer's vision.

His conversation also gradually changes its tone, and instead of mildly inquiring of the porter, on his entering the school of a morning, what is for the day's anatomical demonstration, he talks of "the regular lark he had last night at the Eagle, and how jolly screwed he got!" — a frank admission, which bespeaks the candour of his disposition.

Careful statistics show us that it is about the end of November the new man first makes the acquaintance of his uncle; and observant people have remarked, as worthy of insertion in the Medical Almanack amongst the usual phenomena of the calendar — "About this time dissecting cases and tooth-instruments appear in the windows, and we may look for watches towards the beginning of December."

Thus gradually approaching step by step towards the perfection of his state, the new man's first winter-session passes; and it is not unlikely that, at the close of the course, he may enter to compete for the anatomical prize, which he sometimes gets by stealth, cribbing his answers from a tiny

---

[7] A large anchor carried in the waist of the ship and used as a spare in an emergency, when it's absolutely imperative for the ship not to move (such as when a strong wind is blowing the ship to shore).

manual of knowledge, two inches by one-and-a-half in size, which he hides under his blotting-paper.

This triumph achieved, he devotes the short period which intervenes before the commencement of the summer botanical course to hilarious pastimes; and he writes the following despatch to his governor—

Letter No. II.—(Copy.)

MY DEAR FATHER,—

You will, I am sure, be delighted to learn that I have gained the twenty-ninth honorary certificate for proficiency in anatomy which you will allow is a very high number when I tell you that only thirty are given. I have also the satisfaction of informing you that the various professors have given me certificates of having attended their lectures *very diligently* during the past courses.

I work very hard, but I need not inform you that, with all my economy, I am at some expense for good books and instruments. I have purchased *Liston's Surgery*, Anthony Thompson's *Materia Medica*, Burns and Merriman's *Midwifery*, Graham's *Chemistry*, Astley Cooper's *Dislocations*, and Quain's *Anatomy*, all of which I have read carefully through twice. I also pay a private demonstrator to go over the bones with me of a night; and I have bought a skeleton at Alexander's — a great bargain. This, when I "pass," I think of presenting to the museum of the hospital, as I am under great obligations to the surgeons. I think a ten-pound note will clear my expenses, although I wish to enter to a summer course of dissections, and take some lessons in practical chemistry in the laboratories with Professor Carbon, but these I will endeavour to pay for out of my own pocket. With my best regards to all at home, believe me,

YOUR AFFECTIONATE SON,
JOSEPH MUFF.

Of His Maturity, and Latin Examination.

THE SECOND SEASON ARRIVES, AND our pupil becomes "a medical student" in the fullest sense of the word. He has an indistinct recollection that there are such things as wards in the hospital as well as in a key or the city,[8] and a vague wandering, like the morning's impression of the dreams of the preceding night, that in the remote dark ages of his career he took some notes upon the various lectures, which have long since been converted into pipe-lights or small darts, which, twisted up and propelled from between the forefingers of each hand, fly with unerring aim across the theatre at the lecturer's head, the slumbering student, or any other object worth aiming at — an amusing way of beguiling the hour's lecture, and only excelled by the sport produced, if he has the good luck to sit in a sunbeam, from making a tournament of "Jack-o'-lanthorns" on the ceiling.

His locker in the lobby of the dissecting-room has long since been devoid of apron, sleeves, scalpels, or forceps; but still it is not empty. Its contents are composed of three bellpull-handles, a valuable series of shutter-fastenings, two or three broken pipes, a pewter "go" (which, if everybody had their own, would in all probability belong to Mr. Evans, of Covent Garden Piazza), some scraps of biscuit, and a round knocker, which forcibly recalls a pleasant evening he once spent, with the accompanying anecdotes of how he "bilked the pike"[9] at Waterloo Bridge, and poor Jones got "jug'd" by mistake.

It must not, however, be supposed that the student now neglects visiting the dissecting-room. On the contrary, he is unremitting in his attendance, and sometimes the first there of a morning, more especially when he has, to use his own expression, been "going it rather fast than otherwise" the evening before, and comes to the school very early in the morning to have a good wash and refresh himself previously to snatching a little of the slumber he has forgotten to take during the night, which he enjoys very quietly in the injecting-room down stairs. The dissecting-room is also his favourite resort for

---

[8] A warded lock used obstructions (or wards) to keep the key from turning unless the correct one with the proper-sized slots is inserted. This was replaced by the tumbler locks used today. Wards are also political subdivisions in a city.

[9] Waterloo Bridge was opened in 1817 and operated as a toll bridge until the government took it over in 1878. Bilking in this context meant evading the toll-taker, for which poor Jones was caught and "jugged," e.g., thrown in jail.

refreshment, and he broils sprats and red herrings on the fire-shovel with consummate skill, amusing himself during the process of his culinary arrangements by sawing the corners off the stone mantel-piece, throwing cinders at the new man, or seeing how long it takes to bore a hole through one of the stools with a red-hot poker. Indeed, these luckless pieces of furniture are always marked out by the student as the fittest objects on which to wreak his destructive propensities; and he generally discovers that the readiest way to do them up is to hop steeple-chases upon them from one end of the room to the other—a sporting amusement which shakes them to pieces, and irremediably dislocates all their articulations, sooner than anything else.

Of course these pleasantries are only carried on in the absence of the demonstrator. Should he be present, the industry of the student is confined to poking the fire in the stove and then shutting the flue, or keeping down the ball of the cistern by some abdominal hooks, and then, before the invasion of smoke and water takes place, quietly joining a knot of new men who are strenuously endeavouring to dissect the brain and discover the *hippocampus major*, which they expect to find in the perfect similitude of a sea-horse.

The second or middle course of the three winter sessions which the medical student is compelled to go through is the one in which he most enjoys himself, and indulges in those little outbreaks of eccentric mirth which eminently qualify him for his future professional career.

The only grand project he now undertakes is "going up for his Latin," provided he had not courage to do so upon first coming to London. For some weeks before this period he is never seen without an interlined edition of Celsus and Gregory;[10] not that he debars himself from joviality during the

---

[10] *Lessons in Celsus and Gregory* (1831) by William Cross. The full title continues with typical Victorian flair for detail as *Consisting of passages from those authors syntactically arranged, with copious observations ... and a lexicon of the words. To which is added a succinct and comprehensive grammar.* Aulus Cornelius Celsus (c. 25 BCE-c.50 CE) was a Roman encyclopaedist whose works were lost except for *De Medicina*, which gives us a comprehensive look at the state of medical knowledge in the ancient world. James Gregory

time of his preparation, but he judiciously combines study with amusement — never stirring without his translation in his pocket. Every school possesses circulating copies of these works: they have been originally purchased in some wild moment of industrious extravagance by a new man; and when he passed, he sold them for five shillings to another, who, in turn, disposed of them to a third, until they had run nearly all through the school. The student grinds away at these until he knows them almost by heart, albeit his translation is not the most elegant. He reads — "*Sanus homo*, a sound man; *qui*, who; *et*, also; *bene valet*, well is in health; *et*, and; *suae spontis*, of his own choice; *est*, is," &c.[11]

This, however, is quite sufficient; and, accordingly, one afternoon, in a rash moment, he makes up his mind to "go up." Arrived at Apothecaries' Hall[12] — a building which he regards with a feeling of awe far beyond the Bow-street Police Office — he takes his place amongst the anxious throng, and is at last called into a room, where two examiners politely request that he will favour them by sitting down at a table adorned with severe-looking inkstands, long pens, formal sheets of foolscap, and awfully-sized copies of the light entertaining works mentioned above.

One of the aforesaid examiners then takes a pinch of snuff, coughs, blows his nose, points out a paragraph for the student to translate, and leaves him to do it. He has, with a prudent forethought, stuffed his cribs inside his double-breasted

---

(1753-1821) was a classicist and Scottish physician who was considered the head of his profession. He published a textbook based on his lectures called *Conspectus Medicinae Theoreticae* (1823).

[11] The joke is that the student is translating word by word instead of looking at what the sentence is trying to say and translating with that context in mind. The student translating *Sanus homo, qui et bene valet et suae spontis est...*, as

"A sound man who also well is in health and of his own choice is ...."

when a more accurate translation would be:

"A healthy man who is strong and in control of himself ..."

[12] A society, founded in 1617, that until 1999 was responsible for licensing doctors in England. It wasn't until soon after Palmer's time, however, that doctors were required to meet a set of standards to practice medicine.

waistcoat, but, unfortunately, he finds he cannot use them; so when he sticks at a queer word he writes it on his blotting-paper and shoves it quietly on to the next man. If his neighbour is a brick, he returns an answer; but if he is not, our friend is compelled to take shots of the meaning and trust to chance — a good plan when you are not certain what to do, either at billiards or Apothecaries' Hall.

Of the Grinder and His Class.

ONE FINE MORNING, IN THE October of the third winter session, the student is suddenly struck by the recollection that at the end of the course the time will arrive for him to be thinking about undergoing the ordeals of the Hall and College. Making up his mind, therefore, to begin studying in earnest, he becomes a *pro tempore*[13] member of a temperance society, pledging himself to abstain from immoderate beer for six months: he also purchases a coffee-pot, a reading-candlestick, and *Steggall's Manual*,[14] and then, contriving to accumulate five guineas to pay a "grinder," he routs out his old note-books from the bottom of his box, and commences to "read for the Hall."

Aspirants to honours in law, physic, or divinity, each know the value of private cramming — a process by which their brains are fattened, by abstinence from liquids and an increase of dry food, like the livers of Strasbourg geese. There are grinders in each of these three professional classes; but the medical teacher is the man of the most varied and eccentric knowledge. Not only is he intimately acquainted with the different branches required to be studied, but he is also master of all their minutiae. In accordance with the taste of the examiners, he learns and imparts to his class at what degree of heat water boils in a balloon — how the article of commerce, Prussian blue, is more easily and correctly defined as the Ferrosesquicyanuret of the cyanide of potassium — why the nitrous oxyde, or laughing gas, induces people to make such asses of themselves; and, especially, all sorts of individual

---

[13] Latin for "for the time being." In other words, temporary.

[14] *Dr. Steggall's Manual for Apothecaries' Hall* might be considered the *Doctoring for Dummies* of its day.

inquiries, which, if continued at the present rate, will range from "Who discovered the use of the spleen?" to "Who killed cock robin?" for aught we know. They ask questions at the Hall quite as vague as these.

It is twelve o'clock at noon. In a large room, ornamented by shelves of bottles and preparations, a number of young men are seated round a long table covered with baize, in the centre of whom an intellectual-looking man, whose well-developed forehead shows the amount of knowledge it can contain, is interrogating by turns each of the students, and endeavouring to impress the points in question on their memories by various diverting associations.

"Now, Mr. Muff," says the gentleman to one of his class, handing him a bottle of something which appears like specimens of a chestnut colt's coat after he had been clipped; "what's that, sir?"

"That's cow-itch, sir," replies Mr. Muff.

"Cow what? You must call it at the Hall by its botanical name — dolichos pruriens. What is it used for?"

"To strew in people's beds that you owe a grudge to," replies Muff; whereat all the class laugh.

"That answer would floor you," continues the grinder. "The dolichos is used to destroy worms. How does it act, Mr. Jones?" going on to the next pupil — a man in a light cotton cravat and no shirt collar, who looks very like a butler out of place.

"It tickles them to death, sir," answers Mr. Jones.

"You would say it acts mechanically," observes the grinder. "The fine points stick into the worms and kill them. They say, 'Is this a dagger which I see before me?' and then die. Recollect the dagger,[15] Mr. Jones, when you go up. Mr. Manhug, what do you consider the best sudorific, if you wanted to throw a person into a perspiration?"

Mr. Manhug, who is the wag of the class, winks at the other pupils as much as to say, "See me tackle him, now;" and replies, "The gallery door of Covent Garden on Boxing-night."[16]

---

[15] The grinder quoted from Shakespeare's *Macbeth*. It is the first line from Macbeth's soliloquy in Act II when he is considering murdering the king.

[16] The cheap seats in upper gallery at the Royal Opera House (a.k.a. Covent Garden) were usually crammed, stuffy and hot enough to

"Now, come, be serious for once, Mr. Manhug," continues the teacher; "what else is likely to answer the purpose?"

"I think a run up Holborn-hill, with two Ely-place[17] knockers on your arm, and three policemen on your heels, might have a good effect," answers Mr. Manhug.

"Do you ever think you will pass the Hall, if you go on at this rate?" observes the teacher, in a tone of mild reproach.

"Not a doubt of it, sir," returns the imperturbable Manhug. "I've passed it twenty times within this last month, and did not find any very great difficulty about it; neither do I expect to, unless they block up Union-street and Water-lane."

The grinder gives Mr. Manhug up as a hopeless case, and goes on to the next.

"We have had no chemistry this morning," observes one of the pupils.

"Very well, Mr. Rogers; we will go on with it if you wish. How would you endeavour to detect the presence of gold in any body?"

"By begging the loan of a sovereign, sir," interrupts Mr. Manhug.

"If he knew you as well as I do, Manhug," observes Mr. Jones, "he'd be sure to lend it — oh, yes! — I should rayther think so, certainly," whereupon Mr. Jones compresses his nostril with the thumb of his right hand, and moves his fingers as if he was performing a concerto on an imaginary one handed flageolet.

"Mr. Rapp, what is the difference between an element and a compound body?"

Mr. Rapp is again obliged to confess his ignorance.

"A compound body is composed of two or more elements," says the grinder, "in various proportions. Give me an example, Mr. Jones."

---

cause profuse sweating. Attendees jostled to watch the action onstage through semicircular arches nicknamed "pigeon holes." Boxing night is the evening after Christmas, presumably a time when the theatres were most crowded.

[17] As noted above, wrenching off door-knockers was a favorite sport among medical students. Ely Place is a gated road in London's Camden borough that is still privately owned and managed with its own board of commissioners.

"Half-and-half is a compound body, composed of the two elements, ale and porter, the proportion of the porter increasing in an inverse ratio to the respectability of the public-house you get it from," replies Mr. Jones.

And in like manner the grinding-class proceeds.

Of the Examination at Apothecaries' Hall.

THE LAST TASK THAT DEVOLVES upon our student before he goes up to the Hall is to hunt up his testimonials of attendance to lectures and good moral conduct in his apprenticeship, together with his parochial certificate of age and baptism. The two last he generally writes himself, in the style best consonant with his own feelings and the date of his indenture. His "morality ticket" is as follows:—

(Copy.)

"I hereby certify, that during the period Mr. Joseph Muff served his time with me he especially recommended himself to my notice by his studious and attentive habits, highly moral and gentlemanly conduct, and excellent disposition. He always availed himself of every opportunity to improve his professional knowledge."

(SIGNED)

The certificate of attendance upon lectures is only obtained in its most approved state by much clever manoeuvring. It is important to bear in mind that a lecturer should never be asked whilst he is loitering about the school for his signature of the student's diligence. He may have time to recollect his ignorance of his pupil's face at his discourses. He should always be caught flying — either immediately before or after his lecture — in order that the whole business may be too hurried to admit of investigation.

At last Thursday arrives, and at a quarter to four, any person who takes the trouble to station himself at the corner of Union-street will see groups of three and four young men wending their way towards the portals of Apothecaries' Hall, consisting of students about to be examined, accompanied by friends who come down with them to keep up their spirits. They approach the door, and shake hands as they give and receive wishes of success. The wicket closes on the candidates, and their friends adjourn to the "Retail Establishment" opposite, to *go the odd man*[18] and pledge their anxious companions in dissector's diet-drink—*vulgo*,[19] half-and-half.

We follow our old friend Mr. Joseph Muff. He crosses the paved court-yard with the air of a man who had lost half-a-crown and found a halfpenny. Turning to the left, he ascends a solemn-looking staircase, adorned with severe black figures in niches, who support lamps. On the top of the staircase he enters a room, wherein the partners of his misery are collected. It is a long narrow apartment, commonly known as "the funking-room," ornamented with a savage-looking fireplace at one end, and a huge surly chest at the other. Some of the students are marching up and down the room in feverish restlessness; others, arm in arm, are worrying each other to death with questions.

The clock strikes five, and Mr. Sayer enters the room, exclaiming — "Mr. Manhug, Mr. Jones, Mr. Saxby, and Mr. Collins." The four depart to the chamber of examination, where the medical inquisition awaits them, with every species of mental torture to screw their brains instead of their thumbs, and rack their intellects instead of their limbs.

After an anxious hour, Mr. Jones returns, with a light bounding step to a joyous extempore air of his own composing: he has passed.

In another twenty minutes Mr. Saxby walks fiercely in, calls for his hat, condemns the examiners *ad inferos*,[20] swears he shall cut the profession, and marches away. He has been plucked; and Mr. Muff, who stands sixth on the list, is called on to make his appearance before the awful tribunal.

Of the Sequel to the Hall Examination.

WHILST MR. MUFF FOLLOWS THE beadle from the funking-room

---

[18] Playing a game among three or more persons to decide who pays for a round of drinks. Each person spins a coin. The person who is the only one with heads or tails loses.

[19] Latin for common, as in the "common man", "common language," or in this case, "commonly known as."

[20] Latin for "to the fires," or more accurately "to Hell."

to the Council Chamber, he scarcely knows whether he is walking upon his head or his heels; nor does he recover a sense of his true position until he finds himself seated at one end of a square table, the other three sides whereof are occupied by the same number of gentlemen of grave and austere bearing. The table before him is invitingly spread with pharmacopoeias, books of prescriptions, trays of drugs, and half-dead plants; and upon these subjects, for an hour and a half, he is compelled to answer questions.

We will not follow his examination: nobody was ever able to see the least joke in it; and therefore it is unfitted for our columns. We can but state that after having been puzzled, bullied, "caught," quibbled with, and abused, for the above space of time, his good genius prevails, and he is told he may retire. He has passed the Hall! won't he have a flare-up to-night! — that's all.

As soon as all the candidates have passed, their certificates are given them, upon payment of various sovereigns, and they are let out. The first great rush takes place to the "retail establishment" over the way, where all their friends are assembled — Messrs. Jones, Rapp, Manhug, &c. A pot of "Hospital Medoc" is consumed by each of the thirsty candidates, and off they go, jumping Jim Crow[21] down Union-street, and swaggering along the pavement six abreast, as they sing several extempore variations of their own upon a glee which details divers peculiarities in the economy of certain small pigs, pleasantly enlivened by grunts and whistles, and the occasional asseveration of the singers that their paternal parent was a man of less than ordinary stature. This insensibly changes into "Willy brewed a Peck of Malt,"[22] and finally settles down into "Nix my Dolly,"[23] appropriately danced and

---

[21] A character created by minstrel show performer Thomas D. Rice (1808-1860). A folk trickster created by black slaves, Jim Crow dressed in rags, battered hat, and torn shoes, leapt about and sang "Turn about and wheel about, and do just so. And every time I turn about I jump Jim Crow."

[22] A traditional Scottish drinking song popularized by Robert Burns (1759-1796).

[23] A ballad from *Jack Sheppard* (1834), a play based on the novel by William Harrison Ainsworth (1805-1882) about the burglar. Think of

chorussed, until a policeman, who has no music in his soul, stops their harmony, but threatens to take them into charge if they do not bring their promenade concert to a close.

Arrived at their lodgings, the party throw off all restraint. The table is soon covered with beer, spirits, screws,[24] hot water, and pipes; and the company take off their coats, unbutton their stocks, and proceed to conviviality. Mr. Muff, who is in the chair,[25] sings the first song, which informs his friends that the glasses sparkle on the board and the wine is ruby bright,[26] an allusion to the pewter-pots and half-and half.

Having finished, Mr. Muff calls upon Mr. Jones, who sings a ballad, not altogether perhaps of the same class you would hear at an evening party in Belgrave-square, but still of

---

it as the *Sweeney Todd* of its day. The play was so popular that for years afterward the Lord Chamberlain would censor the title of any play with "Jack Sheppard" in it. "Nix my Dolly" was a canting song because it was filled with thieves' slang ("cant"), as seen in the first verse:

> "In a box of a stone jug I was born,
> Of a hempen widow all forlorn;
> And my old dad, as I've heard say,
> Was a famous merchant in capers gay;
> Nix my dolly, pals, fake away!"

In cant, "stone jug" is a prison cell and "hempen widow" is the wife of a hanged man. The last line has been translated as "Never mind, pals, work away."

[24] Twisted scraps of paper used to light pipes.

[25] In charge of the proceedings. Borrowed from the formal way public meetings and debates were held.

[26] From the song "The Glasses Sparkle" by Thomas Geary, an Irish composer and pianist (1775-1801):

> The glasses sparkle on the board,
> The wine is ruby bright;
> The reign of pleasure is restored,
> Of ease and gay delight;
> The day is gone, the night's our own;
> Then let us feast the soul;
> Should any pain or care remain,
> Why drown it in the bowl.

infinite humour, which is applauded upon the table to a degree that flips all the beer out of the pots, with which Mr. Rapp draws portraits and humorous conceits upon the table with his finger.

The first symptom of approaching cerebral excitement from the action of liquid stimulants is perceived in Mr. Muff himself, who tries to cut some cold meat with the snuffers. Mr. Simpson also, a new man, who is looking very pale, rather overcome with the effects of his elementary screw in a first essay to perpetrate a pipe, petitions for the window to be let down, that the smoke, which you might divide with a knife, may escape more readily.

This proposition is unanimously negatived, until Mr. Jones, who is tilting his chair back, produces the desired effect by overbalancing himself in the middle of a comic medley, and causing a compound, comminuted, and irreducible fracture of three panes of glass by tumbling through them. Hereat, the harmony experiencing a temporary check, and all the half-and half having disappeared, Mr. Muff finds there is no great probability of getting any more, as the servant has long since retired to rest in the back kitchen. An adjournment is therefore determined upon; and the whole party tumble out into the streets at two o'clock in the morning.

"Whiz-z-z-z-t!" shouts Mr. Manhug, as they emerge into the cool air, "there goes a cat!" A volley of hats follow the scared animal, none of which go within ten yards of it, except Mr. Rapp's, who, taking a bold aim, flings his own gossamer[27] over the railings, as the cat jumps between them on to the water-butt. Whereupon Mr. Rapp goes and rings the house-bell, that the domestics may return his property; but not receiving an answer, and being assured of the absence of a policeman, he pulls the handle out as far as it will come, breaks it off, and puts it in his pocket.

After this, they run about the streets, and are eventually separated by their flight from the police, from the safe plan they have adopted of all running different ways when pursued, to bother the crushers.[28]

---

[27] A fashionable hat made of gossamer silk and costing about 4 shillings 9 pence, which also gave it the name "four-and-nine."

[28] Low London slang for a policeman, possibly a reference to their

The Termination of the Hall Examination.

THE MORNING AFTER THE CAROUSAL, the parties are dispersed in various parts of London. Did a modern Asmodeus[29] take a spectator to any elevated point from which he could overlook the Great Metropolis, he would see Mr. Rapp ruminating upon things in general whilst seated on some cabbages in Covent Garden Market; Mr. Jones taking refreshment with a lamplighter and two cabmen at a promenade coffee-stand near Charing Cross, to whom he is giving a lecture upon the action of veratria[30] in paralysis, jumbled somehow or other with frequent asseverations that he shall at all times be happy to see the aforesaid lamplighter and two cabmen at the hospital or his own lodgings; Mr. Manhug, with a pocket-handkerchief tied round his head, not clearly understanding what has become of his latch-key, but rather imagining that he threw it into a lamp instead of the short pipe which still remains in the pocket of his pea-jacket, and, moreover, finding himself close to London Bridge, is taking a gratuitous doze in the cabin of the Boulogne steam-boat, which he ascertains does not start until eight o'clock; whilst Mr. Simpson, the new man, with the usual destiny of such green productions — thirsty, nauseated, and "coming round" — is safely taken care of in one of the small private unfurnished apartments which are let by the night on exceedingly moderate terms in the immediate neighbourhood of the Bow-street Police-office. Where Mr. Muff is — it is impossible to form the least idea.

The reader will now please to shift the time and place to two o'clock P.M. in the dissecting-room, which is full of students, comprising three we have just spoken of, except Mr. Simpson. A message has been received that the anatomical teacher is unavoidably detained at an important case in private practice, and cannot meet his class to day.

Hereupon there is much rejoicing amongst the pupils, who

---

heavy boots. Still used into the 1940s.
[29] A king of demons from Talmudic legends and the Book of Tobit (in Catholic and Orthodox religions). In his classification of demons in 1589, German bishop Peter Binsfeld relied upon the seven deadly sins for his model, and identified Asmodeus as the demon of lust.
[30] A poisonous alkaloid used to treat rheumatism and neuralgia.

gather in a large semicircle round the fireplace, and devise various amusing methods of passing the time. The various arguments are, however, cut short by the entrance of Mr. Muff, who rushes into the room, followed by Mr. Simpson, and throwing off his macintosh cape, pitches a large fluttering mass of feathers into the middle of the circle.

"Halloo, Muff! how are you, my bean — what's up?" is the general exclamation.

"Oh, here's a lark!" is all Mr. Muff's reply. "It's a beautiful patriarchal old hen, that I bottled as she was meandering down the mews; and now I vote we have her for lunch. Who's game to kill her?"

Various plans are immediately suggested, including cutting her head off, poisoning her with morphia, or shooting her with a little cannon Mr. Rapp has got in his locker; but at last the majority decide upon hanging her. A gibbet is speedily prepared, simply consisting of a thigh-bone laid across two high stools; a piece of whip cord is then noosed round the victim's neck; and she is launched into eternity, as the newspapers say — Mr. Manhug attending to pull her legs.

"Depend upon it that's a humane death," remarks Mr. Jones. "I never tried to strangle a fowl but once, and then I twisted its neck bang off. I know a capital plan to finish cats though."

"Throw it off — put it up — let's have it," exclaim the circle.

"Well, then; you must get their necks in a slip knot and pull them up to a key-hole. They can't hurt you, you know, because you are the other side the door.

"Oh, capital — quite a wrinkle," observes Mr. Muff. "But how do you catch them first?"

"Put a hamper outside the leads with some valerian in it, and a bit of cord tied to the lid. If you keep watch, you may bag half-a-dozen in no time; and strange cats are fair game for everybody, — only some of them are rum 'uns to bite."

During the preceding conversation, Mr. Muff cuts down the victim with a scalpel; and, finding that life has departed, commences to pluck it, and perform the usual post-mortem abdominal examinations attendant upon such occasions. Mr. Rapp undertakes to manufacture an extempore spit, from the rather dilapidated umbrella of the new Scotch pupil, which he has heedlessly left in the dissecting-room.

This being completed, with the assistance of some wire from the ribs of an old skeleton that had hung in a corner of the room ever since it was built, the hen is put down to roast, presenting the most extraordinary specimen of trussing upon record. Mr. Jones undertakes to buy some butter at a shop behind the hospital; and Mr. Manhug, not being able to procure any flour, gets some starch from the cabinet of the lecturer on Materia Medica, and powders it in a mortar which he borrows from the laboratory.

"By the way, Muff, where did you get to last night after we all cut?" inquires Mr. Rapp.

"Why, that's what I am rather anxious to find out myself," replies Mr. Muff; "but I think I can collect tolerably good reminiscences of my travels."

"Tell us all about it then," cry three or four.

Essential as sulphuric acid is to the ignition of the platinum in an hydropneumatic lamp; so is half-and-half to the proper illumination of a Medical Student's faculties. All the world inclined towards beer knows that the current price of a pot of half-and-half is fivepence, and by this standard the Medical Student fixes his expenses. He says he has given three pots for a pair of Berlin gloves, and speaks of a half-crown as a six-pot piece.

Mr. Muff takes the goodly measure in his hand, indulges in a prolonged drain, and commences his narrative:—

"You know we should all have got on very well if Rapp hadn't been such a fool as to pull away the lanthorns from the place where they are putting down the wood pavement in the Strand, and swear he was a watchman. I thought the crusher saw us, and so I got ready for a bolt, when Manhug said the blocks had no right to obstruct the footpath; and, shoving down a whole wall of them into the street, voted for stopping to play at duck with them. Whilst he was trying how many he could pitch across the Strand against the shutters opposite, down came the pewlice and off we cut."

"I had a tight squeak for it," interrupts Mr. Rapp; "but I beat them at last, in the dark of the Durham-street arch. That's a dodge worth being up to when you get into a row near the

Adelphi. Fire away, Muff — where did you go?"

"Right up a court to Maiden-lane, in the hope of bolting into the Cider-cellars. But they were all shut up, and the fire out in the kitchen, so I ran on through a lot of alleys and back-slums, until I got somewhere in St. Giles's, and here I took a cab."

"Why, you hadn't got an atom of tin when you left us," says Mr. Manhug.

"Devil a bit did that signify. You know I only took the cab — I'd nothing at all to do with the driver; he was all right in the gin-shop near the stand, I suppose. I got on the box, and drove about for my own diversion — I don't exactly know where; but I couldn't leave the cab, as there was always a crusher in the way when I stopped. At last I found myself at the large gate of New Square, Lincoln's Inn, so I knocked until the porter opened it, and drove in as straight as I could. When I got to the corner of the square, by No. 7, I pulled up, and, tumbling off my perch, walked quietly along to the Portugal-street wicket. Here the other porter let me out, and I found myself in Lincoln's Inn Fields."

"And what became of the cab?" asks Mr. Jones.

"How should I know! — it was no affair of mine. I dare say the horse made it right; it didn't matter to him whether he was standing in St. Giles's or Lincoln's Inn, only the last was the most respectable."

"I don't see that," says Mr. Manhug, refilling his pipe.

"Why, all the thieves in London live in St. Giles's."

"Well, and who live in Lincoln's Inn?"

"Pshaw! that's all worn out," continues Manhug. "I got to the College of Surgeons, and had a good mind to scud some oyster shells through the windows, only there were several people about — fellows coming home to chambers, and the like; so I pattered on until I found myself in Drury-lane, close to a coffee-shop that was open. There I saw such a jolly row!"

"What was it about?" eagerly demand the rest of the circle.

"Why, just as I got in, a gentleman of a vivacious turn of mind, who was taking an early breakfast, had shied a soft-boiled egg at the gas-light, which didn't hit it, of course, but flew across the tops of the boxes, and broke upon a lady's head."

"What a mess it must have made?" interposes Mr. Manhug. "Coffee-shop eggs are always so very albuminous."[31]

"Once I found some feathers in one, and a foetal chick," observes Mr. Rapp.

"Knock that down for a good one!" says Mr. Jones, taking the poker and striking three distinct blows on the mantel-piece, the last of which breaks off the corner. "Well, what did the lady do?"

"Commenced kicking up an extensive shindy, something between crying, coughing, and abusing, until somebody in a fustian coat, addressing the assailant, said, 'he was no gentleman, whoever he was, to throw eggs at a woman; and that if he'd come out he'd pretty soon butter his crumpets on both sides for him, and give him pepper for nothing.' The master of the coffee shop now came forward and said, 'he wasn't a going to have no uproar in his house, which was very respectable, and always used by the first of company, and if they wanted to quarrel, they might fight it out in the streets.'

"Whereupon they all began to barge the master at once, — one saying 'his coffee was all snuff and duckweed,' or something of the kind; whilst the other told him 'he looked as measly as a mouldy muffin;' and then all of a sudden a lot of half-pint cups and pewter spoons flew up in the air, and the three men began an indiscriminate battle all to themselves, in one of the boxes, 'fighting quite permiscus,' as the lady properly observed. I think the landlord was worst off though; he got a very queer wipe across the face from the handle of his own toasting-fork."

"And what did you do, Muff?" asks Mr. Manhug.

"Ah, that was the finishing card of all. I put the gas out, and was walking off as quietly as could be, when some policemen who heard the row outside met me at the door, and wouldn't let me pass. I said I would, and they said I should not, until we came to scuffling, and then one of them calling to some more, told them to take me to Bow-street, which they did; but I made them carry me though. When I got into the office they had not any especial charge to make against me, and the old

---

[31] The albumen is the white of the egg, so one assumes this was undercooked.

bird behind the partition said I might go about my business; but, as ill luck would have it, another of the unboiled ones recognised me as one of the party who had upset the wooden blocks—he knew me again by my d—d Taglioni."

"And what did they do to you?"

"Marched me across the yard and locked me up; when to my great consolation in my affliction, I found Simpson, crying and twisting up his pocket-handkerchief, as if he was wringing it; and hoping his friends would not hear of his disgrace through the *Times*."

"What a love you are, Simpson!" observes Mr. Jones patronisingly. "Why, how the deuce could they, if you gave a proper name? I hope you called yourself James Edwards."

Mr. Simpson blushes, blows his nose, mutters something about his card-case and telling an untruth, which excites much merriment; and Mr. Muff proceeds:—

"The beak wasn't such a bad fellow after all, when we went up in the morning. I said I was ashamed to confess we were both disgracefully intoxicated, and that I would take great care nothing of the same humiliating nature should occur again; whereupon we were fined twelve pots each, and I tossed sudden death with Simpson which should pay both. He lost and paid down the dibs. We came away, and here we are."

Of the College, and the Conclusion.

OUR HERO ONCE MORE UNDERGOES the process of grinding before he presents himself in Lincoln's-inn Fields for examination at the College of Surgeons. Almost the last affair which our hero troubles himself about is the Examination at the College of Surgeons; and as his anatomical knowledge requires a little polishing before he presents himself in Lincoln's-inn Fields, he once more undergoes the process of grinding.

The grinder for the College conducts his tuition in the same style as the grinder for the Hall — often they are united in the same individual, who perpetually has a vacancy for a resident pupil, although his house is already quite full; somewhat resembling a carpet-bag, which was never yet known to be so crammed with articles, but you might put something in besides. The class is carried on similar to the one we have already quoted; but the knowledge required does not embrace the same multiformity of subjects; anatomy and surgery being the principal points.

The examination at the College is altogether a more respectable ordeal than the jalap and rhubarb botheration at Apothecaries' Hall, and par conséquence, Mr. Muff goes up one evening with little misgivings as to his success. Of course, the same kind of scene takes place that was enacted after going up to the Hall, and with the same results, except the police-office, which they manage to avoid.

The next day, as usual, they are again at the school, standing innumerable pots, telling incalculable lies, and singing uncounted choruses, until the Scotch pupil who is still grinding in the museum, is forced to give over study, after having been squirted at through the keyhole five distinct times, with a reversed stomach-pump full of beer, and finally unkennelled. The lecturer upon chemistry, who has a private pupil in his laboratory learning how to discover arsenic in poisoned people's stomachs, where there is none, and make red, blue, and green fires, finds himself locked in, and is obliged to get out at the window; whilst the professor of medicine, who is holding forth, as usual, to a select very few, has his lecture upon intermittent fever so strangely interrupted by distant harmony and convivial hullaballoo, that he finishes abruptly in a pet, to the great joy of his class.

But Mr. Muff and his friends care not. They have passed all their troubles — they are regular medical men, and for aught they care the whole establishment may blow up, tumble down, go to blazes, or anything else in a small way that may completely obliterate it. In another twelve hours they have departed to their homes, and are only spoken of in the reverence with which we regard the ruins of a by-gone edifice, as bricks who were.

Key Dates in William Palmer's Life

1824
Aug. 6: Born in Rugeley to Joseph Palmer and Sarah Bentley.
Oct. 21: Baptized.

1827
Anne Thornton, Palmer's future wife, was born.

1836
Oct. 8: Father Joseph Palmer died, leaving £70,000 in his estate. Palmer receives £7,000.

1844
Studies at Stafford Infirmary.

1846
August: Qualifies as a surgeon.

1847
Oct. 7: Marries Anne Thornton over the objections of her guardians. Moves to home on Market Street in Rugeley.

1849
Jan. 18: Mother-in-law Ann (Mary) Thornton, aged 50, dies at Palmer's house.

1850
May: Leonard Bladen dies at Palmer's house.
October: Anne gives birth to William Brookes Palmer, their first son and the only child to outlive him.

1851
Jan 6: Daughter Elizabeth dies aged 10 weeks.

1852
Jan. 6: Son Henry dies aged one month.
Dec. 19: Son Frank dies 7 hours after birth.

1854
Jan. 27: Son John dies days after birth.

Sept. 29: Wife Anne died. Palmer receives £13,000 from the insurance company and uses it to pay off his more pressing debts

1855

Palmer begins affair with Jane Bergen. Over the next year, she will become pregnant, get an abortion, and use Palmer's letters to blackmail him.

June 26: Eliza Tharm, Palmer's housemaid, gives birth to Palmer's son, Alfred, at his house.

Aug. 16: Palmer's brother Walter dies. Insurance company refuses to pay £13,000 on his policy. Negotiations over it drag on until Cook's death.

Sept. 5: Insurance proposed for Bates.

Nov. 6: Pratt issues writs against Palmer and his mother for £4,000 but withholds serving them while Palmer raises more money.

Nov. 10: Palmer visits Pratt, pays £300.

Nov. 13 (Tuesday): Cook's horse Polestar wins the Shrewsbury Handicap Stakes. Receives between £700 and £800 and promised another £350 plus proceeds from other bets at Tattersall's the following Monday. Palmer returns home to find a letter from Jane demanding money for his letters. Writes letter offering £30. Returns to Shrewsbury. Pratt mails letter to Palmer urging him to come up with £1,000 by Saturday.

Nov. 14 (Wednesday): Cook falls ill drinking brandy at The Raven, Shrewsbury.

Nov. 15 (Thursday): Palmer loses heavily betting on his horse Chicken. Palmer and Cook return to Rugeley at 9:30 p.m. where Cook books Room 10 at the Talbot Arms.

Nov. 16 (Friday): Cook recovers and dines with Palmer and Jeremiah Smith. Palmer writes to Pratt saying a friend will give him £200 the next day and Palmer will visit with the rest on Monday.

Nov. 17 (Saturday): Cook falls ill at the Talbot Arms in Rugeley. Tharme's son Alfred dies aged 5 months (Fletcher says Dec. 13). Palmer's friend gives Pratt a cheque for £200.

Nov. 18 (Sunday): Cook still sick. Chambermaid Mills falls ill after eating broth prepared for Cook.

Nov. 19 (Monday): Palmer travels to London to collect

Cook's winnings. Visits Pratt and Padwick to dispose of £700. Cook's health improves. Palmer returns to Stafford at 8:45 p.m., drives to Rugeley, visits Newton, assistant to surgeon Salt, at 10 p.m., and purchases 3 grains of strychnia. A hour later, gives Cook pills prepared by Dr. Bamford. Around midnight, Cook struck by violent spasms. Palmer sent for and gives him more pills and opium.

Nov. 20 (Tuesday): Cook "comparatively comfortable" in the morning. At 11 a.m., Palmer buys 6 grains of strychnia, prussic acid, and opium from Roberts at Hawkins' establishment. Visits postmaster Cheshire and asks him to write £350 cheque in Cook's name on Weatherby's for his stakes. Cook's friend Jones, a surgeon, arrives from Lutterworth to stay with him. Palmer, Bamford and Jones meet and agree to give Cook more pills over his objections. Bamford makes up pills and gives them to Palmer along with instructions for their use. Palmer and Jones press Cook to take the pills.

Nov. 21 (Wednesday): Cook dies between 12:15 and 1 a.m. in Jones and Palmer's presence. Palmer writes Pratt, apologizing for being unable to attend to business due to Cook's fatal illness and adds "I must have Polestar . . . should any one call upon you to know what money or moneys Cook ever had from you, don't answer the question till I have seen you." Weatherby's, not receiving Cook's stakes, declines to pay cheque.

Nov. 22 (Thursday): Pratt threatens Palmer: "Am greatly disappointed at the non-receipt of the money as promised, and at the vague assurances as to any money. . . . If anything unpleasant occurs you must thank yourself." Palmer visits Pratt and pays £100.

Nov. 23 (Friday): Cook's stepfather, Stevens, arrives in Rugeley. Views body and questions Palmer about betting-book and burial plans before returning to London to seek solicitor's advice. Palmer offers Pratt a plan to repay debts. Visits Cheshire and asks him to witness document with Cook's signature acknowledging £4,000 of bills to have been negotiated by Palmer for Cook. Cheshire refuses. Travels to London.

Nov. 24 (Saturday): Stevens and Palmer meet by accident

at London train station and return to Rugeley. Stevens informs Palmer that post-mortem would be held. Palmer mails final Jane letter paying the remainder of the blackmail money, adding "Please keep letters for me until I send for them."

Nov. 25 (Sunday): Palmer visits Newton to ask how much strychnine could kill a dog and if evidence of it could be found in the body

Nov. 26 (Monday): Post-mortem on Cook. Stevens takes jar to London for analysis by Professor Taylor. Palmer writes Pratt asking to not answer any inquiries about Cook's money. Palmer asks Dr. Bamford for death certificate for Cook claiming apoplexy. Bamford resists, saying Palmer should fill it out himself, but then submits.

Nov. 29 (Thursday): Inquest on Cook opens. After testimony is heard, coroner adjourns hearing to await results of Taylor's analysis of stomach contents.

Nov. 30 (Friday): Cook's funeral

Dec. 5: Postmaster Cheshire opens letter from Taylor to Gardner, Stevens' representative in Rugeley, saying antimony had been found but not strychnine. Cheshire tells Palmer.

Dec. 8: Palmer writes to coroner informing him of Taylor's analysis.

Dec. 12: Inquest on Cook resumes.

Dec. 13: Palmer sends coroner £10.

Dec. 14: Taylor gives evidence at Cook's inquest.

Dec. 15: Inquest rules he was killed through "willful murder." Palmer, who was under house arrest for debt, is removed at 11 p.m. and taken to Stafford Gaol.

Dec. 22: Bodies of Anne Palmer and Walter Palmer exhumed and viewed by jury.

1856

Jan. 9: Inquest held on Mrs. Palmer's death.

Jan. 12: Verdict accuses Palmer in Anne's death.

Jan. 15-16: Inquest held on Walter Palmer's death and hears testimony about Walter's last days and the state of his body. Drs. Alfred Swaine Taylor and George Rees testified that after examining Walter's body, that the cause of death was apoplexy caused by excessive drinking. The hearing was adjured until Jan. 23.

Jan. 21: Palmer testifies in *Padwick v. Mrs. S. Palmer* lawsuit at Westminster that his mother's name were forged on £2,000 in bills by his wife. Jury finds for mother.

Jan. 23: Inquest on Walter Palmer reopens. Drs. Taylor and Rees testify again and change the cause of death from apoplexy to poisoning by prussic acid. The jury indicts William Palmer in Walter's death.

Jan. 26: Cook's body exhumed for another post-mortem.

May 14: Trial opens at the Central Criminal Court, The Old Bailey, London.

May 27: Palmer found guilty.

June 14: Palmer executed at 8 a.m. in Stafford.

1926

April 29: Palmer's surviving son dies of coal gas poisoning aged 76 years. An inquest returned the verdict of death by misadventure.

Bibliography

Aiello, Dawn. "The London Season," from http://www.thehistorybox.com/ny_city/society/printerfriendly/nycity_society_london_season_article0008.htm, accessed March 23, 2016.

Anonymous. "About Dogs," *Putnam's Monthly,* vol. 9, March 1857, pp. 288-292.

Anonymous, "The Infamous Rugeley Poisoner William Palmer." http://palmer.staffscc.net/, accessed June 13, 2014.

Anonymous. "The Metropolis." *The Spectator,* Nov. 28, 1856, pp. 1250-1251.

Anonymous. "The Suspected Poisoning Cases at Rugeley: Inquest on Mr. Walter Palmer." *Association Medical Journal,* Jan. 26, 1856. pp. 77-78.

Anonymous. *The Times Report of the Trial of William Palmer.* Hershey, Pa.: Peschel Press, 2015.

Bates, Stephen. *The Poisoner: The Life and Crimes of Victorian England's Most Notorious Doctor.* New York: Overlook Duckworth, 2014.

Brand, Nadine. "The Concept of the *Sanus Homo* in the *De Medicina* of Celsus." University of Stellenbosch, 2007. https://scholar.sun.ac.za/bitstream/handle/10019.1/2407/brand_concept_2007.pdf, accessed March 11, 2016.

Buckingham, John. *Bitter Nemesis: The Intimate History of Strychnine.* New York: CRC Press, 2008.

Burnand, Francis Cowley. *Records and Reminiscences.* London: Methuen & Co., 1904.

Connor, John. *The Inns and Alehouses of Stafford: Through the North Gate.* Leicestershire: Troubador Publishing, Ltd., 2014.

Edwards, Eliezer. *Words, Facts, and Phrases.* London: Chatto & Windus, 1882.

Farmer, John Stephen and William Henley. *A Dictionary of Slang and Colloquial English.* London: G. Routledge & Sons, 1905.

Fletcher, George, Bill Peschel (editor). *The Life & Career of Dr. William Palmer of Rugeley.* Hershey, Pa.: Peschel Press, 2014.

Green, Jonathon. *Cassell's Dictionary of Slang.* London: Orion Publishing Group, 2005.
Hotten, John Camden. *A Dictionary of Modern Slang, Cant, and Vulgar Word.* London: John Camden Hotten, 1859.
Partridge, Eric. *A Dictionary of the Underworld.* London: Routledge, 2015.
Wikipedia

About the Editor

Bill Peschel is a former journalist who shares a Pulitzer Prize with the staff of *The Patriot-News* in Harrisburg, Pa. He is also a mystery fan who runs the Wimsey Annotations at Planetpeschel.com.

The author of *Writers Gone Wild* (Penguin), he publishes through Peschel Press the 223B Casebook Series of Sherlockian parodies and pastiches and annotated editions of Dorothy L. Sayers' *Whose Body?* and Agatha Christie's *The Mysterious Affair at Styles* and *The Secret Adversary.*

Peschel was born in Warren, Ohio, grew up in Charlotte, N.C., and graduated from the University of North Carolina in Chapel Hill. He lives with his family and animal menagerie in Hershey, where the air really does smell like chocolate.

Visit Bill at Peschel Press (www.peschelpress.com). He can be reached at peschel@Peschelpress.com.

The Complete, Annotated Series

Return to your favorite novels by Agatha Christie & Dorothy L. Sayers, republished with extras that will increase your pleasure, including footnotes describing people, places, events, and idioms, and essays about the author, their creations, and historical events.

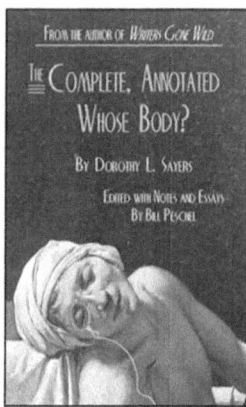

The Complete, Annotated Whose Body?
Dorothy L. Sayers

Her first novel featuring Lord Peter Wimsey comes with 3 maps of London, 10 essays on notorious crimes, anti-Semitism, Sayers and Wimsey, plus a timeline of his cases and Sayers' life. *282 pages.*

The Complete, Annotated Mysterious Affair at Styles
Agatha Christie

Hercule Poirot's debut, updated with revised art, explanation of the murder method, and essays on Poirot, Christie, strychnine, women during the war, plus chronology and book lists. *352 pages.*

The Deluxe Complete, Annotated Secret Adversary
Agatha Christie

Tommy and Tuppence battle socialists plotting to destroy England! This deluxe edition has illustrations from the newspaper edition, plus essays on thrillers, Christie's vanishing and more! *478 pages.*

Don't miss future Peschel Press books: Visit Peschelpress.com or PlanetPeschel.com and sign up for our monthly newsletter.

The 223B Casebook Series

This ongoing multi-volume series reprints classic and newly discovered fanfiction written during the life of Arthur Conan Doyle, with original illustrations and art, plus extensive historical notes.

The Early Punch Parodies of Sherlock Holmes

- Reprints parodies, pastiches, book reviews, cartoons, and jokes from 1890 to 1928.
- Includes 17-story cycle by R.C. Lehmann.
- Two Holmes parodies by P.G. Wodehouse, and a short story by Arthur Conan Doyle.
- Essays on Punch, Lehmann, Wodehouse, and an interview with Conan Doyle. *281 pages.*

Victorian Parodies and Pastiches: 1888-1899 | Edwardian Parodies and Pastiches I: 1900-1904 | Edwardian Parodies and Pastiches II: 1905-1909

Stories by Conan Doyle, Robert Barr, Jack Butler Yeats, and J.M. Barrie. *279 pages.*

Stories by Twain, Finley Peter Dunn, John Kendrick Bangs, and P.G. Wodehouse. *390 pages.*

Stories by 'Banjo' Paterson, Max Beerbohm, Jacques Futrelle, and Lincoln Steffens. *401 pages.*

The Rugeley Poisoner Series

A 3-book series from Peschel Press reprinting seminal works about Victorian poisoner Dr. William Palmer.

 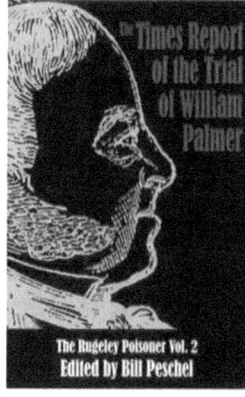 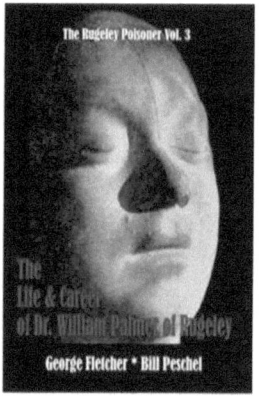

The Illustrated Life and Career of William Palmer *(1856)*

- A book written to cash in on the trial.
- Gossip about Palmer's family, betting scams, and the stews of London.
- More than 50 restored woodcuts.
- Essays on medical training and racing.
- Excerpts from Palmer's love letters. *225 pages.*

The Times Report of the Trial of William Palmer *(1856)*

- A trial transcript created by the *Times* edited, corrected, and annotated.
- More than 50 original woodcuts restored to better-than-new condition.
- Essays on the trial judges and barristers, glossary of medical terms, and index to witnesses. *426 pages.*

The Life and Career of Dr. William Palmer of Rugeley *(1925)*

- Written by a doctor who interviewed witnesses and jurors.
- Rare photos and art not seen since 1925.
- Annotations define medical and legal terms and clarify obscure points.
- Essays on Palmer's impact on culture, strychnine, and Rugeley today. *227 pages.*

PESCHEL PRESS ~ HERSHEY, PA.
WWW.PESCHELPRESS.COM

www.ingramcontent.com/pod-product-compliance
Lightning Source LLC
Chambersburg PA
CBHW030146100526
44592CB00009B/143